Comparative Politics
Using MicroCase ® Explorit

Fourth Edition

Michael K. Le Roy
Whitworth College

THOMSON
✳
WADSWORTH

Australia • Brazil • Canada • Mexico Singapore • Spain • United Kingdom • United States

Printed in the United States of America
1 2 3 4 5 6 7 10 09 08 07 06

Printer: Thomson West

ISBN: 0-495-00761-7
Cover Image: Corbis; Lester Lefkowitz

Thomson Higher Education
10 Davis Drive
Belmont, CA 94002-3098
USA

For more information about our products,
contact us at:
Thomson Learning Academic Resource Center
1-800-423-0563

For permission to use material from this text or
product, submit a request online at
http://www.thomsonrights.com.
Any additional questions about permissions can be
submitted by email to **thomsonrights@thomson.com.**

CONTENTS

ABOUT THE AUTHOR

Michael Le Roy is a Professor of Political Science and Dean of the Faculty at Whitworth College in Spokane, Washington. He received his Ph.D. in Political Science at Vanderbilt University. Between 1992 and 1994, Michael was a Fulbright scholar at Gothenburg University in Sweden and is a recipient of the Faculty Achievement Award for Excellence in Teaching from Wheaton College and the APSA. He teaches comparative politics, international political economy, and research methods in political science. Michael's research on civil society, xenophobia, and the European Union has been published in *Comparative Politics*. He is also the co-author of *Research Methods in Political Science*, 6th Edition (Belmont, CA: Wadsworth, 2006), with the late Michael Corbett. Comments about this book from students and faculty are welcomed and may be sent directly to the author at the following e-mail address: mleroy@whitworth.edu.

ACKNOWLEDGMENTS

I am delighted to acknowledge the efforts of many people who made this workbook possible. John Yoder, my first political science professor, introduced me to the study of comparative politics, and M. Donald Hancock, my advisor in graduate school, persuaded me of the value of empirical comparative research.

I am thankful for the support of Whitworth College and the encouragement of my colleagues in the department including Julia Stronks, Dale Soden, Jim Hunt, Arlin Migliazzo, Patrick Van Inwegen and Corliss Slack. The groundwork for the first edition was laid when I was a faculty member at Wheaton College, so I continue to be indebted to Mark Amstutz, Amy Black, Sandra Joireman, Lyman A. Kellstedt, Helene Slessarev, and Ashley Woodiwiss for their encouragement and support. This workbook would not have been possible, or even desirable, if it were not for the many students who have given feedback and input into the examples used in this text. I particularly wish to thank my student assistants who put in many hours testing the exercises and examples over the years: Sara De Master, David Fabrycky, Sara Gray, Kate Morley, Brittney Peterson, Andrea Saul, Caitlin Storm, Laura Thaut, Ivy Orr, Rob Vickery, and Marjory Winn. In the context of my work as Dean, I now have the benefit of a few other people who keep my feet to the fire and guard my time so that I can still teach, think, and write. I wish to offer my special thanks to Patti Green and Lisa Sem-Rodrigues for their attentiveness to the details of my professional life as I completed this edition. Working with these remarkable people makes my arrival at work each day a pleasure.

I am also very grateful for the careful reading and the many helpful contributions of the reviewers that helped me to prepare the 4th edition. In particular, I would like to thank Gardel Fuertado (The Citadel), Stephen Manning (University of Detroit-Mercy), and Lawrence R. Sullivan (Adelphi University). In addition I am thankful to the reviewers that have helped to improve the book for previous editions, including Donald Baxter (College of William and Mary), Michael L. Bressler (Furman University), Layne Hoppe (Texas Lutheran University), Richard Jankowski (SUNY Fredonia), Kay Knickrehm (James Madison University), Kim Lanegran (Hood College), Jonathon Olsen (University of Wisconsin-Parkside), Margaret E. Scranton (University of Arkansas at Little Rock), and Andreas Sobisch (John Carroll University).

If this workbook achieves any distinction at all, it will be because I stood on the shoulders of giants who came before me. Rodney Stark pioneered the pedagogical use of statistical software in the social sciences and helped teachers better imagine how to engage students in social science research. David Smetters and staff were instrumental in perfecting the software and the instructional resources that accompany it. In particular I wish to thank David for sticking with me through the first edition of the project and giving me the necessary encouragement to bring it to completion.

For the fourth edition I am indebted to Julie Aguilar, Carolyn Merrill, and David Tatom at Wadsworth for their editorial advice and assistance. I am also grateful to Brent Veysey for his high-quality, professional efforts to move my manuscript through the production phase of its development. I continue to appreciate each person's professionalism, patience, and good humor.

I would also like to thank the sources of the data files accompanying this workbook. These data sets represent thousands of hours of work by many unsung heroes who have labored around the world to interview thousands of people, survey the state of human development, and document the state of the politics. In particular I wish to thank Ronald Inglehart at the Institute for Social Research, University of Michigan, for his generosity in making the World Values Survey available to students and scholars. A comparative politics workbook like this would not have been possible if it were not for Professor Inglehart's diligent research over the past thirty years. I am pleased to thank the study staff at the CSES Secretariat, based in the Center for Political Studies, University of Michigan, for its very exciting work on Comparative Study of Electoral Systems.

The collection of cross-national data sets has grown exponentially since I first started writing in the MicroCase series in 1994. A special thanks is reserved for Andrew Kohut of the Pew Research Center for making the Pew Global Attitudes Data available to students and scholars in the field of Comparative Politics.

Finally, no academic project can ever go forward without the support of the people we love who give us the space to work and the time to think and travel. I thank my family: my wife Andrea, my son Dana, and daughters Hannah and Astrid. As always, I am indebted to them for their patience and support throughout the development of this book.

PREFACE

ny illusion that we need not concern ourselves with the internal politics of other nations came crashing down as I sat writing the second edition of this text on September 11, 2001. This brutal attack on thousands of innocent people was instigated by political forces far from our shores, but hit the United States just as hard as it would have had it been hatched in our own backyard. The world is indeed a smaller place. And we must know more about it.

Even if you've never traveled abroad, you too have probably noticed how the world has grown smaller over the past ten years. Think about it. Someone in the United States can now pick up the phone and call Bangkok and pay just pennies a minute. A person in Great Britain can wake up someone in Hawaii with equal effort and cost. We have faxes, e-mail, the Internet, and a host of other telecommunications pulling us closer and closer every day.

We are witnessing the unification of economies and currencies in Europe. We are nervously watching political and economic transition in the former Soviet Union. The Asian tigers are roaring one day, silent the next, and then roaring once again with ever more determination and might. The Middle East keeps pumping oil under a cloud of violence, and Africa keeps struggling. With so many different countries in the world, how does one make sense of it all? What political systems are most stable? Which countries have the best records for respecting human rights? Which political systems are the most corrupt? What factors lead to internal and external war? Which countries have the weakest infrastructures for dealing with education, health, and population growth?

The answers to these and many other questions can be found by comparing one nation to another. And that's exactly what these materials will teach you to do: compare nations. This workbook and its accompanying software allow you to explore the real world of comparative politics, using the same data and analytical tools used by professional researchers. This book allows you to download the software needed to complete your work in this book. In addition, you will find an incredibly rich assortment of data files, such as the GLOBAL data file, which contains more than 450 variables for the 172 largest countries in the world. There are also regional files providing aggregate data for Asia, Europe, Africa, and Latin America. All data are from the best sources available, such as the World Values Survey, the Pew Global Attitudes Survey, the World Bank, and the United Nations. The fourth edition is a significant revision thanks to the proliferation of new data sources. The most recent edition of the World Values Survey is incorporated with new data from India in addition to the many other countries included in earlier editions.

When I was in college, I had a political science professor who continually pushed us to "think beyond the water's edge." Sometimes it was difficult to meet this challenge because it required analytical tools that were not easily accessible to college students. It also called for the analysis of data sets that were not readily available. Times have changed. The software and workbook materials you are holding in your hands are unlike anything ever available for comparative politics courses. I wish I could say that

I came up with this instructional concept myself, but I didn't. I undertook this project only after seeing how easily students in an introductory American government course were able to do real analysis using Wadsworth's software-based workbook, *American Government: An Introduction Using ExplorIt*. The workbook and software considerably simplify what had previously been considered too complex for college freshmen, and did so without compromising or dumbing down the content. If you've never encountered the Student ExplorIt or Student MicroCase software, you'll be amazed at how easily you can generate maps, analyze survey data, and do many other things.

When I started work on this project, a primary goal was to develop a set of materials that would allow undergraduate students to explore the real world of comparative politics research. The exercises in this workbook provide a great deal of guidance and structure, and I promise you will find nothing difficult about these materials if you simply read the text and follow the step-by-step instructions. However, I encourage you to do more than just try to get the "right answers" for the worksheet sections. With a little application and exploration, you'll discover that comparative politics is much more than learning facts and figures about distant lands.

I hope you enjoy this workbook. I took great pleasure in developing these materials. If I have been successful at my task, you too will experience the excitement of exploring politics beyond the water's edge.

Michael K. Le Roy
Spokane, Washington

GETTING STARTED

INTRODUCTION

Welcome to ExplorIt! With the easy-to-use software available for this workbook, you will have the opportunity to learn about comparative politics by exploring more than 170 countries and dozens of political issues with data from around the world.

Each chapter in this workbook deals with a theme in the study of comparative politics or the study of the countries in a specific region of the world. The preliminary section of each chapter uses data provided with the workbook to illustrate key issues related to the topic in question. You can easily create all the graphics in this part of the chapter by following the ExplorIt Guides you'll be seeing. Doing so will take just a few clicks of your computer mouse and will help you become familiar with ExplorIt. The ExplorIt Guides are described in more detail below.

Each chapter also has a worksheet section where you'll do your own data analysis. This section usually contains about a dozen questions that will either follow up on examples from the preliminary section or have you explore some new issues. You'll use the Student ExplorIt software to answer these questions.

SYSTEM REQUIREMENTS

- Windows 98 (or higher)
- 64 MB RAM (minimum)
- 20 MB of hard drive space
- Internet Access (broadband recommended)

Macintosh Note: This software was designed for use with a PC. To run the software on a Macintosh, you will need PC emulation software or hardware installed. Many Macintosh computers in the past few years come with PC emulation software or hardware. For more information about PC emulation software or hardware, review the documentation that came with your computer or check with your local Macintosh retailer.

NETWORK VERSIONS OF STUDENT EXPLORIT

A network version of Student ExplorIt is available at no charge to instructors who adopt this book for their course. We strongly recommend installing the network version if students may be using this software on lab computers. The network version is available from the Instructor Companion page for this book at http://www.thomsonedu.com/politicalscience.

INSTALLING STUDENT EXPLORIT

A card has been packaged with this book. This card contains a PIN code and a website address from which you can download the Student ExplorIt software needed to complete the worksheet sections in this book. You must have this card to obtain the software. Only one person may use this card.

To install Student ExplorIt to a hard drive, you will need to follow the instructions on the card to register for access. Once you are on the download screen, follow these steps in order:

1. Select DOWNLOAD to begin downloading the software.

2. You will then be selected with a choice:

   a. Run this program from its current location. This is the recommended option, and this option will allow the installation to begin as soon as the file is downloaded to your computer.

   b. Save this program to disk. This option will allow you to save the downloaded file to your computer for later installation. This option also provides you a file that will reinstall the software in the event this is needed. If you select this option, you will then need to specify where to save the file. Be sure to select a location where you can easily find the file. This file is named STU0495007617.exe. Once the file has downloaded, locate the downloaded file and open or double-click the file name.

3. A security warning may appear next. Select [Yes].

4. The next screen will display the name of this book. Click [OK] to continue.

5. The next screen shows where the files needed for the installation will be placed. We strongly recommend you accept the default location, but if desired, you can specify a new location. Click [Unzip] to begin the install.

6. During the installation, you will be presented with several screens, as described below. In most cases you will be required to make a selection or an entry and then click [Next] to continue.

   The first screen that appears is the **License Name** screen. Here you are asked to type your name. It is important to type your name correctly, because it cannot be changed after this point. Your name will appear on all printouts, so make sure you spell it completely and correctly! Then click [Next] to continue.

   A **Welcome** screen now appears. This provides some introductory information and suggests that you shut down any other programs that may be running. Click [Next] to continue.

   You are next presented with a **Software License Agreement**. Read this screen and click [Yes] if you accept the terms of the software license.

   The next screen has you Choose the Destination for the program files. You are strongly advised to use the destination directory that is shown on the screen. Click [Next] to continue.

7. The Student ExplorIt program will now be installed. At the end of the installation, you will be asked if you would like a shortcut icon placed on the Windows desktop. We recommend that you select [Yes]. You are now informed that the installation of Student ExplorIt is finished. Click the [Finish] button and you will be returned to the opening Welcome Screen. To exit completely, click the option "Exit Welcome Screen."

STARTING STUDENT EXPLORIT

There are two ways to run Student ExplorIt: (1) from a hard drive installation or (2) from a network installation. Both methods are described below.

Starting Student ExplorIt from a Hard Drive Installation

If Student ExplorIt is installed to the hard drive of your computer (see earlier section "Installing Student ExplorIt"), locate the Student ExplorIt "shortcut" icon on the Windows desktop, which looks something like this:

To start Student ExplorIt, position your mouse pointer over the shortcut icon and double-click (that is, click it twice in rapid succession). If you did not permit the shortcut icon to be placed on the desktop during the install process (or if the icon was accidentally deleted), you can follow these directions to start the software:

Click [Start] from the Windows desktop.

Click [Programs].

Click MicroCase.

Click Student ExplorIt - CP.

After a few seconds, Student ExplorIt will appear on your screen.

Starting Student ExplorIt from a Network

If the network version of Student ExplorIt has been installed to a computer network, double-click the Student ExplorIt icon that appears on the Windows desktop to start the program. You will need to enter your name each time you start the network version. Anything you print from software will display the name you enter and the current date. (Note: Your instructor may provide additional information that is unique to your computer network.)

MAIN MENU OF STUDENT EXPLORIT

Student ExplorIt is extremely easy to use. All you do is point and click your way through the program. That is, use your mouse arrow to point at the selection you want, and then click the left button on the mouse.

The main menu is the starting point for everything you will do in Student ExplorIt. Look at how it works. Notice that not all options on the menu are always available. You will know which options are available at any given time by looking at the colors of the options. For example, when you first start the software, only the Open File option is immediately available. As you can see, the colors for this option are brighter than those for the other tasks shown on the screen. Also, when you move your mouse pointer over this option, it becomes highlighted.

EXPLORIT GUIDES

Throughout this workbook, "ExplorIt Guides" provide the basic information needed to carry out each task. Here is an example:

> ➤ *Data File:* **GLOBAL**
>   ➤ *Task:* **Mapping**
> ➤ *Variable 1:* **12) POPULATION**
>   ➤ *View:* **Map**

Each line of the ExplorIt Guide is actually an instruction. Let's follow the simple steps to carry out this task.

Step 1: Select a Data File

Before you can do anything in Student ExplorIt, you need to open a data file. To open a data file, click the Open File task. A list of data files will appear in a window (e.g., AFRICA, ASIA, EUROPE). If you click on a file name once, a description of the highlighted file is shown in the window next to this list. In the ExplorIt Guide shown above, the ➤ symbol to the left of the Data File step indicates that you should open the GLOBAL data file. To do so, click GLOBAL and then click the [Open] button (or just double-click GLOBAL). The next window that appears (labeled File Settings) provides additional information about the data file, including a file description, the number of cases in the file, and the number of variables, among other things. To continue, click the [OK] button. You are now returned to the main menu of Student ExplorIt. (You won't need to repeat this step until you want to open a different data file.) Notice that you can always see which data file is currently open by looking at the file name shown on the top line of the screen.

Step 2: Select a Task

Once you open a data file, the next step is to select a program task. Seven analysis tasks are offered in this version of Student ExplorIt. Not all tasks are available for each data file, because some tasks are appropriate only for certain kinds of data. Mapping, for example, is a task that applies only to ecological data, and thus cannot be used with survey data files.

In the ExplorIt Guide we're following, the ➤ symbol on the second line indicates that the MAPPING task should be selected, so click the Mapping option with your left mouse button.

Step 3: Select a Variable

After a task is selected, you will be shown a list of the variables in the open data file. Notice that the first variable is highlighted and a description of that variable is shown in the Variable Description window at the lower right. You can move this highlight through the list of variables by using the up and down cursor keys (as well as the <Page Up> and <Page Down> keys). You can also click once on a variable name to move the highlight and update the variable description. Go ahead—move the highlight to a few other variables and read their descriptions.

If the variable you want to select is not showing in the variable window, click on the scroll bars located on the right side of the variable list window to move through the list. See the following figure:

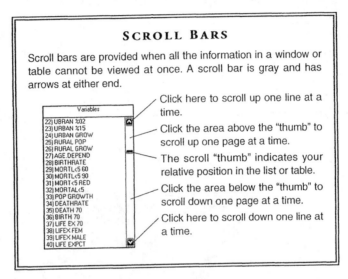

By the way, you will find an appendix at the back of this workbook that contains a list of the variable names for key data files provided in this package.

Each task requires the selection of one or more variables, and the ExplorIt Guides indicate which variables should be selected. The ExplorIt Guide example indicates that you should select 12) POPULATION as Variable 1. On the screen, there is a box labeled Variable 1. Inside this box, there is a vertical cursor that indicates this box is currently an active option. When you select a variable, it will be placed in this box. Before selecting a variable, be sure that the cursor is in the appropriate box. If it is not, place the cursor inside the appropriate box by clicking the box with your mouse. This is important because in some tasks the ExplorIt Guide will require more than one variable to be selected, and you want to be sure that you put each selected variable in the right place.

To select a variable, use any one of the methods shown below. (Note: If the name of a previously selected variable is in the box, use the <Delete> or <Backspace> key to remove it—or click the [Clear All] button.)

- Type the **number** of the variable and press <Enter>.

- Type the **name** of the variable and press <Enter>. Or you can type just enough of the name to distinguish it from other variables in the data—POPU would be sufficient for this example.

- Double-click the desired variable in the variable list window. This selection will then appear in the variable selection box. (If the name of a previously selected variable is in the box, the newly selected variable will replace it.)

- Highlight the desired variable in the variable list, and then click the arrow that appears to the left of the variable selection box. The variable you selected will now appear in the box. (If the name of a previously selected variable is in the box, the newly selected variable will replace it.)

Once you have selected your variable (or variables), click the [OK] button to continue to the final results screen.

Step 4: Select a View

The next screen that appears shows the final results of your analysis. In most cases, the screen that first appears matches the "view" indicated in the ExplorIt Guide. In this example, you are instructed to look at the Map view—that's what is currently showing on the screen. In some instances, however, you may need to make an additional selection to produce the desired screen.

POPULATION – Total population in thousands. (UNPD, 2005)

(OPTIONAL) Step 5: Select an Additional Display

Some ExplorIt Guides will indicate that an additional "Display" should be selected. In that case, simply click on the option indicated for that additional display. For example, this ExplorIt Guide may have included an additional line that required you to select the Legend display.

Step 6: Continuing to the Next ExplorIt Guide

Some instructions in the ExplorIt Guide may be the same for at least two examples in a row. For instance, after you display the map for population in the example above, the following ExplorIt Guide may be given:

> Data File: **GLOBAL**
> Task: **Mapping**
> ➤ Variable 1: **62) CAP PUN 06**
> ➤ View: **Map**

Comparative Politics

Notice that the first two lines in the ExplorIt Guide do not have the ➤ symbol located in front of the items. That's because you already have the data file GLOBAL open and you have already selected the MAPPING task. With the results of your first analysis showing on the screen, there is no need to return to the main menu to complete this next analysis. Instead, all you need to do is select CAP PUN 06 as your new variable. Click the [[⟳]] button located in the top left corner of your screen and the variable selection screen for the MAPPING task appears again. Replace the variable with 62) CAP PUN 06 and click [OK].

To repeat: You need to do only those items in the ExplorIt Guide that have the ➤ symbol in front of them. If you start from the top of the ExplorIt Guide, you're simply wasting your time.

If the ExplorIt Guide instructs you to select an entirely new task or data file, you will need to return to the main menu. To return to the main menu, simply click the [Menu] button located at the top left corner of the screen. At this point, select the new data file and/or task that is indicated in the ExplorIt Guide.

That's all there is to the basic operation of Student ExplorIt. Just follow the instructions given in the ExplorIt Guide and point and click your way through the program.

ADDITIONAL SHORTCUTS

There are some additional ways to navigate through the software that you may find helpful.

- If you are frequently switching between 2–4 data files, you can quickly change files from any screen by clicking [File] on the drop-down menu. The last four files opened will appear at the bottom of the drop-down list. You can select the desired file from this list, the file will open automatically, and you will be returned to the main menu to select the desired task.

- Again, by clicking [File] on the drop-down menu, you can select [Open] to open any data file from any screen. When you open a new file, you will automatically return to the main menu.

- To switch to a different statistical task, instead of returning to the main menu, select [Statistics] from the drop-down menu and select the desired task. NOTE: If you select a task that is not enabled on the main menu, a message box will open alerting you that this task is not available.

- You can open a list of variables in the open file at any time by pressing the <F3> key.

ONLINE HELP

Student ExplorIt offers extensive online help. You can obtain task-specific help by pressing <F1> at any point in the program. For example, if you are performing a scatterplot analysis, you can press <F1> to see the help for the SCATTERPLOT task.

If you prefer to browse through a list of the available help topics, select Help from the pull-down menu at the top of the screen and select the **Help Topics** option. At this point, you will be provided a list of topic areas. A closed-book icon represents each topic. To see what information is available in a given topic area, double-click on a book to "open" it. (For this version of the software, use only the "Student ExplorIt" section of help; do not use the "Student MicroCase" section.) When you double-click on a book graphic, a list of help topics is shown. A help topic is represented by a graphic with a piece of paper with a question mark on it. Double-click on a help topic to view it.

If you have questions about Student ExplorIt, try the online help described above. If you are not familiar with software or computers, you may want to ask a classmate or your instructor for assistance.

EXITING FROM STUDENT EXPLORIT

If you are continuing to the next section of this workbook, it is not necessary to exit from Student ExplorIt quite yet. But when you are finished using the program, it is very important that you properly exit the software—do not just walk away from the computer. To exit Student ExplorIt, return to the main menu and select the [Exit Program] button that appears on the screen.

World Map

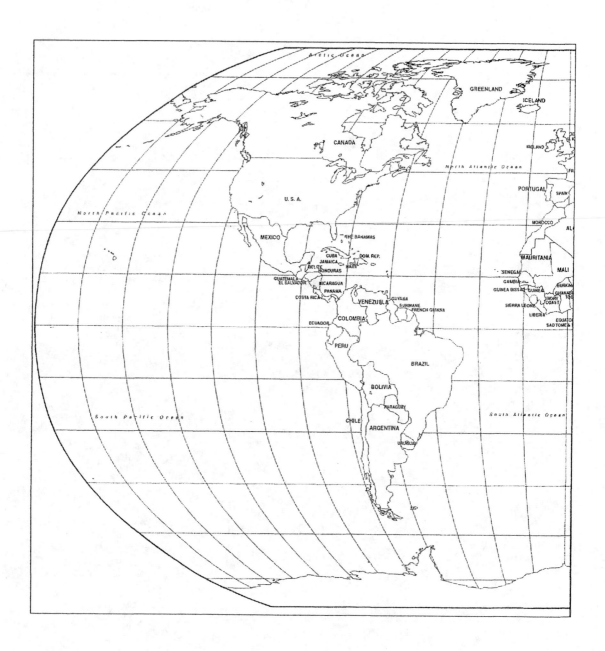

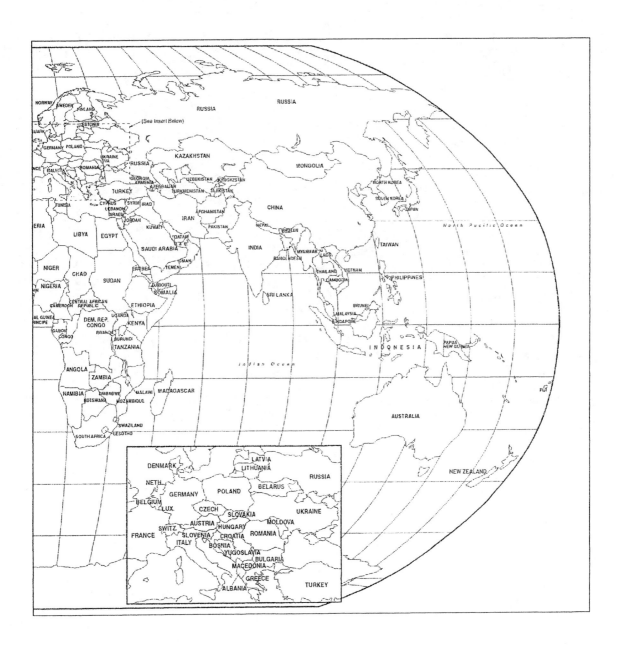

Part I

DOING COMPARATIVE POLITICS WITH EXPLORIT

CHAPTER 1

THE NATION-STATE

Without a country, I am not a man.

NAWAF AL-NASIR AL-SABAH
KUWAITI DEFENSE MINISTER, 1990

Tasks: Mapping, Univariate, Historical Trends
Data Files: GLOBAL, PGAP02-NIGERIA, WVS02–NIGERIA, HISTORY, WVS02–MEXICO, WVS02–USA

One of the great challenges associated with learning comparative politics in the post–Cold War era is the task of making some kind of order from the apparent chaos of the world in which we live. Each of the world's more than 190 countries has its own distinct political, social, and economic systems. You may have traveled abroad and done comparisons of your own. Someday you may be sent to a country you have never heard of to close a business deal or to keep the peace. You might meet an immigrant from a country different from your own or send a check to stop deforestation in a tropical country. You will be better equipped to do any of these things if you know more about our world.

The objective of comparative politics is to explain similarities and differences among nation-states. But good exploration usually begins with curiosity. For example, curious people will want to know why capital punishment (the death penalty) is used so frequently in Asia and Africa and so rarely in Europe. In a standard textbook, a statement like this might be accompanied by instructions that direct you to look at a table listing various countries according to their laws on capital punishment. In fact, as you will soon see, graphics of this type appear throughout this workbook. But the difference between this workbook and an ordinary textbook is that you can *explore* the original data yourself—not just read about what other researchers have found.

As shown in the "Getting Started" section (if you haven't yet gone through that section, do so now), the software provided with this workbook contains numerous data sets. Many of the data sets have *variables* that can be mapped. For example, if we want to check the status of nuclear weapons development in the countries of Asia, we can use the ASIA data file to view a map showing the countries having the most (and least) developed nuclear weapons programs. If we want to look at economic growth across the countries of Africa, we can open the AFRICA file and map a variable that shows this too. To look at the number of political parties in each European country, we would select the appropriate variable from the EUROPE file, and so on. We will examine hundreds of these types of analyses throughout this workbook. To begin, we'll return to the topic of capital punishment. Using the GLOBAL data file, look at the variation in capital punishment across the world.

> ➤ *Data File:* **GLOBAL**
> ➤ *Task:* **Mapping**
> ➤ *Variable 1:* **62) CAP PUN 06**
> ➤ *View:* **Map**

To reproduce this graphic on the computer screen using ExplorIt, review the instructions in the "Getting Started" section. For this example, open the GLOBAL data file, select the MAPPING task, and select 62) CAP PUN 06 for Variable 1. The first view shown is the Map view. (Remember, the ➤ symbol indicates which steps you need to perform if you are doing all the examples as you follow along in the text. So, in the next example below, you only need to select a new view—that is, you don't need to repeat the first three steps because they were already done in this example.)

The nations in this map of the world appear in several colors from very dark to very light. The darker a country is, the more prevalent its use of capital punishment. The lighter a country is, the less likely it is to use capital punishment. Let's see what the different colors actually mean.

> *Data File:* **GLOBAL**
> *Task:* **Mapping**
> *Variable 1:* **62) CAP PUN 06**
> *View:* **Map**
> ➤ *Display:* **Legend**

As indicated by the ➤ symbol, if you are continuing from the previous example, select the [Legend] button. (It is not necessary to reselect the MAPPING task and 62) CAP PUN 06 variable.) Sometimes, as in this case, the description for a map is too long for it to fit on the screen with the map. If you want to see the complete description for a map, click on the [˅] button. A window will appear that gives you the complete description for the map.

Now you will see that the lightest colors actually mean that capital punishment has been abolished in those countries. The legend also indicates that 70 of the 172 countries in our GLOBAL file have abolished capital punishment for all crimes. The second category, colored orange, indicates that capital punishment has been abolished for all crimes except those that are treasonable or those committed during wartime. The third category, in red, indicates that the death penalty still exists in these countries but has not been used recently. The fourth category, the darkest color, indicates those countries that retain capital punishment and still use it. Sixty-nine of the 172 countries in the GLOBAL file are in this last category. Finally, you will notice that the label for the yellow box at the top of the legend is missing. The label is missing because the variable being examined has only four categories. If there were five categories, all five colors would have a label.

But what percentage of all nations has abolished the death penalty? The map legend gives you the *number* of countries that have abolished the death penalty (70), but not the proportion or percentage. If we want to find this out, we will need to approach it another way.

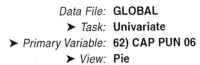

Data File: **GLOBAL**
➤ Task: **Univariate**
➤ Primary Variable: **62) CAP PUN 06**
➤ View: **Pie**

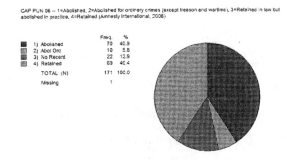

CAP PUN 06 -- 1=Abolished, 2=Abolished for ordinary crimes (except treason and wartime), 3=Retained in law but abolished in practice, 4=Retained (Amnesty International, 2006)

	Freq.	%
1) Abolished	70	40.9
2) Abol Ord	10	5.8
3) No Recent	22	12.9
4) Retained	69	40.4
TOTAL (N)	171	100.0
Missing	1	

To reproduce this new view on your screen, you will need to click the [Menu] button at the top of the screen. Then click the UNIVARIATE task, select the 62) CAP PUN 06 variable, and click [OK]. (It is not necessary to reselect the GLOBAL file.)

You should now see a pie chart on your screen that indicates the legal status of the death penalty in 172 nations around the world. However, this view also calculates the percentage of countries that have abolished the death penalty (40.9%), the percentage of countries that permit the death penalty in exceptional cases (5.8%), the percentage of countries that allow the death penalty under law, but have not used it in more than ten years (12.9%), and finally, the percentage of countries that still use the death penalty (40.4%). Like the map, you will also notice that the description above the pie chart explains the variable and each category in more detail. The description also tells you where the data come from. In this case, these data come from Amnesty International's 2006 website report. More detailed information on the source of the variable is always available in the bibliography of sources for all data in the back of this workbook.

NATION-STATES

So far we have referred to countries as nations, but this term is not quite accurate for our purposes. The term *nation* is used to describe a specific ethnic group. In the United States or Canada, this use of the term is often misunderstood because in these nations there is not one dominant ethnic group. However, you may have heard someone ask you what your *nationality* is. When this question is asked in the United States or Canada, it is very likely that people reflect on the origins of their family prior to coming to North America. Perhaps they came from Ireland, Japan, or Italy, in which case one explains that his or her *nationality* is Irish, Japanese, or Italian even though the person is clearly a U.S. or Canadian citizen. If one's nationality refers to an ethnic identity, a state refers to all of the institutions of government that have sovereignty over a group of people whether they constitute a nation or not. *Nation-states*—that is, people of a particular *nationality* (or *nationalities*) governed by an autonomous state—are one of the key units we study in comparative politics.

The notion of a nation-state did not come into being until the 1648 Treaty of Westphalia, which recognized the legitimacy of the nation-state as the fundamental entity in international relations. This concept is not without its problems. One problem is that states rarely govern single ethnic groups, or nationalities.

Data File: **GLOBAL**
➤ Task: **Mapping**
➤ Variable 1: **461) MULTI-CULT**
➤ View: **Map**

MULTI-CULT -- MULTI-CULTURALISM:ODDS THAT ANY 2 PERSONS WILL DIFFER IN
THEIR RACE, RELIGION, ETHNICITY (TRIBE),OR LANGUAGE GROUP (STARK)

If you are continuing from the previous example, click [Menu], and then select the MAPPING task. Select 461) MULTI-CULT as the new Variable 1. (Again, it is not necessary to reselect the GLOBAL file.)

This map indicates the chances out of 100 that two citizens in a nation-state will be of a different race, religion, ethnicity, or language group. The darker a nation-state, the greater the chance that a person in the nation has a chance of meeting someone of a different cultural background.

Data File: **GLOBAL**
Task: **Mapping**
Variable 1: **461) MULTI-CULT**
➤ View: **List: Rank**

MULTI-CULT: Multi-culturalism: Odds that any 2 persons will differ in their race, religion, ethnicity (tribe), or language group

RANK	CASE NAME	VALUE
1	India	91
1	Congo, Dem. Republic	91
3	Bolivia	90
4	Uganda	89
4	Cameroon	89
6	Nigeria	88
7	South Africa	87
8	Côte d'Ivoire	86
9	Bhutan	85
9	Congo, Republic	85

If you are continuing from the previous example, simply select the [List: Rank] option. The number of rows shown on your screen may be different from that shown here. Use the cursor keys and scroll bar to move through this list if necessary.

You will notice that in a nation-state like India, one's chances of meeting someone of a different cultural background are 91 out of 100. If you scroll to the bottom of the list, you will see that in Japan one's chances of encountering someone of a different cultural background are 1 in 100. But even Japan, one of the most ethnically homogeneous countries in the world, still has within it minority ethnic groups who are not Japanese.

The definition of a nation-state itself (people governed by an independent government) implies that nation-states are fairly autonomous in terms of economics, politics, and culture. But in fact, nation-states are affected by factors outside their borders, such as environmental pollution and changes in the international economy. States' autonomy is also constrained by domestic particularities unique to each country, such as political conflict between ethnic groups or geographic isolation. For example, in Canada the autonomy of the state is constrained by ethnic political rivalry between French-speaking Canadians, English-speaking Canadians, and indigenous Canadians. This makes it very difficult for the nation-state to act in any particular way without considering the demands of the different peoples and their interests.

Nigeria is another example of a nation-state that is characterized by strong divisions between its "many nations." A 2002 survey asked Nigerians to describe their national identity. What ethnic group or nationality is descriptive of each citizen? To see what the people of Nigeria had to say, we can look at the results of the Nigerian Global Attitudes Survey.

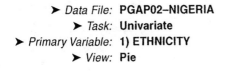

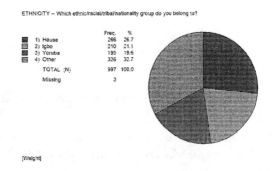

ETHNICITY – Which ethnic/racial/tribal/nationality group do you belong to?

	Freq.	%
1) Hausa	266	26.7
2) Igbo	210	21.1
3) Yoruba	195	19.6
4) Other	326	32.7
TOTAL (N)	997	100.0
Missing	3	

[Weight]

> *Data File:* **PGAP02–NIGERIA**
> *Task:* **Univariate**
> *Primary Variable:* **1) ETHNICITY**
> *View:* **Pie**

If you are continuing from the previous example, you will need to select a new data file. Simply click [Open File] and open the file titled PGAP02–NIGERIA. Now click the UNIVARIATE task and select 1) ETHNICITY as the primary variable.

You will quickly notice that 26.7% of the citizens surveyed indicate that they see themselves as Hausa, Igbo (21.1%), Yoruba (19.6%), or the member of another ethnic group (32.7%). The nation-state of Nigeria is a nation-state composed of many "nations."

POLITICAL INDEPENDENCE

Political independence in the modern era represents the "coming of age" of a nation-state. For a very small number of countries (e.g., the United Kingdom, Russia, France, Spain, and Portugal), this coming of age occurred gradually as kings sought to consolidate their hold over peoples and territories in geographic proximity to their centers of power. Since the Treaty of Westphalia, national groups dominated by other nation-states have endeavored to form their own states in an effort to achieve national independence. This trend has accelerated from the 19th century to the present such that new nationalities seeking their own state seem to be discovered by the media almost every year. Be they Québecois, Kurdish, Hutu, Chechnyan, or Pashtun, these nationalities believe that statehood guarantees them a degree of security that they should not be without. To help you better understand the history of the nation-state, the section that follows will explore comparatively the patterns of political independence worldwide.

➤ *Data File:* **GLOBAL**
➤ *Task:* **Mapping**
➤ *Variable 1:* **455) IND DATE**
➤ *View:* **Map**
➤ *Display:* **Legend**

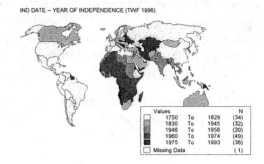

If you are continuing from the previous example, return to the variable selection screen. Select 455) IND DATE as the new Variable 1. When the map appears, click [Legend].

As you can see, the countries shown in darker colors have become independent relatively recently. The most recent countries are in Central Asia and Eastern Europe. The next most recent group is in Africa. Let's use the rank option to see which nation-states achieved independence most recently.

Data File: **GLOBAL**
Task: **Mapping**
Variable 1: **455) IND DATE**
➤ *View:* **List: Rank**

IND DATE: Year of independence

RANK	CASE NAME	VALUE
1	Eritrea	1993
1	Slovak Republic	1993
1	Czech Republic	1993
4	Bosnia and Herzegovina	1992
4	Yugoslavia (Serbia/Montenegro)	1992
6	Lithuania	1991
6	Latvia	1991
6	Belarus	1991
6	Estonia	1991
6	Kyrgyzstan	1991

Eritrea, the Slovak Republic, and the Czech Republic all became independent in 1993. Scrolling down the list to the nation-states with the longest standing independence, we see that European countries like Russia, Spain, and France were independent by 1750, as were Asian countries such as Japan, China, and Thailand. The GLOBAL data set contains a second version of this variable in which the dates of independence for nation-states are grouped into historically relevant time periods. This map has the additional advantage of showing a clearer regional pattern to independence, particularly in South and East Asia.

Data File: **GLOBAL**
Task: **Mapping**
➤ *Variable 1:* **456) IND PERIOD**
➤ *View:* **Map**
➤ *Display:* **Legend**

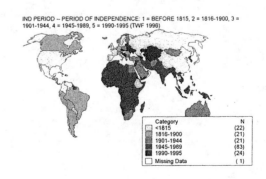

When the mapping function displays countries by the "period" of their independence, we can see the regional patterns of independence that emerge for the individual nation-states. It makes sense to view the map in terms of periods rather than dates because the historical events that occur in different periods mark the rise and fall of the empires that gave birth to the new nations. You will notice that many countries of Western and Northern Europe, the United States, and parts of South and East Asia achieved independence or had a tradition of independence before 1815. Many of the powerful countries that were independent before 1815 had set up *colonies* throughout much of the world. A *colony* is a settlement of foreigners established and protected in a territory by the foreigners' government. The first colonizers were Portugal and Spain, which began their colonial expansion and conquest around 1450. They were followed in the 17th and 18th centuries by Britain, France, and Russia. In the 19th century, Holland, Germany, Italy, and Belgium sought the territories that were left. By 1900 every region of the world was colonized. Only a few countries in Asia (Afghanistan, China, Japan, Nepal, and Thailand) escaped colonial domination.

As you examine the map and its accompanying legend, you will probably notice that the first wave of independence after 1815 occurred in South and Central America. The Spanish and Portuguese empires collapsed in the early part of the 19th century, which precipitated a wave of independence movements throughout the former colonies of Latin America. By the beginning of the 20th century, there were more than 40 independent nation-states worldwide. Around 1920 a few states in the Middle East began agitating their colonial powers to obtain independence. However, the wave of independence between 1900 and 1945 is not significant. Only 21 nation-states achieved independence during this period, and many of these acquired independence as a result of changes in the European map and Axis colonial holdings at the end of World War I.

From an examination of your map, you will notice that independence expanded at a very rapid pace at the end of World War II in 1945. Political independence since then has occurred in two distinct phases. The first phase began in 1947 as Britain and France started to recognize that they were incapable of carrying the financial burden of their colonial holdings. In addition to these peaceful withdrawals, colonial rebellion characterized independence movements between 1947 and 1975 as the number of nation-states worldwide nearly doubled during this period. The second phase of independence began in 1989 as the Soviet Union collapsed. All of the former republics of the vast Soviet empire were given their political independence. The 20th century was indeed the age of the nation-state. In 1900 there were fewer than 50 independent nation-states. At the beginning of the 21st century there are more than 190 independent nation-states, an increase of more than 400% during a single century! Our examination of the map helps us to see that there is clearly a regional pattern to independence that is strongly related to the decline of European colonial empires (Spain, Portugal, Great Britain, Germany, France, and the Soviet Union). The same general pattern can be seen historically.

➤ *Data File:* **HISTORY**
  ➤ *Task:* **Historical Trends**
➤ *Variables:* **2) IND NATION**

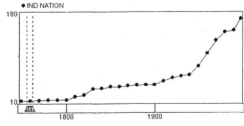

Number of independent nation-states, 1750–1998

The ➤ symbol on the Data File line indicates that you must return to the main menu and open a new data file. Now select the HISTORICAL TRENDS task and choose the variable 2) IND NATION.

As you can see, the number of countries that became independent between 1945 and 1985 more than doubled the total number of nation-states in the world. You can associate the increase in the number of independent nations with significant world events by clicking on a period that interests you or by scrolling through the world events at the bottom of your screen. Scroll up to World War II and click on it. World War II lasted for six years, so the red lines on the graph indicate the range of years in which the event occurs. You will notice that the number of independent countries increased significantly in the years following WWII. Below is a slightly different graphical representation of the same data. This variable shows the number of countries that became independent in each decade since 1750.

<table>
<tr><td align="right">Data File:</td><td>HISTORY</td></tr>
<tr><td align="right">Task:</td><td>Historical Trends</td></tr>
<tr><td align="right">➤ Variables:</td><td>3) IND/DECADE</td></tr>
</table>

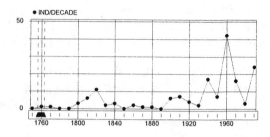

Number of countries that achieved independence in each decade

Be sure to delete the previously selected variable before selecting 3) IND/DECADE. The easiest way to do this is to click the [Clear All] button.

This graphical representation of the number of countries becoming independent in each decade helps us to see historical patterns more clearly. The last jump in the number of independent countries comes since 1989. Click on the year 1990. Notice that the scroll bar changes to display a series of events occurring in the early 1990s. It also displays a series of events that were critical during the end of the Cold War. If you scroll to 1991, you will see that the resignation of Mikhail Gorbachev and the collapse of the USSR correspond to another increase in the number of independent nations.

Now let's see how the distinct patterns of nation-state independence might be related to other phenomena. Most people are aware that some nation-states have a great deal more wealth than others. What causes such variation? Could the time at which a nation-state attains independence be a significant factor in determining its national wealth? Let's return to the GLOBAL data file and the MAPPING task to find out.

<table>
<tr><td align="right">➤ Data File:</td><td>GLOBAL</td></tr>
<tr><td align="right">➤ Task:</td><td>Mapping</td></tr>
<tr><td align="right">➤ Variable 1:</td><td>135) GDP</td></tr>
<tr><td align="right">➤ View:</td><td>Map</td></tr>
<tr><td align="right">➤ Display:</td><td>Legend</td></tr>
</table>

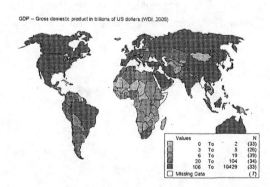

Now you can examine nation-states from the highest to the lowest gross domestic product from 2005, which is the total domestic economic output for a nation-state. But from this map it is hard to tell

which countries have the highest levels of wealth. We can visualize the magnitude of a nation-state's wealth more clearly by selecting the [Spot Fill] option.

Data File: **GLOBAL**
Task: **Mapping**
Variable 1: **135) GDP**
View: **Map**
➤ Display: **Legend**
Spot

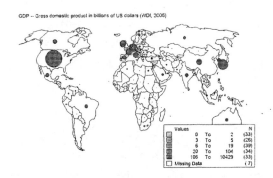

If you are continuing from the previous example, select the [Spot Fill] display option.

The size of each spot is proportional to the value of each state on the variable being mapped. Thus the United States, Japan, and several countries in Europe have the largest spots. The color keys remain as they were when the whole country was colored in, but the small spots are difficult to see because the level of GDP in the wealthiest countries is so much larger than it is in the poorer countries.

One problem with using GDP is that it is closely linked to the population of a country. You can see this by ranking the nations by GDP.

GDP: Gross domestic product in billions of U.S. dollars

Data File: **GLOBAL**
Task: **Mapping**
Variable 1: **135) GDP**
➤ View: **List: Rank**

RANK	CASE NAME	VALUE
1	United States	10429
2	Japan	3972
3	Germany	1986
4	United Kingdom	1564
5	France	1437
6	China	1271
7	Italy	1186
8	Canada	725
9	Spain	655
10	Mexico	648

You will notice that China, which has the largest population in the world (1.3 billion), has the sixth largest GDP in the world. If you scroll down the ranking, you will also see that the country of Luxembourg has a GDP ranking of 64 out of 161 nations. Analysis of gross domestic product alone indicates that China may be wealthier than Luxembourg, but this interpretation is misleading. A better measure of national wealth is GDP per capita.

GDPCAP PPP: Gross domestic product per capita

Data File: **GLOBAL**
Task: **Mapping**
➤ Variable 1: **133) GDPCAP PPP**
➤ View: **List: Rank**

RANK	CASE NAME	VALUE
1	Luxembourg	57741
2	Norway	35734
3	Ireland	35352
4	United States	34557
5	Denmark	29730
6	Switzerland	29205
7	Canada	28728
8	Iceland	28566
9	Austria	28223
10	Netherlands	27932

We use per capita (or "per person") figures instead of the actual GDP because this measure adjusts for nations having large or small populations. In this instance you will see that Luxembourg's GDP per capita is $57,741 (in U.S. dollars), which ranks it 1st among all nation-states. China is an example of the other extreme. China's GDP per capita of $4,379 (again, in U.S. dollars) puts it at 82nd in the ranked list. Because we are more interested in the average amount of economic output a person generates within a nation-state, the GDP per capita figure is the better measure for our purposes.

If you want to see where a particular country stands in terms of its ranking on GDP per capita, you can identify it by selecting the [Find Case] option that appears on the mapping screen. An alphabetical list of all countries will appear, and you can select the country you're interested in. Select the box next to Canada and click [OK]. The map now highlights the country you selected (Canada) and shows its value and rank on the variable at the bottom of the screen. If you know the location of the country you're interested in, you can also click on the country. For example, click on the United States and you will see its value and rank on the GDP per capita variable.

ExplorIt's MAPPING task allows you to examine two maps at once. This is extremely useful if you are trying to determine if regional patterns for one variable are similar to regional patterns of another variable. Let's continue to use GDPCAP PPP as Variable 1, but add IND DATE as our second variable.

Data File: **GLOBAL**
Task: **Mapping**
Variable 1: **133) GDPCAP PPP**
➤ Variable 2: **455) IND DATE**
➤ Views: **Map**
➤ Display: **Legend**

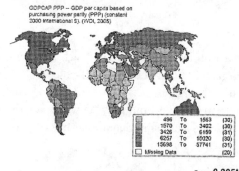

GDPCAP PPP -- GDP per capita based on purchasing power parity (PPP) (constant 2000 International $). (WDI, 2005)

496	To	1563	(30)
1570	To	3402	(30)
3426	To	6169	(31)
6257	To	16020	(30)
15698	To	57741	(31)
Missing Data			(20)

r = −0.385**

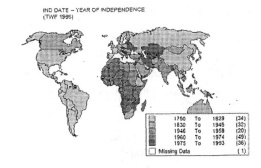

IND DATE – YEAR OF INDEPENDENCE
(TWF 1995)

1750	To	1829	(34)
1830	To	1945	(32)
1946	To	1959	(20)
1960	To	1974	(49)
1975	To	1993	(36)
Missing Data			(1)

If you are continuing from the previous example, return to the variable selection screen. Select 455) IND DATE for Variable 2.

We saw the lower map showing independence dates earlier. As you'll recall, the darker countries in the IND DATE map are those that achieved independence most recently; the lighter countries have been independent the longest. Now, compare the top map (GDP per capita) to the independence date map. Although the pattern is not perfect, the maps are almost mirror opposites of one another. Start by comparing North America on both maps. Notice how on the top map it is dark and on the bottom map it is light. Then move to South America, and notice that these nations are darkly colored in the GDPCAP PPP map and lightly colored in the IND DATE map. If you make the same comparisons for Europe, Asia, and Africa, the same general pattern of opposition continues from region to region. That means the more established a country is, the more likely it is to have generated significant wealth per capita. Conversely, countries that have been independent a shorter period of time have less wealth per capita. Indeed, there appears to be a relationship between the year a country became independent and the relative degree of wealth a country has.

You can also use the [List: Rank] option to show the distributions for both of these variables.

Data File: **GLOBAL**
Task: **Mapping**
Variable 1: **133) GDPCAP PPP**
Variable 2: **455) IND DATE**
➤ Views: **List: Rank**

GDPCAP PPP: Gross domestic product per capita

RANK	CASE NAME	VALUE
1	Luxembourg	57741
2	Norway	35734
3	Ireland	35352
4	United States	34557
5	Denmark	29730

IND DATE: Year of independence

RANK	CASE NAME	VALUE
1	Eritrea	1993
1	Slovak Republic	1993
1	Czech Republic	1993
4	Bosnia and Herzegovina	1992
4	Yugoslavia (Serbia/Montenegro)	1992

If you do some tallying for the 172 countries in our GLOBAL file, you'll see that 13 of the 20 countries ranked highest on GDP per capita were independent nation-states before 1900. Nineteen of the top 20 were independent by the early 1940s. Looking at the bottom of the GDP per capita list, the opposite trend is clearly visible. Of the 20 countries ranked lowest in terms of GDP per capita, 19 obtained their independence since 1960.

Sometimes people who are trying to understand the underlying reasons for social problems in certain countries, such as overpopulation, child poverty, or unemployment, may wish to compare variables to understand these problems better. In addition to national wealth, we can compare the map of national independence with other social factors, such as the fertility rate, across nations.

    Data File: **GLOBAL**
        Task: **Mapping**
➤ *Variable 1:* **456) IND PERIOD**
➤ *Variable 2:* **44) FERTILITY**
  ➤ *Views:* **Map**
➤ *Display:* **Legend**

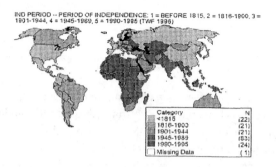

IND PERIOD -- PERIOD OF INDEPENDENCE: 1 = BEFORE 1815, 2 = 1816-1900, 3 = 1901-1944, 4 = 1945-1989, 5 = 1990-1995 (TWF 1996)

Category	N
<1815	(22)
1816-1900	(21)
1901-1944	(21)
1945-1989	(83)
1990-1995	(24)
Missing Data	(1)

r = 0.190**

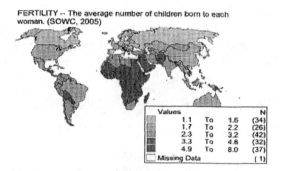

FERTILITY -- The average number of children born to each woman. (SOWC, 2005)

Values			N
1.1	To	1.6	(34)
1.7	To	2.2	(26)
2.3	To	3.2	(42)
3.3	To	4.8	(32)
4.9	To	8.0	(37)
Missing Data			(1)

Once again, the darkest countries in the top map are the nation-states that have become independent most recently. The second map shows the average number of children born per woman in her lifetime for each country. Look at Africa on each map. Notice that on both maps Africa is mostly shaded with the two darkest shades of color on the legend. Now look at North America and Europe on each map. With some exceptions in Europe, where former communist nation-states achieved recent independence from the Soviet Union, European and North American nations are generally shaded more lightly on both maps. These maps are similar, which indicates that younger countries tend to have much higher rates of fertility than older countries.

The modern nation-state has clearly matured in the 20th century. Our examination of patterns of independence revealed that nation-states have proliferated at an accelerating pace since 1900. We have also witnessed that the year a country became independent may have a lot to do with its national characteristics such as wealth and fertility.

Before you start on the worksheet section that follows, I'd like to show you another feature in ExplorIt that you will find very useful. Return to the variable selection screen for the MAPPING task and click the [Search] button. If you want to find a variable in the data set but don't know its number or location (or even if such a variable exists), this option lets you search variable names and descriptions for key words. Type in the word REGION and click [OK]. An abbreviated list of variables is now shown, and each variable having the word REGION in either its variable name or description is listed. It is obvious why the variables 463) REGION and 464) REGION2 were found in this search, but it is not immediately clear why the variable 458) WAR is listed. Click once on the variable WAR and examine the variable description in the window at the lower right. Sure enough, a variant of the word "region" ("regional") appears in the variable description. If you wanted to conduct another search, you would click on the [Full List] button to return to the full list of variables. But instead, select the variable REGION and click [OK] to view the map. (Remember to clear all of your previously selected variables.) Then click the [Legend] option.

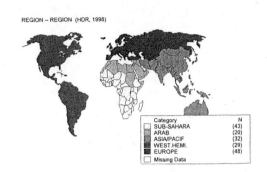

Data File: **GLOBAL**
Task: **Mapping**
➤ Variable 1: **463) REGION**
➤ Views: **Map**
➤ Display: **Legend**

This map shows the regions of the world broken down into five categories: sub-Saharan Africa, Arab nation-states, Asia/Pacific, the Western Hemisphere, and Europe. There are many different ways to classify the regions of the world, but we will often use this particular grouping to keep things simple. Likewise, if you encounter a question in the workbook that requires you to refer to a particular region of the world, you can use this region variable for guidance.

Speaking of workbook questions, you are now ready for the first worksheet section in this book.

Terms and Concepts

Nation-state
Capital punishment
Nation
Multiculturalism
Political independence
Gross domestic product
Gross domestic product per capita
Fertility

NAME: Ramona Khan

COURSE:

DATE:

If you have not already done so, review the instructions in the "Getting Started" section.

REVIEW QUESTIONS

Based on the first part of this chapter, answer True or False to the following items:

1. A nation-state is a term used to describe a specific ethnic group. T F

2. A nation-state with a multicultural rating of 2 is very homogeneous. T F

3. For the most part, nation-states in Central Asia and Eastern Europe are relatively recent independent states. T F

4. Compared to other nation-states, the United States is a fairly new independent state. T F

5. Japan, China, and Thailand were colonies until the late 1800s, at which time they obtained their independence. T F

6. The number of nation-states more than doubled in the last half of the 20th century. T F

7. For our purposes, the GDP *per capita* is a better measure than the actual GDP because it adjusts for variations in national population. T F

8. A key advantage of ExplorIt's MAPPING task is that you can see how political boundaries were formed by natural terrain, such as mountains and rivers. T F

9. According to the preliminary section of this chapter, nation-states that have early dates of independence generally tend to be _____ than nation-states with later dates of independence. (circle one of the following)

   a. larger
   b. wealthier
   c. poorer
   d. more ethnically diverse

Chapter 1: The Nation-State

10. According to the preliminary section, nation-states that have early dates of independence generally have lower rates of _____ than nation-states with later dates of independence. (circle one of the following)

   a. crime

   b. diversity

   c. war

   (d.) fertility

EXPLORIT QUESTIONS

> You will need to use the ExplorIt software for the following questions. Make sure you have already gone through the "Getting Started" section that is located prior to the first chapter. If you have any difficulties using the software to obtain the appropriate informa- tion, or if you want to learn about additional features of ExplorIt's MAPPING task, refer to the online help topics on MAPPING under the Help menu.

I. Earlier in this chapter we looked at the relationship between a country's date of independence and its GDP per capita and fertility rate. Let's pursue this analysis to see if the independence date of a coun- try is related to other important social factors. We might theorize that the longer a nation-state has been an independent and sovereign entity, the more likely it is able to pursue the benefits of a good society (i.e., higher levels of education, health, and wealth). A statement such as this is known as a hypothesis. A hypothesis is a statement of probability. It does not seek to determine whether some- thing is "true" or "false" but, rather, whether a relationship is likely to exist based on the evidence. In the first few analyses below, we will study the relationship between the length of time a nation-state has been independent and other social factors that might evidence a good society. Variable 339) EDUC INDEX combines a country's literacy rate and school enrollment rate to come up with an index between 0 and 1.00 for the level of education in a country. A number like .15 (Niger) would mean that there is a relatively low level of education in a nation-state while a number like .99 (New Zealand) means that there is relatively high education.

> ➤ Data File: **GLOBAL**
> ➤ Task: **Mapping**
> ➤ Variable 1: **339) EDUC INDEX**
> ➤ Variable 2: **455) IND DATE**
> ➤ View: **Map**

11. Compare the continent of Africa in both maps. Are the majority of countries on the maps of Africa similar, opposite, or neither? [By opposite, we mean that countries that are light on one map appear in a darker color on the other map, and vice versa.] (circle one)

   a. Similar

   (b.) Opposite

   c. Neither

12. Which of the following is the best interpretation of the education/independence maps of Africa? (circle one)

     a. The countries of Africa tend to have early independence dates and higher levels of education.

     b. The countries of Africa tend to have early independence dates and lower levels of education.

     (c.) The countries of Africa tend to have more recent independence dates and lower levels of education.

II. In the first column below, list the top five nation-states in terms of the education index. In the second column, indicate the year in which each country became independent. (Hint: Use the [List: Alpha] option for the bottom map to list the countries in alphabetical order.)

EDUCATION INDEX	INDEPENDENCE DATE
New Zealand	~~12~~ 1907
Finland	1917
United kingdom	1801
Australia	1901
Netherlands	1750

Now list the lowest ranked nation-states in terms of the education index. Also list their independence date. (Exclude nation-states that don't have any data listed for them.)

EDUCATION INDEX	INDEPENDENCE DATE
Niger	1960
Sierra Leone	1961
Burkina Faso	1960
Guinea	1958
Ethiopia	1750

13. Which of the following statements most closely resembles the patterns that you have examined above?

    a. Nation-states with earlier independence dates tend to have lower education index ratings.

    b. Nation-states with later independence dates tend to have lower education index ratings.

    c. Nation-states with earlier independence dates tend to have higher education index ratings.

    d. Nation-states with later independence dates tend to have higher education index ratings.

    e. Both b and c are correct.

III. The variable 127) HUMAN DEV02 is a composite measure of the level of human development for a nation. It combines GDP per capita, educational attainment, and life expectancy, and it ranges from .27 (low) to .960 (high).

14. Based on our earlier findings, do you predict that nations that achieved early independence will be ranked low or high on this measure?

    a. Low

    b. High

Let's test your prediction.

> Data File: **GLOBAL**
> Task: **Mapping**
> ➤ Variable 1: **127) HUMAN DEV02**
> ➤ Variable 2: **455) IND DATE**
> ➤ View: **Map**

15. One region at a time, take a look at North America, South America, Western Europe, and Africa. Comparing region to region, do these maps look similar, opposite, or neither? (circle one)

    a. Similar

    b. Opposite

    c. Neither

16. Which of the following statements is the best interpretation of the human development/independence maps?

    a. Countries that tend to have early independence dates also have higher levels of human development.

    b. Countries that tend to have later independence dates also have lower levels of human development.

    c. Countries that tend to have later independence dates also have higher levels of human development.

    d. Both a and b are true.

17. In terms of human development, how many of the ten highest ranked nation-states obtained independence prior to the end of World War II (1945)? _____

18. In terms of human development, how many of the ten lowest ranked nation-states
    obtained independence after the end of World War II?   _____

IV. A basic goal of a nation-state is to ensure that there is sufficient food for its people. Use ExplorIt's
    search function to locate a variable that measures the daily available calories that are available to
    members of a society.

   19. Which variable did you select?   _____

   20. Based on our earlier findings, do you predict that nations that achieved
       early independence will be ranked low or high on this measure?   _____

Use the MAPPING task to compare the variable you selected with the map of independence date.

   21. Look at the two maps in your comparison. Start by comparing Europe and North America in
       one map to Europe and North America in the other map. Do they look like they are similar,
       opposite, or neither? (circle one)

       a. Similar

       b. Opposite

       c. Neither

   22. Now make the same comparison with Africa in both maps. Do they look like they are similar,
       opposite, or neither? (circle one)

       a. Similar

       b. Opposite

       c. Neither

   23. Does your prediction seem to be supported by the analysis? (circle one)

       a. Yes

       b. No

V. Earlier in this chapter we examined a map showing the level of multiculturalism for each nation of
   the world. As you will recall, the variable 461) MULTI-CULT indicates the odds that any two persons
   in a nation-state will differ in their race, religion, ethnicity, or language group. Let's take a brief look
   at how the level of multiculturalism in a nation-state might be related to how individuals in Nigeria,
   Mexico, and the United States feel about their national identity. Your task here is to determine if the
   members of an ethnically diverse nation-state are more or less likely to identify with the nation-
   state (e.g., "I am very proud to be an American"). These are the steps you should follow:

   1. Create a map of 461) MULTI-CULT from the GLOBAL file.

   2. Obtain a ranked list of 461) MULTI-CULT. Print out this ranked list and turn it in with your assignment.

   3. Create pie charts for each of the following countries. (If you don't remember how to do this, please refer
      to the preliminary part of the chapter.) Print out each pie chart and turn it in with your assignment.

DATA FILE	VARIABLE
WVS02–MEXICO	223) PROUD
WVS02–NIGERIA	174) PROUD
WVS02–USA	215) PROUD

4. As your final step, use the printouts to fill in the table below. For the column on multiculturalism, indicate the ranking of the nation-state (e.g., 1st, 2nd, 45th, 90th). For the column labeled %PROUD, indicate the percentage that identify themselves as "very proud" to be a Mexican, Nigerian, or American.

NATION-STATE	MULTI-CULTURAL RANK	%VERY PROUD
MEXICO	_____	_____%
NIGERIA	_____	_____%
UNITED STATES	_____	_____%

24. Which of the following is the best interpretation of the results of our analysis of these three countries? (circle one)

    a. Nation-states that are ranked high for cultural diversity have a greater percentage of citizens who identify with the nation-state (as Mexicans, Nigerians, or Americans).

    b. Nation-states that are ranked high for cultural diversity have a lower percentage of citizens who identify with the nation-state (as Mexicans, Nigerians, or Americans).

    c. Cultural diversity does not seem to be related to the percentage of the population that identifies with the nation-state.

VI. Civil liberties are basic freedoms that include such things as freedom of speech, press, religion, and assembly. An international organization known as Freedom House has created an index that scores every nation in terms of civil liberties from 1 (most free) to 7 (least free). Let's use this index to look at the relationship between multiculturalism and civil liberties. Because nations having high levels of multiculturalism tend to have more internal struggles, let's predict that civil liberties will be lowest in nation-states having high levels of multiculturalism.

Data File:	**GLOBAL**
Task:	**Mapping**
Variable 1:	**461) MULTI-CULT**
➤ Variable 2:	**305) CIV LIBS04**
➤ View 1:	**List: Rank**
➤ View 2:	**List: Alpha**

25. Less than half of the ten nation-states having the highest levels of multiculturalism scored less than a 4 on the civil liberties index.   T   F

26. More than half of the eleven nation-states having the lowest levels of multiculturalism scored a 1 or 2 on the civil liberties index.   T   F

IN YOUR OWN WORDS

The goal of this section of the worksheet is to link the statements that you make to actual evidence from the results of your analysis. In your own words, please answer the following questions and be sure to use evidence to support your claims.

1.   Summarize the relationship between the age of the nation-state and its level of human development.

2.   In a brief paragraph, explain why you think the relationship between civil liberties and multiculturalism exists (or does not exist).

CHAPTER 2

PEOPLE, POPULATIONS, AND STATE CAPACITY

An empty stomach is not a good political advisor.
ALBERT EINSTEIN

Tasks: Mapping, Scatterplot
Data Files: GLOBAL

In the previous chapter you learned to compare maps to identify similarities and differences between nation-states. As you'll recall, we looked briefly at several basic economic and political indicators such as gross domestic product per capita, capital punishment, and political independence. When political scientists or, broadly speaking, social scientists consider the overall concept of "development," the examination extends well beyond the general wealth and democracy of nation-states. Development includes the entire realm of social factors such as population growth, infant mortality rates, employment, health care, education, and nutrition. In a basic sense, these are problems that all governments must address in one way or another. *State capacity* refers to a state's ability to use resources to achieve social and economic change. States with a high capacity are relatively more effective in achieving policy goals than those states with low capacity. Human development and state capacity will be the focus of this chapter.

Let's begin by looking at a common, albeit important, social indicator: population growth rates.

> ➤ *Data File:* **GLOBAL**
> ➤ *Task:* **Mapping**
> ➤ *Variable 1:* **33) POP GROWTH**
> ➤ *View:* **Map**
> ➤ *Display:* **Legend**

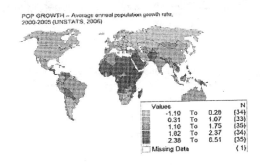

This map shows the annual population growth for nation-states across the world. From this map we can see that populations are growing most rapidly in Africa and the Islamic nation-states. Population growth rates pose a very serious problem to some developing nations. For example, an annual population growth rate of 4% per year means that a nation's population will double every 16.6 years. This creates serious problems for governments in the developing world that would be challenged to keep order and encourage development under conditions of zero population growth. In the chapter that follows, we will examine population growth as an example of one problem that states must manage.

POP GROWTH: Average annual population growth rate, 2000-2005 (UNSTATS, 2006).

Data File: **GLOBAL**
Task: **Mapping**
Variable 1: **33) POP GROWTH**
➤ View: **List: Rank**

RANK	CASE NAME	VALUE
1	United Arab Emirates	6.51
2	Qatar	5.86
3	Afghanistan	4.59
3	Eritrea	4.26
5	Sierra Leone	4.07
6	Kuwait	3.73
7	Chad	3.42
8	Uganda	3.40
9	Niger	3.39
10	Gaza and West Bank	3.23

The United Arab Emirates (6.51%), Qatar (5.86%), Afghanistan (4.59%), Eritrea (4.26%), and Sierra Leone (4.07%) all experienced average annual growth of more than 4% per year. At the bottom of the list we see that 16 nation-states are actually declining in population on an average annual basis. During the 2000–2005 period, Ukraine (-1.10%) and Georgia (-1.07%) declined at a rate of more than 1% per year. Most advanced industrial democracies are either holding steady (growth rates around 0%) or growing their populations at a rate of close to 1% per year.

What causes the variation in population growth across nation-states? The most obvious answer is the birth rate. As the birth rate increases, so does the population. Notice that almost all the nation-states at the bottom of the list were from the former Soviet Union or its satellite states. Was there something about the breakup of the Soviet Union that led to these declines, or did the pattern of low population growth exist before this time? Perhaps nation-states having people with higher life expectancies experience higher levels of population growth. Along this line of thinking, we might attribute the level of health care for a country as an indirect contributor to population growth. Perhaps nations with high infant mortality rates have lower population growth. We can investigate many of these questions with ExplorIt.

The most obvious answer to our population growth question is birth rates. Let's start there.

Data File: **GLOBAL**
Task: **Mapping**
Variable 1: **33) POP GROWTH**
➤ Variable 2: **28) BIRTHRATE**
➤ Views: **Map**
➤ Display: **Legend**

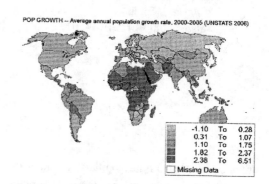

POP GROWTH -- Average annual population growth rate, 2000-2005 (UNSTATS 2006)

-1.10	To	0.28
0.31	To	1.07
1.10	To	1.75
1.82	To	2.37
2.38	To	6.51
Missing Data		

r = 0.703**

BIRTHRATE -- Crude birth rate indicates the number of live births occurring during the year, per 1,000 population estimated at midyear. (WDI, 2005)

8.16	To	11.50
11.60	To	18.36
18.41	To	26.03
26.82	To	35.24
35.37	To	50.28
Missing Data		

These two maps are clearly similar. We see that sub-Saharan Africa and the Arab nation-states are also the highest in terms of birth rate. Use the [List: Rank] option to list the results for the BIRTHRATE variable. In terms of birth rates, Angola is the highest with 50.28 births per 1,000 population, followed by Somalia (49.99) and Guinea-Bissau (48.56). At the bottom of the birth rate list we find Georgia (8.16), Bulgaria (8.40), and Slovenia (8.60). Again, the Eastern European nations are at the bottom of the list.

In the previous chapter you used comparison maps to determine whether one variable is similar to another. If two maps are very similar to (or mirror opposites of) one another, it is fairly easy to determine the relationship. But, as you examine maps that are less alike, it is more difficult to identify the patterns. Comparing ranked lists of nation-states is also cumbersome, especially when you have to keep track of 172 nations. While comparison maps are helpful, there is another method that is more precise and informative in describing the similarity of two maps. The method was invented about 100 years ago in England by Karl Pearson. Once you see how he did it, you will find it very easy to apply to your own analysis. To understand Pearson's method, we draw a horizontal line to represent the BIRTHRATE map. On the left end of the line we write 8.16 to represent the nation-state with the lowest birth rate (Georgia); on the right end of the line we write 50.28 to represent the nation-state with the highest birth rate (Angola).

8.16   BIRTHRATE   50.28

Starting at the left end of the horizontal line, we now draw a vertical line of equal length up the left side of the paper to represent the population growth. At the bottom of this line we write –1.10 to represent Ukraine's population growth rate, and at the top of the line we write 6.51 to represent the population growth rate for the United Arab Emirates.

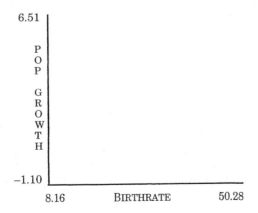

What we end up with are two lines having an appropriate scale to represent each map. The bottom line representing the birth rate is called the x-axis; the vertical line representing growth rate is called the y-axis. The next step is to obtain the value for each nation-state and locate it on each line according to its score. Let's start with Angola. Because it has the highest birth rate of 50.28 per 1,000 population, it's easy to locate its place on the horizontal line. Place a small mark on the horizontal line to indicate Angola's location. Next, we need to find Angola's location on the vertical line. Angola's annual growth rate is 2.83%, so we place a mark on the vertical line at its approximate location. Now, we draw a line up from the mark for Angola on the horizontal line and draw another line out from its mark on the vertical line. Where these two lines intersect we place a dot. This dot represents the combined values for the population growth rate and the birth rate for Angola.

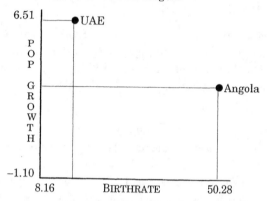

Let's also locate the United Arab Emirates (UAE). To find the UAE on the line representing birth rates, estimate where 17.29 is located and make a mark on the horizontal line. The UAE is easy to locate on the vertical line because its value of 6.51% is the highest of all nation-states. So make a mark at the top of the vertical line. Again, draw a line up from the horizontal line and out from the vertical line. Where these two lines meet is the combined location for the UAE. Don't worry, you'll never have to complete this process for all 172 nations in the data set—ExplorIt can do this for you. But do recognize that if we followed this procedure for all nations, we would have all 172 nations located within the space defined by the vertical and horizontal lines representing the two maps. What you would have created is known as a scatterplot. Use ExplorIt to create a complete scatterplot using these same two variables.

> Data File: **GLOBAL**
> ➤ Task: **Scatterplot**
> ➤ Dependent Variable: **33) POP GROWTH**
> ➤ Independent Variable: **28) BIRTHRATE**

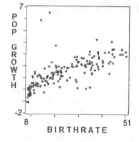

r = 0.703** Prob. = 0.000 N = 169 Missing = 3

Special Feature: When the scatterplot is showing, you may obtain information on any dot by clicking on it. A little box will appear around the dot, and the values of 33) POP GROWTH (or the y-axis variable) and 28) BIRTHRATE (or the x-axis variable) will be shown. To deselect the case, click the [Find Case] box.

Each of the dots shown here represents a nation-state. To identify a dot, just point at it with your mouse and click. Start by clicking on the dot at the top of the scatterplot. As expected, ExplorIt will identify it as the United Arab Emirates, which had the highest average annual population growth rate between 2000 and 2005. When you click on a dot, information about its exact coordinates on the x-axis and y-axis appears to the left of the scatterplot. Here we see that the UAE's X value (birth rate) is 17.29 per 1,000 population; its Y value (population growth) is 6.51%. Now, click on the dot located farthest to the right on the graph. Angola is identified as the case, and its values on both variables are shown on the left side of the screen.

Once Pearson created a scatterplot, his next step was to calculate what he called the regression line.

<table>
<tr><td align="right">Data File:</td><td>GLOBAL</td></tr>
<tr><td align="right">Task:</td><td>Scatterplot</td></tr>
<tr><td align="right">Dependent Variable:</td><td>33) POP GROWTH</td></tr>
<tr><td align="right">Independent Variable:</td><td>28) BIRTHRATE</td></tr>
<tr><td align="right">➤ View:</td><td>Reg. Line</td></tr>
</table>

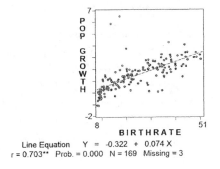

Line Equation   Y = -0.322 + 0.074 X
r = 0.703** Prob. = 0.000 N = 169 Missing = 3

To show the regression line, select the [Reg. Line] option from the menu.

The regression line represents the best effort to draw a straight line that minimizes the distance between all of the dots. It is unnecessary for you to know how to calculate the regression line since the program does it for you. The line alerts us to a pattern in the data. In our comparison of the birth rate and population growth, the line slopes upward. The regression line tells us that as the birth rate increases, population growth also increases. If you would like to see how the regression line looks if the maps are identical, then all you need to do is examine a scatterplot of identical maps. So, if you create a scatterplot using POP GROWTH as both the dependent and independent variables, you will be comparing identical maps and the dots representing countries on the regression line will look like a string of beads. However, because the maps for POP GROWTH and BIRTHRATE are only very similar, but not identical, most of the dots are scattered near, but not on, the regression line. Pearson's method for calculating how much alike are any two maps or lists is very easy once the regression line has been drawn. What it amounts to is measuring the distance out from the regression line to every dot. To do this, simply click on [Residuals].

<table>
<tr><td align="right">Data File:</td><td>GLOBAL</td></tr>
<tr><td align="right">Task:</td><td>Scatterplot</td></tr>
<tr><td align="right">Dependent Variable:</td><td>33) POP GROWTH</td></tr>
<tr><td align="right">➤ Independent Variable:</td><td>28) BIRTHRATE</td></tr>
<tr><td align="right">➤ View:</td><td>Reg. Line/Residuals</td></tr>
</table>

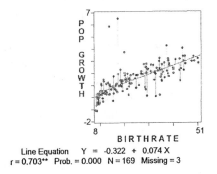

Line Equation   Y = -0.322 + 0.074 X
r = 0.703** Prob. = 0.000 N = 169 Missing = 3

To show the residuals, select the [Residuals] option. Keep the [Reg. Line] option selected too.

See all of the little lines. If you added them all together, you would have a sum of the deviation of all the dots from the regression line. The smaller this sum is, the more alike are the two maps. For example, when the maps are identical and all the dots are on the regression line, the sum of the deviations is 0. In order to make it simple to interpret results, Pearson invented a procedure to convert the sums into a number called the correlation coefficient. The correlation coefficient varies from 0.0 to 1.0. When maps are identical, the correlation coefficient will be 1.0. When they are completely unalike, the correlation coefficient will be 0.0. Thus, the closer the correlation coefficient is to 1.0, the more alike the two maps or lists. Pearson used the letter r as the symbol for his correlation coefficient. Look at the lower left of the screen and you will see r = 0.703**. The number indicates that the maps are quite similar and that the relationship between the two variables is strong. The meaning of the asterisks will be discussed later in this chapter.

Correlation coefficients can be either positive or negative. This correlation is positive: where birth rates are higher, the population growth rate is higher. That is, as one rises so does the other; they tend to rise or fall in unison. If nation-states are trying to reduce their population growth rates, they might first attempt to reduce their birth rates. A successful solution for reducing the birth rate should be negatively correlated with the birth rate. For example, we might expect that as the percentage of women in the population who use contraception increases, the birth rate would decrease. Hence, we are looking for a negative correlation between contraception use and birth rates. We expect that as contraception use increases, birth rates will fall.

Data File:	**GLOBAL**
Task:	**Scatterplot**
➤ Dependent Variable:	**28) BIRTHRATE**
➤ Independent Variable:	**104) CONTRACEPT**
➤ View:	**Reg. Line**

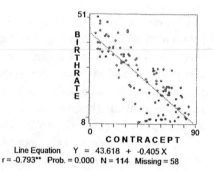

Line Equation   Y = 43.618 + -0.405 X
r = -0.793**   Prob. = 0.000   N = 114   Missing = 58

Here we see a very clear relationship between the use of contraception and the birth rates in nation-states. As the percentage of women using contraception increases, the birth rate decreases. Notice that in this case, the regression line slopes downward from left to right, rather than upward. That always indicates a negative correlation. Also notice that a minus sign now precedes the correlation coefficient (r = –0.793**). Incidentally, you will rarely see a correlation coefficient this high. It suggests that the negative correlation between these two variables is very close to the perfect value of 1.0.

The purpose of calculating correlation coefficients isn't simply to say how alike or unalike two maps are. The point of comparing two maps or creating a scatterplot is to search for links, or connections, between variables. Ultimately, we are looking for causal relationships. Only when such links exist can we propose that there is a causal relationship between them. Thus, implicit in our first two uses of the scatterplot is the assumption that one variable *might* be the cause of the other. Whenever social scientists become interested in a variable, the first thing they do is ask what causes it to vary. And the *first* test of any proposed answer to the question is to demonstrate the existence of a correlation between the variable to be explained and its proposed cause. In this instance we have demonstrated that contraception use in a society is related to the birth rate in a society since the two are highly correlated. By itself, correlation does not establish that a causal relationship exists. But without a correlation there can be no causal relationship. That helps us explain the distinction between independent and dependent variables. In the SCATTERPLOT task, the software asks for the dependent variable and then asks for the independent variable. If we think something might be the cause of something else, we say that the cause is the independent variable and that the consequence (or the thing that is being caused) is the dependent variable. Put another way, the dependent variable depends on the independent variable.

Suppose a researcher thought that population growth rates might be related to the death rates in countries. If population growth is high, perhaps it's related to the fact that not enough people are dying to offset other factors that contribute to population growth. Let's create a scatterplot using annual population growth and the number of deaths per 1,000 population per year.

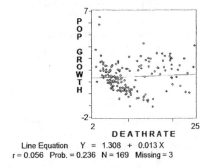

> Data File: **GLOBAL**
> Task: **Scatterplot**
> ➤ Dependent Variable: **33) POP GROWTH**
> ➤ Independent Variable: **34) DEATHRATE**
> ➤ View: **Reg. Line**

Line Equation   Y = 1.308 + 0.013 X
r = 0.056 Prob. = 0.236 N = 169 Missing = 3

The correlation is positive, but it's not very strong (r = 0.056). Also notice that the result is not significant (there are no asterisks). According to this analysis, there is no relationship between population growth and the death rate. While this is certainly the case for all 169 countries in this analysis, it is also possible that there is a pattern that is not at first apparent. Click on two or three of the countries in the far upper-left corner of the scatterplot. These countries have very high population growth rates and low death rates. You should notice that most of these countries are Islamic oil-producing countries in the Middle East and South Asia. These are unique cases because they are wealthy societies that are able to promote public health (and have a low death rate), but they are also Islamic societies that have a high birth rate for religious reasons. For these reasons we might consider that these societies are what are called outliers in our analysis. When doing comparative analysis, it is sometimes necessary to exclude outliers from the analysis so that they don't substantially exaggerate (or dampen) the overall results. If there is a reasonable explanation for removing an outlier, it is often justified for these reasons. Click on the option labeled [Outlier] and notice that the case located far above the rest in terms of population growth is highlighted. This is the nation of United Arab Emirates, located on the coast of the Arabian Peninsula. Because of this special situation, let's remove United Arab Emirates from the analysis. To do this, simply click the [Remove] button located to the left of the scatterplot. United Arab Emirates is now removed and the scatterplot is rescaled to adjust the new range of values. Notice too that the correlation coefficient (r) has risen to 0.093.

Notice that there is very little slope to the regression line. Moreover, the dots are not located very close to the regression line. This is what it looks like when two variables have almost no correlation. So population growth does not seem to be related to the death rate. Notice, however, that the value is not at absolute zero (with the outlier removed, r = 0.093). So, how are we able to say that these two variables aren't correlated? We can say it because the odds are very high that this correlation is nothing but a random occurrence—in short, an accident.

If we think about the relationship between population growth and death rates a little more, this result is a little puzzling. After all, wouldn't the death rate have some kind of relationship to population growth rates? If you click around on the nations to the right of the scatterplot, you will notice that almost all of them are in Africa. If you have been following the news in recent years, you may remember hearing that HIV/AIDS, along with a number of civil wars, has ravaged the continent of Africa. Because of these unique circumstances, it might be appropriate to do an analysis of death rates and population growth without African countries in the mix. Let's see what happens when we do this.

<table>
<tr><td align="right">Data File:</td><td>GLOBAL</td></tr>
<tr><td align="right">Task:</td><td>Scatterplot</td></tr>
<tr><td align="right">Dependent Variable:</td><td>33) POP GROWTH</td></tr>
<tr><td align="right">Independent Variable:</td><td>34) DEATHRATE</td></tr>
<tr><td align="right">➤ Subset Variable:</td><td>464) REGIONAL</td></tr>
<tr><td align="right">➤ Subset Category:</td><td>Exclude: 1) Africa</td></tr>
<tr><td align="right">➤ View:</td><td>Reg. Line</td></tr>
</table>

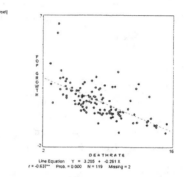

If you are working from the previous example, click the arrow button [⟲] and add the subset variable called 464) REGIONAL. Select 1) Africa from the list. Also check the option "Exclude selected categories."

This will give you the same scatterplot as before, but without African countries, which seem to be unique. You will notice that the new correlation coefficient is 0.637**. This result is very strong, and it is significant. This suggests that there is a strong and significant relationship between population growth and the death rate in non-African countries.

Many correlations are so small that we treat them as if they were zero. The software automatically does the calculation for you and gives you the results. If you look back at the correlation between birth rate and contraception use, you will see that there are two asterisks following the value of r (r = –0.793**). Two asterisks mean that there is less than 1 chance in 100 that this correlation is a random accident. One asterisk means that the odds against a correlation being random are 1 in 20 (or 5 out of 100). Whenever there are no asterisks following a correlation, the odds are too high that it could be random. Thus, the result is not significant.

That's how we know that the original correlation between the population growth and death rate (before we exclude African countries) is too small to matter: there are no asterisks. Treat all correlations without asterisks as if they were zero correlations.

When r has at least one asterisk, it indicates a statistically significant relationship. In assessing the strength of a correlation coefficient, treat an r smaller than ±.30 as a weak relationship, an r between ±.30 and ±.60 as a moderate relationship, and an r greater than ±.60 as a strong relationship. Also remember to examine whether the relationship is positive or negative. Remember that a negative correlation is not the same thing as a weak correlation.

As you will find in Chapter 4, statistical significance in survey data helps us to assess whether or not a relationship exists in the population from which the survey sample was drawn. In ecological data sets, such as the GLOBAL file, statistical significance helps us determine whether the existing relationship is a result of chance factors. This rule of thumb does not apply in the use of survey data. A rule of thumb for interpreting correlation coefficients in survey data is discussed in Chapter 4.

Finally, keep in mind that correlation and causation are *not* the same thing. It is true that without correlation there can be no causation, but correlations often occur between two variables without one being a cause of the other. And we are often interested in correlations between two variables even when we don't think that one causes the other. For example, we might wonder if nation-states that have more cigarette consumption also have higher rates of life expectancy.

To see if these two variables are correlated, we will go back to the MAPPING task.

<table>
<tr><td align="right">Data File:</td><td>**GLOBAL**</td></tr>
<tr><td align="right">➤ Task:</td><td>**Mapping**</td></tr>
<tr><td align="right">➤ Variable 1:</td><td>**71) CIGARETTES**</td></tr>
<tr><td align="right">➤ Variable 2:</td><td>**40) LIFE EXPCT**</td></tr>
<tr><td align="right">➤ Views:</td><td>**Map**</td></tr>
<tr><td align="right">➤ Display:</td><td>**Legend**</td></tr>
</table>

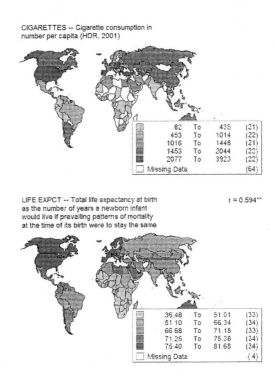

CIGARETTES -- Cigarette consumption in number per capita (HDR, 2001)

	62	To	435	(21)
453	To	1014	(22)
1016	To	1448	(21)
1453	To	2044	(22)
2077	To	3923	(22)
☐ Missing Data			(64)

LIFE EXPCT -- Total life expectancy at birth as the number of years a newborn infant would live if prevailing patterns of mortality at the time of its birth were to stay the same

$r = 0.594^{**}$

36.48	To	51.01	(33)
51.10	To	66.34	(34)
66.68	To	71.18	(33)
71.25	To	75.38	(34)
75.40	To	81.68	(34)
☐ Missing Data			(4)

The maps here look very similar, and teach us an important lesson about correlation. CIGARETTES is high in the Northern Hemisphere and low in the Southern Hemisphere, and LIFE EXPCT is high in the Northern Hemisphere and low in the Southern Hemisphere. Pearson's r ($r = 0.594^{**}$) is already calculated for you in the map comparison. The calculation is the same in both the MAPPING task and the SCATTERPLOT task. The two asterisks show that this is a significant correlation, but they do not show that one variable is causing another. If you aren't careful here, it might lead you to believe that countries with populations full of high cigarette consumers lead people to live longer. Or stranger than this, one might conclude that nation-states with citizens who live for a long time also smoke more. Neither of these interpretations are correct, though. It is far more likely that a third variable is causing both of these phenomena to be high: A high level of wealth allows consumers to purchase more cigarettes than people in poor countries, and high wealth also leads people to live longer.

The SCATTERPLOT task and Pearson's correlation coefficient are powerful tools. In the worksheet section that follows, you'll use these tools to examine a number of issues related to social development and state capacity.

Terms and Concepts

Population growth	Causal relationship	Correlation and causation
Negative population growth	Negative correlation	Death rate
Birth rate	Positive correlation	Life expectancy
Scatterplot	Significance	State capacity
Regression line	Strong correlation	Outlier
Correlation	Weak correlation	

NAME: *Ramona Khan*

COURSE:

DATE: *2/26/07*

2

REVIEW QUESTIONS

Based on the first part of this chapter, answer True or False to the following items:

1. Sub-Saharan Africa and the Arab nation-states have the highest population growth rates.   (T)   F

2. The United Arab Emirates' high population growth rate is caused by an exceptionally high birth rate.   (T)   F

3. The correlation coefficient produced by the scatterplot is more accurate than the one produced by the compare map function.   T   F

4. If one variable causes another, then they must be correlated.   T (T) (F)

5. When a correlation is followed by two asterisks, we treat the results as statistically significant.   (T)   F

6. State capacity refers to a state's ability to use resources to achieve social and economic change.   (T)   F

7. The last two maps in the preliminary section of the chapter tell us that people who smoke cigarettes live longer.   T   (F)

8. Using our rule of thumb, a Pearson's *r* of –0.708** is considered weak.   T   (F)

9. In a causal relationship, the ___*independent*___ variable is said to be the cause of something and the consequence is the ___*dependent*___ variable.   *independent*   *dependent*

10. The _____ represents the best effort to draw a straight line that connects all the dots in a scatterplot.   *regression*

11. A(n) _____ is an oddball case in a scatterplot that is located far from all other cases.   *outlier*

EXPLORIT QUESTIONS

If you have any difficulties using the software to obtain the appropriate information, or if you want to learn about additional features of ExplorIt's SCATTERPLOT task, refer to the online help under the Help menu.

I.   In the preliminary part of this chapter, we examined several factors that were related to population growth. One way that we can begin to understand state capacity is to analyze the relationship between basic government-sponsored programs and public health. Let's pursue this analysis by looking at the issue of child health worldwide. The hypothesis is: Countries with higher government commitment to health care will have better public health. First let's look at the effect of immunization programs on child health. In the analysis below we will use the following variables: 32) MORTAL<5; 108) IM:DPT; 109) IM:MEASLES. We assume that a state's child vaccination rate is an indicator of state capacity. In other words, states with high vaccination coverage for children have higher state capacity than those without high rates of child vaccination.

> ➤ *Data File:* **GLOBAL**
> ➤ *Task:* **Scatterplot**
> ➤ *Dependent Variable:* **32) MORTAL<5**
> ➤ *Independent Variable:* **108) IM:DPT**
> ➤ *View:* **Reg. Line**

12. From the variable description for 32) MORTAL<5, we see that this variable is a measurement of (circle one of the following)

  a.   the probability that a newborn baby will live past his/her fifth birthday.

  b.   the probability that a newborn baby will die before his/her fifth birthday.

  c.   the death of fewer than 5 people out of every 1,000.

  (d.) It's not possible to tell from the graph.

13. From the variable description for 108) IM:DPT, we see that this variable is a measurement of

  a.   the probability that a child will be immunized against diphtheria, pertussis, and tetanus.

  b.   the rate of vaccination coverage for diphtheria, pertussis, and tetanus for children aged 12–23 months.

  c.   the immortality rate of people exposed to DPT.

  (d.) It's not possible to tell.

14. The countries that are the highest on 32) MORTAL<5 should appear as dots at the

  a.   right of the scatterplot.

  b.   left of the scatterplot.

  c.   top of the scatterplot.

  (d.) bottom of the scatterplot.

  e.   It's not possible to tell without looking at the values.

15. The dots that appear farthest to the right side of the scatterplot represent those countries that have the (circle one of the following)
    a. highest rates of mortality under age 5.
    b. highest rates of vaccination coverage for DPT.
    c. lowest rates of mortality under age 5.
    (d.) lowest rates of vaccination coverage for DPT.
    e. The location of the dots tells us nothing about the values of the cases or these variables.

16. What is the correlation coefficient for these results?   r = -0.781

17. Is the relationship positive or negative?   ~~pos~~ negative

18. According to our rule of thumb for interpreting correlation coefficients, this relationship is considered (circle one of the following)
    (a.) strong.
    b. moderate.
    (c) weak.

19. Are these results statistically significant?   (Yes) No

20. What is the name of the outlier in this scatterplot?   Rwanda

21. Remove the outlier and indicate the new correlation coefficient.   r = ~~0.78~~ -0.794

22. Are these new results statistically significant?   (Yes) No

23. Do these results support the hypothesis that countries with higher levels of immunization for DPT have lower rates of child mortality for children under age 5?   (Yes) No

Now analyze the relationship between 109) IM:MEASLES and 32) MORTAL<5.

Data File:	**GLOBAL**
Task:	**Scatterplot**
Dependent Variable:	**32) MORTAL<5**
➤ Independent Variable:	**109) IM:MEASLES**
➤ View:	**Reg. Line**

24. What is the correlation coefficient for these results?   r = -0.749

25. Is the relationship positive or negative?   negative

26. According to our rule of thumb for interpreting correlation coefficients, this relationship is considered (circle one of the following)
    a. strong.
    b. moderate.
    (c.) weak.

27. Are these results statistically significant?   (Yes) No

28. What is the name of the outlier in this scatterplot?   MAlta

29. Remove the outlier and indicate the new correlation coefficient.   r = -0.759

30. Are these new results statistically significant?   (Yes) No

31. Do these results support the hypothesis that countries with higher levels
    of immunization for measles have lower rates of child mortality for children
    under age 5?   (Yes) No

II. The state's use of the education system is another way to achieve significant change in a society. In
     the following analysis, we assume that high-capacity states have stronger education systems than
     low-capacity states. In the preliminary part of the chapter, we saw that birth rates were substantially
     lower in countries with higher percentages of women using contraception. For contraceptives to be
     effective, people must first learn how to use them. So it would seem that nations with a strong educa-
     tion infrastructure would be best equipped for distributing information about contraceptives. So our
     hypothesis is: Citizens in nation-states with higher levels of education will be more likely to use con-
     traceptives. In the analysis that follows, we will assess the relationship between the variables
     104) CONTRACEPT and 339) EDUC INDEX.

             Data File: **GLOBAL**
                 Task: **Scatterplot**
   ➤ Dependent Variable: **104) CONTRACEPT**
   ➤ Independent Variable: **339) EDUC INDEX**
             ➤ View: **Reg. Line**

32. Identify the two countries that are highest on 104) CONTRACEPT.   China
                                                                       U.K

33. What percentage of married women of childbearing age use contraception in   84   %
    the above listed countries?

34. Identify a country that is highest on 339) EDUC INDEX.   Austria

35. What is the education index number for the above listed country?   87.4

36. What is the correlation coefficient for this scatterplot?   r = 0.796

37. Are the results statistically significant?   (Yes) No

38. Do these results offer support to our hypothesis?   (Yes) No

Let's see if there are other variables that might be related to contraception rates. Create a scatterplot
between 104) CONTRACEPT and each variable listed below. For each analysis, fill in the correlation
coefficient and indicate whether the results are statistically significant. Then answer the series of questions that follow. (Note: Be sure to examine each variable description before you select it for analysis.)

	DEPENDENT	INDEPENDENT		
39.	104) CONTRACEPT and 132) CALORIES	r = 0.581	Significant?	Yes (No)
40.	104) CONTRACEPT and 22) URBAN %02	r = 0.566	Significant?	(Yes) No
41.	104) CONTRACEPT and 338) M/F EDUC.	r = 0.579	Significant?	(Yes) No
42.	104) CONTRACEPT and 212) F/M EMPLOY	r = -0.018	Significant?	Yes (No)

43. Nation-states with higher percentages of women using contraception are likely to have greater amounts of calories (food) available per person.   (T) F

44. There is a moderate relationship between contraceptive use and the percentage of the population who live in urban areas.   (T) F

45. Countries with higher percentages of contraceptive use are more likely to have greater proportions of women who are educated.   (T) F

46. Countries with higher percentages of contraceptive use are more likely to have greater levels of female employment.   T (F)

47. Each of the results in the analysis of contraception is statistically significant.   T (F)

III. Does religion play a role in development? Is development affected by the predominant religion in a nation-state? Let's compare nation-states having high percentages of Muslims with those having high percentages of Christians. The first variable listed is dependent.

48.	104) CONTRACEPT and 440) %MUSLIM	r = -0.281	Significant?	(Yes) No
49.	28) BIRTHRATE and 440) %MUSLIM	r = 0.281	Significant?	(Yes) No
50.	339) EDUC INDEX and 440) %MUSLIM	r = -0.400	Significant?	Yes (No)
51.	338) M/F EDUC. and 440) %MUSLIM	r = -0.521	Significant?	(Yes) No
52.	212) F/M EMPLOY and 440) %MUSLIM	r = -0.344	Significant?	(Yes) No
53.	104) CONTRACEPT and 441) %CHRISTIAN	r = 0.720	Significant?	(Yes) No
54.	28) BIRTHRATE and 441) %CHRISTIAN	r = -0.228	Significant?	(Yes) No
55.	339) EDUC INDEX and 441) %CHRISTIAN	r = 0.424	Significant?	(Yes) (No)
56.	338) M/F EDUC. and 441) %CHRISTIAN	r = 0.499	Significant?	(Yes) No
57.	212) F/M EMPLOY and 441) %CHRISTIAN	r = 0.127	Significant?	Yes (No)

IN YOUR OWN WORDS

The goal of this section of the worksheet is to learn to connect the statements that you make to actual evidence from the results of your analysis. In your own words, please answer the following questions.

Sample Question: What is the relationship between immunization rates for DPT and measles, and the mortality rates of children under age 5? What does a positive (or negative) relationship mean?

Sample Answer: Immunization rates for DPT and measles seem to be strongly correlated with infant mortality rates for children under age 5. The variable 32) MORTAL<5 has a strong negative relationship with immuniza-tion for DPT (r = –0.771) and measles (r = –0.759). The negative correlation means that an increase in the immunization rate in a country is correlated with a decrease in deaths under age 5.

1. From the results of your analysis in Questions 48–57, how does religion relate to patterns of social development? Be sure to support your response with evidence. From this analysis, can you conclude that variations in social development are caused by religious differences?

    Religion does seem to play a
    role in social development for
    for example we see that the
    level of education for those who
    are Muslim generally tend to show
    little significance.

2. Using the GLOBAL file, analyze the relationship between the dependent variable 32) MORTAL<5 and the independent variables 326) MIL %GDP, 325) MIL/BUDGET, and 328) MIL PERSON. Carefully examine both variable descriptions before you answer. Remove one outlier from each analysis and con-sider the following: Often a country chooses between building up a large army and promoting the health of its citizens. Based on this analysis (without the outlier), is there a relationship between a state's sup-port for the military and the health of citizens? Be sure to support your answer with evidence.

ORGANIZING POLITICAL SYSTEMS: FIRST, SECOND, AND THIRD WORLDS?

As the long forgotten peoples of the respective continents rise and begin to reclaim their ancient heritage, they will discover the meaning of the lands of the ancestors.

VINE VICTOR DELORIA, JR.
NATIVE AMERICAN HISTORIAN
AND ACTIVIST

Tasks: Mapping, Univariate, Cross-tabulation
Data Files: GLOBAL

If one of the primary objectives of comparative politics is to study the differences and similarities of countries, then how do we make order out of the apparent chaos of all the nation-states in the world? Political philosophers throughout Western history have sought to organize political systems into categories to aid in the understanding of the most basic questions of political organization: Why do some governments fail while others do not? Why are some nations democratic while others are not? Why have some states been easier to conquer than others? Aristotle collected the constitutions of about 150 city-states in an attempt to answer the question of which government system was most stable. From his analysis he generated a classification scheme to organize the various political models that were operative in ancient Greece (Table 3.1).

Table 3.1 Aristotle's Classification of Regimes

Rule by	Virtuous Form	Degenerative Form
One	Monarchy	Tyranny
Few	Aristocracy	Oligarchy
Many	Polity	Democracy

The key variable that Aristotle identified in his attempt to explain or understand government instability was the number of people involved in governing the state or regime. In addition, he recognized that these governments were sometimes capable of governing virtuously, and thus have just, fair, and efficient forms, and that they were also capable of governing selfishly, which produced degenerative forms.

In his quest to understand the cause of political instability, or a state's movement from the virtuous form to the degenerative form, he examined the effects of social and economic factors that supported or undermined the stability of the regimes. Based on this examination of real cases in ancient Greece, Aristotle concluded that democracy and oligarchy were the least stable forms of political organization, whereas systems that combined these two forms tended to be the most stable.

Those who study comparative politics are still in pursuit of answers to the same questions Aristotle asked in ancient Greece. We also must have the means to classify nation-states into groups with similar characteristics so that we might better understand the factors that are responsible for the similarities and differences of the various groups. From the end of World War II until 1989, it was commonplace for teachers and students of comparative politics to classify nation-states according to the Three Worlds classification schema. To see how these categories appear geographically, map the following procedure:

➤ *Data File:* **GLOBAL**
➤ *Task:* **Mapping**
➤ *Variable 1:* **129) THREEWORLD**
➤ *View:* **Map**

THREEWORLD -- CLASSIFICATION OF COUNTRIES INTO THREE WORLDS MODEL: 1 = FIRST WORLD, 2 = SECOND WORLD, 3 = THIRD WORLD (LE ROY, 1998)

You will notice that this categorization of nation-states is most useful for geographers. With the exception of Japan, Australia, and New Zealand, this classification locates all First World countries in Europe and North America. Almost all Second World countries are located in Eastern Europe and Asia, and all Third World nation-states are located to the south of the First and Second Worlds.

Political scientists have found it very useful to organize or classify countries according to their political system, economic system, size, geopolitical power, wealth, and region. The Three Worlds was the dominant classification method used during the Cold War. This system of organization classified countries according to their political and economic systems. People classified First World countries according to their form of political organization (i.e., democratic) and their economic system (i.e., free-market capitalist). In contrast, Second World countries were organized according to a totalitarian form of government (i.e., communist) and their centrally planned, state-dominated economies. The classification was a little broader for Third World countries because this tended to include almost all countries that were former colonies of First World nations that were not easily classified in either of the other two categories.

Politically speaking, Third World countries tended to be authoritarian rather than totalitarian. The difference between authoritarianism and totalitarianism is that in totalitarian systems the leadership seeks to extend its authority to all domains, such as religion, family life, and economic activity. Authoritarian regimes are usually concerned only with controlling those domains specifically related to political activity. Economically, Third World nation-states were characterized by a wide variety of economic systems. Some, such as Cuba and Vietnam, have a state-dominant economy, whereas others, including Chile and Brazil, chose a capitalist economy. A large number of countries, such as India, Egypt, and Tunisia, also tried to experiment with a "mixed economy." That is, they sought to draw from both economic traditions. Table 3.2 shows that First World and Second World countries have very distinct political and economic systems, but Third World countries tend to vary a great deal.

Table 3.2 Three Worlds by Economic and Political System

	Polity		
Economy	Democratic	Totalitarian	Authoritarian
Capitalist	First World Great Britain	N/A	Third World Chile
State-Dominant	N/A	Second World U.S.S.R.	Third World Iraq
Mixed	Third World India	Third World China	Third World Egypt

As you can see in the table, there were five types of nations that were classified as Third World and only one type classified as either First or Second World. This means that a large number of nation-states were bound to be classified in the third category and relatively few would be classified in the other two groups.

No classification system is perfect, but the Three Worlds approach worked well during the Cold War because it highlighted the differences between the two major superpowers. However, in the 1970s, this classification system came under attack by scholars who thought it was important to more carefully classify the countries of the Third World. We can see the reason for this when we examine the number of countries in each of these categories in the map legend below.

Data File: **GLOBAL**
Task: **Mapping**
Variable 1: **129) THREEWORLD**
View: **Map**
➤ Display: **Legend**

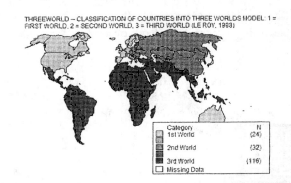

With the legend showing on the screen, notice the numbers that appear to the right side of the legend window. The "N" is a symbol that represents the number of cases for each category. We see that there are 24 nation-states categorized as First World, 32 categorized as Second World, and 116 categorized as Third World.

Remember that we can also examine the number of countries in each of these categories through a procedure called univariate analysis, which allows us to view these same numbers in the form of a pie chart or bar graph.

Data File: **GLOBAL**
➤ Task: **Univariate**
➤ Primary Variable: **129) THREEWORLD**
➤ View: **Pie**

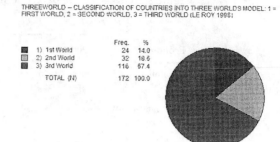

THREEWORLD – CLASSIFICATION OF COUNTRIES INTO THREE WORLDS MODEL: 1 = FIRST WORLD, 2 = SECOND WORLD, 3 = THIRD WORLD (LE ROY 1998)

		Freq.	%
■	1) 1st World	24	14.0
▦	2) 2nd World	32	18.6
▦	3) 3rd World	116	67.4
	TOTAL (N)	172	100.0

Return to the main menu of ExplorIt and select the UNIVARIATE task. Select 129) THREEWORLD as your variable.

Using the UNIVARIATE task, you get a pie chart that shows you the distribution of countries according to their classification in the Three Worlds schema. Notice that the numbers to the right of the pie chart match those provided by the map legend. Additional information is also provided, such as the percentage of nation-states that fall into each category. Here we see that 14.0% of countries are categorized as First World countries, 18.6% are Second World, and 67.4% are Third World countries. While this classification schema may provide some insight to the economic and political characteristics of First World and Second World nation-states, it is problematic when you consider that over two-thirds of all countries fit into one category (Third World). Are two-thirds of the nation-states really that similar?

With the ExplorIt software, we can test the validity of the Three Worlds classification method. To do this, we will use a variable that places all the countries of the world into one of three categories, according to their gross domestic product per capita.

Data File: **GLOBAL**
Task: **Univariate**
➤ Primary Variable: **134) GDPCAP PP3**
➤ View: **Pie**

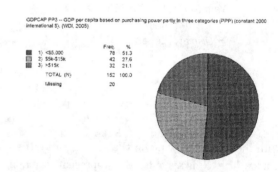

GDPCAP PP3 -- GDP per capita based on purchasing power parity in three categories (PPP) (constant 2000 international $) (WDI, 2005)

		Freq.	%
■	1) <$5,000	78	51.3
▦	2) $5k-$15k	42	27.6
▦	3) >$15k	32	21.1
	TOTAL (N)	152	100.0
	Missing	20	

Here we see that 51.3% of the nations in this analysis have a GDP per capita of less than $5,000; 27.6% are located in the $5,000 to $15,000 range; and another 21.1% of nations have a GDP per capita of over $15,000. Notice that the percentage distributions of these categories are fairly equal to those for the Three Worlds variable. Hence, if the Three Worlds classification works for the purpose of economic differentiation, we would expect First World nations to be concentrated in the highest GDP per capita category, Second World nations to be found mainly in the middle GDP category, and Third World nations to be located primarily in the lowest GDP category.

Let's use ExplorIt's subset feature to see how the nation-states of the First World are distributed according to their wealth per capita.

Comparative Politics

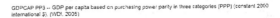

GDPCAP PP3 -- GDP per capita based on purchasing power parity in three categories (PPP) (constant 2000 international $). (WDI, 2005)

Data File:	**GLOBAL**
Task:	**Univariate**
Primary Variable:	**134) GDPCAP PP3**
➤ Subset Variable:	**129) THREEWORLD**
➤ Subset Category:	**Include: 1) 1st World**
➤ View:	**Pie**

		Freq.	%
3) >$15k		24	100.0
TOTAL (N)		24	100.0

The option for selecting a subset variable is located on the same screen you use to select other variables. For this example, select 129) THREEWORLD as a subset variable. A window will appear that shows the categories of the subset variable. Select 1) 1st World as your subset category and choose the [Include] option. Then click [OK] and continue as usual.

With this particular subset, the results will be limited to the First World countries in the data file. Note that the subset selection continues until you delete the subset variable, or use the [Clear All] button to remove all variable selections, or exit the task completely.

The subset category we selected limits the analysis to countries categorized as First World. All of the nations classified as First World fall into the top wealth category.

We could repeat this analysis using the subset option to limit analyses to countries categorized as Second World, and then do a third analysis including only Third World countries. But this is a time-consuming process and there is, in fact, an easier way to obtain the same results in one step by using ExplorIt's CROSS-TABULATION task.

Data File:	**GLOBAL**
➤ Task:	**Cross-tabulation**
➤ Row Variable:	**134) GDPCAP PP3**
➤ Column Variable:	**129) THREEWORLD**
➤ View:	**Tables**
➤ Display:	**Column %**

GDPCAP PP3   by   THREEWORLD
Cramer's V: 0.607**

		THREEWORLD			
		1st World	2nd World	3rd World	TOTAL
GDPCAP PP3	<$5,000	0	13	65	78
		0.0%	44.8%	65.7%	51.3%
	$5k-$15k	0	14	28	42
		0.0%	48.3%	28.3%	27.6%
	>$15k	24	2	6	32
		100.0%	6.9%	6.1%	21.1%
	Missing	0	3	17	20
	TOTAL	24	29	99	152
		100.0%	100.0%	100.0%	

To construct this table, return to the main menu and select the CROSS-TABULATION task. Then select 134) GDPCAP PP3 as the row variable and 129) THREEWORLD as the column variable. When the table appears, select the [Column %] option.

For each row of a cross-tabulation, always compare the column percentages horizontally. Let's focus on the bottom row of the table (the one representing nations having GDP per capita of greater than $15,000). Reading across the bottom row of the table, we see that 100% of First World countries fall into the highest category for GDP per capita. Notice that this is the same result we found in our previous analysis. Continuing across this same row, we see that only 6.9% of the Second World countries falls into this category, while 6.1% of Third World nations are located in the highest GDP per capita category.

It is also important to note how we have described these results. In this workbook we will always use column percentages. When we do, the sentences that describe our results almost always take the same

Chapter 3: Organizing Political Systems: First, Second, and Third Worlds?

49

form: "6.1% of Third World countries have a GDP higher than $15,000." We always refer to the percentage of the column variable first, and the row variable second. This is important because if we reversed the logic of the sentence, it would not have the same meaning: "6.1% of countries with GDP higher than $15,000 are Third World." Not only does this not have the same meaning, it is not accurate! We will talk about this in greater detail in Chapter 4, but for now, just be sure that you understand how we describe what we find in the table.

Continuing on, let's look at the row for $5,000 to $15,000 GDP per capita. Here we see that none of the First World nations fall into this category, compared to 48.3% of Second World nations and 28.3% of Third World nations. The pattern of the results is somewhat along the line of what we might expect, but there is not a clear-cut distinction between Second World and Third World nations in terms of GDP per capita.

As we move to the top row (less than $5,000 GDP per capita), a similarly muddled picture appears: 44.8% of Second World nations and 65.7% of Third World nations have less than $5,000 GDP per capita. We would expect far fewer poor countries in the Second World category than we see here. As it turns out, there is not a clear economic distinction between Second World and Third World nation-states.

In addition to economic classification, the Three Worlds approach was used to describe the political makeup of a nation-state. In the 1960s, during the Cold War, the Three Worlds classification worked well because it illuminated the conflict between democratic capitalism (the First World) and communism (the Second World) and the attempt of both groups to win over the other countries (the Third World). Some countries, like China, Vietnam, Cuba, and Angola, were clearly in the communist camp due to their Marxist-Leninist commitments and one-party political systems. So they were classified as Second World nations, even though many were preindustrial and very poor. There were also a number of nation-states, such as Saudi Arabia, Kuwait, and Oman, that were neither democratic nor communist (hence, classified Third World) although they had relatively high GDP per capita due to oil income. As the Cold War wound down in the late 1980s and many communist countries became "postcommunist," it became increasingly apparent that making political distinctions based on the Three Worlds categories was not very useful.

The Three Worlds classification is clearly problematic. But what can we use to place nation-states into groups? Aristotle would agree with most contemporary political scientists that it's essential to place nation-states into groupings that allow systematic study. This need is made even more clear by the fact that institutions like the United Nations, the World Bank, the International Monetary Fund, governments of wealthy nations, and nongovernmental organizations (NGOs) must decide how to focus their efforts to serve less developed countries based on some type of criteria. Which groups of nations are the most in need of economic assistance? Which nations are successfully developing? What factors have led to development failures? Leaders from one country may wish to give aid only to stable, democratic governments. How do they do this without a means of identifying the groups of countries that fit this criterion? All of these questions demand methods of classification to organize nation-states in an intellectually coherent manner.

In order to develop a proper classification schema, social scientists must consider at least three major forces that shape a nation-state: political factors, economic factors, and social factors. (By social factors, we are referring to the ethnic, linguistic, and cultural factors that characterize a society.) If you emphasize just one of the three factors, you overlook the important role the other two play in shaping the nation-state.

A political scientist by the name of John McCormick has argued for an alternative classification scheme that attempts to incorporate political, social, and economic factors.[1] Nation-states are categorized as follows: (1) liberal democracies, (2) communist or postcommunist, (3) newly industrialized countries (NICs), (4) less developed countries (LDCs), (5) Islamic world, (6) marginal states, and (7) microstates. Each one of the seven worlds is defined with examples for your reference in Table 3.3.

Table 3.3 Definitions of Seven Worlds of Comparative Politics

Type	Definition	Example
Liberal Democracy	Liberal democracies have well-defined, predictable democratic political institutions and processes, and a high degree of political legitimacy. They also tend to be wealthier than most other types of nation-states and have a relatively high regard for civil rights and civil liberties.	Great Britain United States Japan
Communist/ Postcommunist	This category could now also be described as "states in transition," but they are all linked by a common experience of Marxist-Leninist government and economy. Most of these states turned their backs on communism at the end of the Cold War. Eventually many of these nation-states will probably disperse into other categories like liberal democracies, newly industrializing countries, or the Islamic states.	Russia, Poland, China, North Korea, Cuba, Vietnam
Newly Industrializing Countries (NICs)	Most of these states are undergoing economic, political, and social transformation as a result of industrialization like the kind experienced in Europe in the 18th and 19th centuries. Their political systems are stabilizing, and the economy of these states is industrializing rapidly.	Mexico, India, Brazil, Taiwan, South Africa
Less Developed Countries (LDCs)	This group of countries may be found in Central and South America as well as sub-Saharan Africa. These nation-states have some potential to build political, economic, or social stability, but face many long-term obstacles. Some have stable political systems, but poor economies. Some have growing economies but unstable government due to corruption and questionable human rights records.	Ecuador, Tanzania, Nigeria, Nicaragua
Islamic World	This group of countries is characterized by the dominance of the religion of Islam in these societies. This is distinct because the Islamic faith informs all other aspects of a nation-state's character including political organization, economics, and social values.	Iran, Saudi Arabia, Pakistan, Turkey
Marginal States	This group is the most "transitory" of all the nation-states that we might study because these nations are in fact "failed states" because of political, social, or economic upheaval due to extended warfare, environmental disaster, or political and economic isolation.	Angola, Liberia, Afghanistan, Ethiopia, Myanmar
Microstates	These nations are put into a single category because their size seems to be the most important factor that distinguishes them from the rest of the countries in the world. They have populations ranging from 50,000 to 250,000. They are usually highly dependent on larger neighboring countries for trade, protection, and other natural resources.	Luxembourg, Bahamas, Monaco, Vatican City

[1] John McCormick, *Comparative Politics in Transition* (New York: Wadsworth, 1995), pp. 5–17.

Let's examine this Seven Worlds classification using the UNIVARIATE task.

Data File: **GLOBAL**
➤ Task: **Univariate**
➤ Primary Variable: **130) WORLDS.7**
➤ View: **Pie**

WORLDS.7 – CLASSIFICATION OF COUNTRIES INTO "SEVEN WORLDS" OR CATEGORIES: 1 = LIBERAL DEMOCRACY, 2 = COMMUNIST/POST-COMMUNIST, 3 = NEWLY INDUSTRIALIZED COUNTRY, 4 = LESS DEVELOPED COUNTRY, 5 = ISLAMIC, 6 = MARGINAL, 7 = MICRO (McCORMICK 1995)

	Freq.	%
1) Lib Democ	24	14.0
2) Comm/P-Com	34	19.8
3) NICs	21	12.2
4) LDCs	36	20.9
5) Islamic	26	15.1
6) Marginal	25	14.5
7) Micro	6	3.5
TOTAL (N)	172	100.0

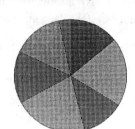

Look at the distribution of these countries. Communist/postcommunist nation-states and the LDCs are the largest categories with around 20% each. Liberal democracies, NICs, Islamic countries, and marginal countries each make up about 12%–15%. The smallest group is those countries classified as micro (3.5%).

Let's return to the CROSS-TABULATION task and repeat the earlier analysis using GDP per capita. This time, however, we'll use the Seven Worlds variable.[2]

Data File: **GLOBAL**
➤ Task: **Cross-tabulation**
➤ Row Variable: **134) GDPCAP PP3**
➤ Column Variable: **130) WORLDS.7**
➤ View: **Tables**
➤ Display: **Column %**

GDPCAP PP3   by   WORLDS.7
Cramer's V: 0.696**

		Lib Democ	Comm/P-Com	NICs	LDCs	Islamic	Marginal	Micro	TOTAL
GDPCAP PP3	<$5,000	0	15	3	28	11	19	2	78
		0.0%	48.4%	15.8%	80.0%	61.1%	100.0%	33.3%	51.3%
	$5k-$15k	0	14	13	7	5	0	3	42
		0.0%	45.2%	68.4%	20.0%	27.8%	0.0%	50.0%	27.6%
	>$15k	24	2	3	0	2	0	1	32
		100.0%	6.5%	15.8%	0.0%	11.1%	0.0%	16.7%	21.1%
	Missing	0	3	2	1	8	6	0	20
	TOTAL	24	31	19	35	18	19	6	152
		100.0%	100.0%	100.0%	100.0%	100.0%	100.0%	100.0%	

Although the 21 cells of this table can be overwhelming at first, it provides more useful information than the earlier table that used the Three Worlds variable. Let's start with the bottom row (>$15,000). Again, 100% of liberal democracies fall into this category, compared to 15.8% of NICs and 11.1% of Islamic nation-states. There are only two communist/postcommunist countries in this category, no LDCs or marginal states.

Skipping to the top row (<$5,000), we see that all of the marginal countries (or 100%) fall into this category, followed by LDCs (80.0%), communist/postcommunist (48.4%), micro countries (33.3%), and Islamic countries (61.1%). In the center row ($5,000–$15,000), the most notable result is that 68.4% of newly industrialized countries are in this category.

Let's look at a bar graph of these results.

---

[2] There are some instances in this chapter (and in the worksheet section that follows) where the cross-tabulation results using the GLOBAL file produce the statement "Warning: Potential significance problem." This is to alert you that the statistical significance value may not be reliable due to the small number of nations used in the analysis. This is not a problem for the type of analysis that we are currently conducting. For our purposes in this chapter, we will often ignore this warning.

Data File: **GLOBAL**
Task: **Cross-tabulation**
Row Variable: **134) GDPCAP PP3**
Column Variable: **130) WORLDS.7**
➤ View: **Bar**

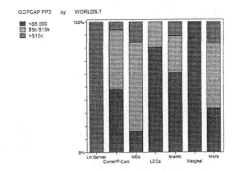

You'll recall that one of the problems with the Three Worlds variable was that there wasn't much differentiation between Second World and Third World countries in terms of GDP per capita (and many other variables, as it turns out). But the Seven Worlds variable provides substantially more information. Marginal societies are clearly different from both communist/postcommunist societies and NICs. Islamic countries and NICs have fairly sizable numbers in each GDP category, whereas several of the other types of nation-states do not.

We will use the Seven Worlds variable often throughout this workbook. Although this classification is not perfect, it does provide better insight to the social, political, and economic differences among nation-states than does the Three Worlds system.

Now it's your turn to test the Seven Worlds variable in the worksheet section that follows.

Terms and Conditions

Aristotle's classification
Three Worlds classification
Seven Worlds classification
Liberal democracies
Communist/postcommunist nation-states
NICs
LDCs
Islamic world
Marginal states
Microstates

NAME: Ramona Khem

COURSE:

DATE: 2/26/07

REVIEW QUESTIONS

Based on the first part of this chapter, answer True or False to the following items:

1. Aristotle's reason for studying types of governments was to understand how war could be avoided.   T (F)

2. One of the most important objectives of comparative politics is to understand what accounts for the differences and similarities between nation-states.   (T) F

3. The Three Worlds classification is based on the Old World of Europe (e.g., Great Britain, France), the New World (e.g., United States, Canada, Australia), and the developing world (e.g., Africa, Asia, South America).   T (F)

4. The Three Worlds classification seemed to have its greatest validity during the Cold War era.   (T) F

5. The First World classification holds up rather well in an analysis of GDP per capita because most of these nation-states are concentrated in the highest levels of GDP.   (T) F

6. The Second World and Third World classifications don't hold up well in an analysis of GDP per capita because there is not much differentiation between the two types of nation-states.   T (F)

7. The subset feature of ExplorIt's UNIVARIATE task allows you to limit analysis to a particular category of a second variable.   (T) F

8. ExplorIt's CROSS-TABULATION task allows you to create pie charts and maps.   T (F)

EXPLORIT QUESTIONS

> **If you have any difficulties using the software to obtain the appropriate information, or if you want to learn about additional features of ExplorIt's CROSS-TABULATION task, refer to the ExplorIt help topics under the Help menu.**

I. The GLOBAL file contains a variable named 312) POL RIGT04 that measures the level of political freedom individuals have within a given nation. The political organization, Freedom House, surveys each country and compiles a set of scores on a number of criteria, such as the right of all adults to vote, the right to compete for public office, and the right for elected representatives to have a decisive vote on public policies. Nation-states that meet all the criteria are given a score of 1 (most free), whereas those that meet none of the criteria are given a score of 7 (least free). The POL RIGT04 variable contains a complete set of scores for the nations in the GLOBAL data file.

> *Data File:* **GLOBAL**
> *Task:* **Univariate**
> *Primary Variable:* **312) POL RIGT04**
> *View:* **Pie**

9. Freedom House gave a score of 1 or 2 to more than a third of all nations.   F

10. More nation-states received a score of 7 than any other score. T

To simplify things a bit, it's possible to create a second variable that places all nation-states with a score of 1 or 2 in a "free" category; nation-states that scored a 3, 4, or 5 in a "partially free" category; and nation-states that scored a 6 or 7 in a category called "not free." We'll use this second version of the variable, 313) POL RIGHT, to examine the Seven Worlds classification.

> *Data File:* **GLOBAL**
> *Task:* **Cross-tabulation**
> *Row Variable:* **313) POL RIGHT**
> *Column Variable:* **130) WORLDS.7**
> *View:* **Tables**
> *Display:* **Column %**

11. In terms of political rights, which nation-state categories had less than half of their countries scored as "free"? (circle all that apply)
    a. Liberal democracies
    b. Comm/P-Com
    c. NICs
    d. LDCs
    e. Islamic
    f. Marginal
    g. Micro

12. Which nation-state grouping has the lowest percentage of its countries in the free category? *Islamic*

13. Which nation-state grouping has the highest percentage of its countries in the free category? *lib. Democ.*

14. In terms of political rights, newly industrialized countries are more similar to
    a. liberal democracies.
    b. less developed countries.

15. Print a bar graph of these two variables and turn it in with this assignment. *See attachment*

NAME *Ramora Khan* | **CHAPTER 3**

II.   In the first chapter we examined another Freedom House measure for civil liberties. As a reminder, civil liberties include such things as freedom of speech, press, religion, and assembly. Freedom House also scored nation-states on a scale of 1 (high protection of civil liberties, or most free) to 7 (no protection of civil liberties, or least free). However, for the following analysis, we will use a second version of the variable that combines categories 1–2 (for "free"), 3–5 (for "partially free"), and 6–7 (for "not free").

>   *Data File:* **GLOBAL**
>   *Task:* **Cross-tabulation**
> ➤   *Row Variable:* **306) CIV LIBS**
> ➤   *Column Variable:* **130) WORLDS.7**
>   ➤ *View:* **Tables**
>   ➤ *Display:* **Column %**

16.   In terms of civil liberties, which nation-state categories had less than half of their countries scored as "free"? (circle all that apply)

     a.   Liberal democracies
     (b.)   Comm/P. Comm
     c.   NICs
     d.   LDCs
     e.   Islamic
     f.   Marginal
     g.   Micro

17.   Which nation-state grouping had the lowest percentage of its countries in the free category?   *Islamic*

18.   Which nation-state grouping had the highest percentage of its countries in the free category?   *lib. dem.*

19.   In terms of civil liberties, are communist/postcommunist countries more similar to liberal democracies or marginal states?   *neither*

20.   Print a bar graph of these two variables and turn it in with this assignment.   *See attachment*

III. Is there a geographic pattern to the Seven Worlds classification of nation-states? For example, do liberal democracies tend to be located in a particular region? What about other regions of the world? The variable 463) REGION shows you the five key regions used by the United Nations Development Program (UNDP). If you map this variable, you can see them: 1. sub-Saharan Africa, 2. Arab states, 3. Asia and the Pacific, 4. the Western Hemisphere, and 5. Europe. Now let's try to see if our nation-state categories are concentrated in a specific region.

>   *Data File:* **GLOBAL**
>   *Task:* **Cross-tabulation**
> ➤   *Row Variable:* **463) REGION**
> ➤   *Column Variable:* **130) WORLDS.7**
>   ➤ *View:* **Tables**
>   ➤ *Display:* **Column %**

Chapter 3: Organizing Political Systems: First, Second, and Third Worlds?   57

21. What percentage of liberal democracies are in Europe?   **75.0** %

22. A majority of LDCs and marginal states are located in _Sub-Saharan Africa_

23. Most communist/postcommunist states are located in __Europe.__

24. Most Islamic states are located in __Arab__.

25. NICs are mostly located in two regions: _Asia_ and _West-Hemisphere_

Now that we understand where each type of nation-state is concentrated, let's see if these regions tend to be dominated by certain types of regimes. For example, does Europe tend to be dominated by a particular type of nation-state? To do this, we just reverse the variables in our analysis.

> Data File: **GLOBAL**
> Task: **Cross-tabulation**
> ➤ Row Variable: **130) WORLDS.7**
> ➤ Column Variable: **463) REGION**
> ➤ View: **Tables**
> ➤ Display: **Column %**

26. What percentage of European countries are communist or postcommunist? **56.3** %

Use either the bar graph or the table (with column percentaging) to answer the following questions:

27. _Marginal_ has every type of nation-state in the Seven Worlds represented. _____

28. Ninety percent of the nation-states in the _Arab_ region are _Islamic_

29. What are the two most common types of nation-states in the Western Hemisphere?   _LDC's_   _NIC's_

30. The most common types of nation states in Europe are _____ and _____.   _Com.P.com_   _Lib.Dem._

IV. Warfare is the most violent and costly interaction among nation-states. Civil wars are also prevalent within many nation-states. Are certain types of nation-states more likely to experience warfare than other types?

> Data File: **GLOBAL**
>   Task: **Cross-tabulation**
> ➤ Row Variable: **458) WAR**
> ➤ Column Variable: **130) WORLDS.7**
>   ➤ View: **Tables**
>   ➤ Display: **Column %**

Use both the [Column %] and the [Bar] option to answer the following questions:

31. What is the correct way to express the result found in the upper-left corner of the table?
  a. 70.8% of countries that experienced no warfare from 1990 to 2002 are liberal democracies.
  b. 20.0% of liberal democracies experienced no warfare from 1990 to 2002.
  c. 70.8% of liberal democracies experienced no warfare from 1990 to 2002.
  d. none of the above.

32. Which type of nation-state did not experience any form of warfare in the period 1990 to 2002?

micro

33. Which type of nation-state is most likely to have experienced civil war between 1990 and 2002?

marginal

34. Which two types of nation-states are the most likely to have experienced interstate war between 1990 and 2002?

LDC's
Islamic

35. Which two types of nation-states have experienced the most warfare?

marginal
Islamic

IN YOUR OWN WORDS

In your own words, please answer the following questions. Be sure to support your statements with evidence from your analysis.

1. Imagine that you are a representative of a human rights organization concerned with political rights and civil liberties. Which category of countries shows the most promise for improving political rights and civil liberties to the level of liberal democracies and microstates? In a brief paragraph, describe the similarities and/or differences between the results you found in the political rights analysis and the civil liberties analysis. Be sure to support your claims with evidence.

Comm./P-Com. & NIC's

2. In the Three Worlds classification, NICs and LDCs would be placed in the same Third World category. What are the differences between these two groups of countries with respect to per capita wealth (use GDPCAP PP3), war, civil liberties, and political rights? Are they different enough to warrant separate categories?

Part II

POLITICS AND GOVERNMENT IN LIBERAL DEMOCRACIES

CHAPTER 4

POLITICAL CULTURE IN LIBERAL DEMOCRACIES

The ruling ideas of each age have ever been the ideas of its ruling class.

KARL MARX AND FRIEDRICH
ENGELS, 1848

Tasks: Mapping, Cross-tabulation, Univariate, Auto-Analyzer
Data Files: GLOBAL, WVS02all, WVS02–ANALYZER, WVS02–UK, WVS02–GERMANY,
WVS02–JAPAN, WVS02–SWEDEN, WVS02–USA

In Chapter 3 we learned that there are different types of nation-states in the international system. Some scholars refer to these differences according to the traditional Three Worlds classification, while others are more specific in their characterization of these nation-states. We also learned that these differences in classification are most pronounced when we are trying to characterize the differences in developing nations. But both characterizations seem to agree that liberal democracies have very distinct characteristics *vis-à-vis* other nation-states throughout the world: they are all democratic, they are relatively wealthy, and they are relatively stable compared to most other categories of nation-states.

In the previous chapter, we looked at the factors that distinguish countries from each other at the nation-state level. Most of us would agree that liberal democracies have different levels of wealth, education, and health, but are the political values and ideas of citizens in these countries different? This chapter continues with the topic of liberal democracies but relies primarily on individual-level data for citizens. As such, you'll use the CROSS-TABULATION task and learn several new techniques that will be useful throughout the remainder of the workbook. But before we jump into analysis of survey data with the CROSS-TABULATION task, let's start with an example using our familiar GLOBAL file and the MAPPING task.

➤ *Data File:* **GLOBAL**
➤ *Task:* **Mapping**
➤ *Variable 1:* **393) TRUST?**
➤ *View:* **List: Rank**

TRUST?: Percent who say that most people can be trusted

RANK	CASE NAME	VALUE
1	Denmark	66.5
2	Sweden	66.3
3	Iran	65.3
3	Norway	65.3

Over the past several decades, political scientists have studied social trust among the citizens from a wide variety of nation-states. Most of these studies conclude that social trust helps to make democracy

63

work because it increases social unity and makes citizens feel like the government will respond to their needs if they choose to express a concern.

The TRUST? variable is based on data from surveys that were conducted in 70 countries as part of the World Values Survey. What is shown here is the *average* response given by a sampling of the population in each country to the following survey question: "Generally speaking, would you say that most people can be trusted or that you can't be too careful in dealing with people?" As you can see, 66.5% of people interviewed in Denmark indicate that they trust most people. At the bottom of the list is Brazil, in which only 2.8% of survey respondents indicate that they trust other people.

This example and most others in the first three chapters of this workbook used the "nation-state" as the *unit of analysis*. The term *unit of analysis* refers to the "things" or "cases" being analyzed. Because we are comparing data across nation-states, we say that nation-states are the unit of analysis. Of course, political scientists use other units of analysis besides nation-states and individuals. For example, a researcher in the United States might analyze the laws of the 50 U.S. states, and therefore the state would be her unit of analysis (each variable would list one value for each state). Or she might use the 254 counties of Texas, or the census tracts of New York City, or the neighborhood areas of Chicago, and so on. Perhaps the most widely used unit of analysis is individuals. When a political scientist conducts a survey or poll, the analyses are usually based on the combined responses that individuals gave during the survey (e.g., "In a national survey of Swedes, 66.3% indicate that most people can be trusted."). It's important that you always recognize the unit of analysis that is being used.

In the last example, you used a variable in the GLOBAL file that is based on the World Values Survey. Did you wonder how the "average response" for each nation was obtained? That is, what process was used to come up with the value of 65.3% for Norway? As it happens, there is a very large data file used by researchers that contains the responses of all 118,519 people interviewed in more than 70 countries that were part of the World Values Survey. This data file is a bit overwhelming for our purposes, but you have a smaller version named WVS02all that includes all 16,462 people interviewed in 8 of the 70 countries. Although only a few of the original survey questions are included in this file, it will give you a good sense of how this source of data (where the *individual* is the unit of analysis) can be used to create data where the nation-state is the unit of analysis. Let's look at the same survey question above (trust in fellow citizens) using individual-level data for eight countries.

➤ Data File: **WVS02all**
➤ Task: **Cross-tabulation**
➤ Row Variable: **3) TRUST PEOP**
➤ Column Variable: **1) COUNTRY**
➤ View: **Tables**
➤ Display: **Column %**

TRUST PEOP by COUNTRY
Cramer's V: 0.201 **

		Germany	USA	Japan	Russia	S Korea	Mexico	Turkey	Nigeria	TOTAL
	Can trust	727	431	540	579	328	327	727	512	4171
		37.5%	36.3%	43.1%	24.0%	27.3%	21.8%	16.0%	25.6%	26.0%
	Be careful	1210	757	714	1836	872	1170	3820	1489	11868
		62.5%	63.7%	56.9%	76.0%	72.7%	78.2%	84.0%	74.4%	74.0%
	Missing	99	12	108	85	0	38	60	21	423
	TOTAL	1937	1188	1254	2415	1200	1497	4547	2001	16039
		100.0%	100.0%	100.0%	100.0%	100.0%	100.0%	100.0%	100.0%	

Note that this task uses a new data file. To create these results, open the file named WVS02all. Then select the CROSS-TABULATION task and 3) TRUST PEOP as the row variable and 1) COUNTRY as the column variable. When the table is showing, select the [Column %] option. You may need to scroll the table to view all the columns.

The top row of this table shows the percentage of people in each of the eight countries who indicate that you "can trust" people. The second row shows the percentage of people who indicate that you should "be careful." The eight countries included in this data set are listed across the top of the columns. As you learned in Chapter 3, the easiest way to read a cross-tabulation result is to pick a row and read it from left to right (just like a book). If you read across the top row, you'll see that 37.5% of citizens in Germany are apt to trust people, compared to 36.3% in the USA and 43.1% in Japan. As you work your way across the table, you'll also find the percentages for Russia (24.0%), South Korea (27.3%), Mexico (21.8%), Turkey (16.0%), and Nigeria (25.6%). So this is the answer to our original question: In order to obtain the response for each nation-state on a survey question, you simply create a table like this to determine the percentaged results of individuals in each category. In fact, if you repeat the opening analysis of this chapter, you'll see that the values you obtained with the GLOBAL file match those shown here.

We can also get the table we just examined by using the AUTO-ANALYZER task. This task combines the univariate and cross-tabulation procedures you have already seen in this book. It first shows you the distribution of a *primary variable* you select and then allows you to choose one of seven demographic variables—country, the Seven Worlds typology, gender, age, class, income, and education—to see what difference, if any, this demographic variable makes. It then gives you the appropriate cross-tabulation and actually tells you what is happening in the table. Let's see how it works.

➤ *Data File:* **WVS02–ANALYZER**
➤ *Task:* **Auto-Analyzer**
➤ *Row Variable:* **18) TRUST PEOP**
➤ *View:* **Univariate**

TRUST PEOP -- Generally speaking, would you say that most people can be trusted or that you need to be very careful in dealing with people?

	%
Can trust	26.0%
Be careful	74.0%
Number of cases	16039

Among all respondents, 26.0% of the sample say that most people can be trusted.

To obtain these results, return to the main menu and select the AUTO-ANALYZER task. Then select 18) TRUST PEOP as your variable and click [OK].

Here is the univariate distribution for 18) TRUST PEOP in the eight nation-states that are part of this data file (the same countries that are used in WVS02all). Now let's see what difference a person's country makes in their answer to this question.

Data File: **WVS02–ANALYZER**
Task: **Auto-Analyzer**
Row Variable: **18) TRUST PEOP**
➤ *View:* **Country**

TRUST PEOP -- Generally speaking, would you say that most people can be trusted or that you need to be very careful in dealing with people?

	Germany	USA	Japan	Russia	S Korea	Mexico	Turkey	Nigeria
Can trust	37.5%	36.3%	43.1%	24.0%	27.3%	21.8%	16.0%	25.6%
Be careful	62.5%	63.7%	56.9%	76.0%	72.7%	78.2%	84.0%	74.4%
Number of cases	1937	1188	1254	2415	1200	1497	4547	2001

Japanese are most likely (43.1%) to say that most people can be trusted and Turks (16.0%) are least likely. The difference is statistically significant.

If you are continuing from the previous example, simply select [country] to see the results.

These results are identical to the ones we obtained using the CROSS-TABULATION task from the main menu, and the textual summary points to a country difference in the level of social trust. Use this summary to better understand the results of your analysis. The textual summary also notes that this result is *significant* (more about this later).

The eight countries selected for the WVS02all data set were not arbitrary. In fact, they will be the focus of many discussions in the second half of this workbook. These countries were selected because they represent five of the seven major categories of nation-states:

Liberal Democracies: Germany, USA, Japan
Communist or Postcommunist: Russia
NICs: S. Korea, Mexico
Islamic: Turkey
LDC: Nigeria

We are unable to include any marginal or microstates in this analysis. In the case of marginal states, it is too difficult to conduct reliable surveys in states torn apart by civil war. Microstates were not included in the analysis because the World Values Survey focuses most of its resources on the most populous nations. These countries were also selected because they contain some of the best illustrations of the themes we will explore in the chapters that follow. In fact, let's see if there is a difference in trust between these different categories.

Data File: **WVS02-ANALYZER**
Task: **Auto-Analyzer**
Row Variable: **18) TRUST PEOP**
➤ View: **worlds 7**

TRUST PEOP -- Generally speaking, would you say that most people can be trusted or that you need to be very careful in dealing with people?

	Lib Democ	Comm/P-Com	NICs	LDCs	Islamic	Marginal	Micro
Can trust	38.8%	24.0%	24.3%	25.6%	16.0%	0.0%	0.0%
Be careful	61.2%	76.0%	75.7%	74.4%	84.0%	0.0%	0.0%
Number of cases	4379	2415	2697	2001	4547	0	0

Those from liberal democracies are most likely (38.8%) to say that most people can be trusted and those from Islamic countries (16.0%) are least likely. The difference is statistically significant.

If you are continuing from the previous example, simply select [worlds 7] to see the results.

As AUTO-ANALYZER indicates, there is a difference in citizens' level of trust in others across the different types of nation-states. Liberal democracies have the highest degree of trust in others (38.8%); the communist/postcommunist state is lower with only 24.0% of the population saying that you can trust others. NICs are slightly higher (24.3%), the Islamic state has the lowest (16.0%), and the LDC comes close to this result for NICs and communist/post communist states (25.6%). This result is statistically significant.

We have now established that liberal democracies have relatively higher levels of social trust than the other categories. One of the leading hypotheses on the development of democracy suggests that stable democracies must also be ideologically centrist. That is, a majority of the population must identify with the political center rather than the left or the right. Let's go back to the WVS02all data file to examine political ideology across these five categories.

➤ *Data File:* **WVS02all**
➤ *Task:* **Cross-tabulation**
➤ *Row Variable:* **5) LT-RT-3**
➤ *Column Variable:* **2) WORLDS 7**
➤ *View:* **Tables**
➤ *Display:* **Column %**

LT-RT-3   by   WORLDS 7
Cramer's V: 0.130**

		WORLDS 7					
		Lib Democ	Comm/P-Com	NICs	LDCs	Islamic	TOTAL
L T - R T - 3	Left	943	490	559	656	944	3592
		24.6%	31.0%	24.6%	33.4%	22.0%	25.8%
	Center	1859	798	820	537	1888	5902
		48.4%	50.5%	36.1%	27.3%	44.0%	42.3%
	Right	1035	292	890	773	1460	4450
		27.0%	18.5%	39.2%	39.3%	34.0%	31.9%
	Missing	761	920	466	56	315	2518
	TOTAL	3837	1580	2269	1966	4292	13944
		100.0%	100.0%	100.0%	100.0%	100.0%	

To see the entire table, click the right arrow of the bottom scroll bar.

Let's focus our attention in this analysis on the political center in the second row of the table. Here we see that 48.4% of the population in the three liberal democracies in our study identify themselves with the political center. It is also worth noting that the left and right are fairly evenly balanced within liberal democracies. As we move across the table into the other categories, we can see that the identification with the moderate political perspective found in the political center changes. 50.5% of the population of the communist/postcommunist country in our study identifies with the center, but only 36.1% of NICs align themselves with the political center. Only 27.3% of the population in the LDC aligns with centrist ideas and 44.0% of the population of the Islamic country aligns with centrist ideas. If we use 45% as the threshold for what constitutes a "centrist political culture," then we can see that liberal democracies and our postcommunist country fit this criterion, but NICs, LDCs, and Islamic states have not yet crossed this threshold. Certainly we would have to do a lot more analysis to test the ideology hypothesis, but based on the analysis we have done here, ideological centrism does seem to be a valid indicator of democratic development. If you want to continue practicing the analysis of tables, go back to the WVS02all file and create the same table, but with 1) COUNTRY as the row variable. Or you could return to the WVS02-Analyzer file and create the same table that we just created here. The text guides will direct you in the interpretation of the results.

Now we used an arbitrary threshold for what constitutes the difference between a centrist political culture and a noncentrist political culture. How do we know that the difference between the percentage of people that identify with the center in Mexico and Germany is meaningful? To understand the answer to this question, we have to understand a bit more about polling itself.

Most people are familiar with public opinion polling because it is widely used in the news media. But did you ever wonder how a survey of 1,000 people can be used to represent the opinions among more than 298 million Americans, 128 million Japanese, or more than 1 billion Chinese? The answer is found in the *laws of probability*.

Just as a sophisticated gambler can calculate the odds involved in a particular bet, so too political scientists know how to calculate the odds that findings based on a sample of the population can yield an accurate portrait of the entire population. And just as gamblers assume that they are participating in a random game (that the deck has not been stacked or the dice loaded), so too the odds on a sample being accurate depend on the sample being selected at random from the population.

Thus, the first principle of accurate polling is that people in the sample are selected by *random techniques*. For example, in advanced industrial democracies, interviewers conducting telephone polls often use random dialing software to place their calls. This produces a random sample of all telephones (including those with unlisted numbers) and a random sample of households (except for the percentage of the population without phones). Often, the media will report surveys of public opinion that consist of percentages in favor of or against something—usually something controversial. Unfortunately these surveys are often not based on randomly selected samples, such as when people are invited to register their opinions by dialing a phone number, "hitting" a Web page, or faxing in a response. If the sample is selected at random, we can use the laws of probability to calculate the odds that what we find accurately reflects the population from which the sample was drawn. These odds are determined by two factors: the size of the sample and the size of the observed differences within the sample.

First of all, the sample must be sufficiently large. Obviously, we couldn't use a sample of two people as the basis for describing the population of Great Britain (59 million). If we did so, there is a very high probability that they would both be female and then the population would appear to be entirely female. For this reason, survey studies include enough cases (individuals) so that they can accurately reflect the population in terms of variations in such characteristics as age, sex, education, religion, and the like. The accuracy of a sample is a function of its size: the larger the sample, the more accurate it is. Oddly enough, accuracy depends *only* on the size of the sample, not on the size of the sample relative to the size of the population from which the sample is drawn. Thus, a sample of 1,000 people will yield an equally accurate description of the populations of Luxembourg (465,000) and the United States (298 million).

We can use the UNIVARIATE task to see how many people were included in each of the eight surveys for the WVS02all file.

Data File: **WVS02all**
➤ Task: **Univariate**
➤ Primary Variable: **1) COUNTRY**
➤ View: **Bar - Freq.**

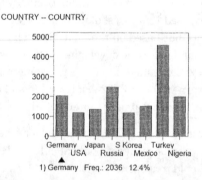

COUNTRY -- COUNTRY

1) Germany Freq.: 2036 12.4%

Click on any of the bars to see the number of people surveyed in each country and the percentage of the population in this survey from each country.

Good survey samples include around 1,000 people. For the eight nations included here, we see that the sample from Germany includes 2,036 people while the Turkish survey includes 4,607. The United States and South Korea have the smallest number of people surveyed (1,200), but all of the countries in this file have more than 1,000 people surveyed so we have a relatively high degree of confidence in our results. Generally it is good practice to have a higher number of people in a sample from a nation where there is a great deal of diversity. Japan, a relatively homogeneous society, has a smaller sample than Nigeria, where there is a high degree of religious and ethnic diversity.

While the GLOBAL and WVS02all files are great for quick examinations of attitudes across different countries, they are not especially useful for examining issues within nations. For example, from the analysis of the GLOBAL file we know that the Danes are more trusting of fellow citizens than are the Brazilians, but we don't know whether older people in these two countries are more trusting than

Comparative Politics

younger people, or whether women are more trusting than men, or whether those who are wealthy are more trusting than those who are poor. In order to do this type of analysis, it's necessary to examine the survey data for the individual nations. Your book came with numerous data files that allow you to do just that.

Also, we have seen that the political culture in liberal democracies is very different from that of other types of nation-states, so in this chapter, and the two chapters that follow, we will focus our analysis on liberal democracies. Let's start with Germany

> *Data File:* **WVS02–GERMANY**
> *Task:* **Univariate**
> *Primary Variable:* **151) LT-RT-3**
> *View:* **Pie**

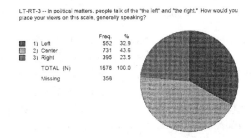

LT-RT-3 -- In political matters, people talk of the "the left" and "the right." How would you place your views on this scale, generally speaking?

		Freq.	%
1)	Left	552	32.9
2)	Center	731	43.6
3)	Right	395	23.5
	TOTAL (N)	1678	100.0
	Missing	358	

This is the ideology distribution for the people surveyed in Germany. Of course, these numbers should (and do) match those obtained above with the eight-country data set: 32.9% are leftists, 43.6% are centrists, and 23.5% are rightists. Now, let's say that you want to know whether people in Germany who identify themselves as being on the political right are more likely to be male or female. It is increasingly the case in liberal democracies that gender is associated with ideology, but is this the case in Germany?

Data File: **WVS02-GERMANY**
> *Task:* **Cross-tabulation**
> *Row Variable:* **151) LT-RT-3**
> *Column Variable:* **304) GENDER**
> *View:* **Tables**
> *Display:* **Column%**

LT-RT-3   by   GENDER
Cramer's V: 0.145 **

		GENDER		
		Male	Female	TOTAL
LT-RT-3	Left	251	301	552
		33.1%	32.7%	32.9%
	Center	296	435	731
		39.1%	47.3%	43.6%
	Right	211	184	395
		27.8%	20.0%	23.5%
	Missing	119	239	358
	TOTAL	758	920	1678
		100.0%	100.0%	

Read across the top row and you'll see that 33.1% of males identify themselves with the political left compared to 32.7% of females. On the left there is really not much of a difference, but when we move to the center row we start to see some change. 39.1% of males identify themselves with the political center in Germany compared to 47.3% of females. The pattern on the right is also distinct. 27.8% of males identify themselves with the political right, while only 20.0% of females do so. There does seem to be a pattern to these results: men are more likely than women to identify with the political right in Germany, while women are more likely than men to identify with the ideology of the political center. But how do we know that the differences in political ideology between males and females are really meaningful?

Assuming that a random sample is used to select the respondents for a survey, pollsters want to determine the probability that the data they collect is representative of the entire population. As explained earlier in this chapter, the first factor that impacts the probability level is the number of people included in the survey. The second factor that has an impact on the probability level is the size of the differences observed within a cross-tabulation result. Simply put, if the difference between the percentaged results is high (e.g., 90% of rich people are rightists, compared to 30% of poor people), then the odds that a difference also exists in the entire population are very good. But if the percentage differences are very similar (e.g., 65% of rich people are rightists, compared to 62% of poor people), then there is an increased chance that these differences are simply due to randomness, rather than some actual difference in the population. Think about it this way. Suppose you have a bag containing 1,000 marbles. If after drawing out 100 of the marbles, you find that 90 are black and 10 are white, you will feel pretty confident in stating that many more black marbles remain in the bag than white marbles. However, if you draw out 55 black marbles and 45 white marbles, you will be less confident in stating that there are substantially more black marbles than white marbles remaining in the bag.

These two limits of survey data (i.e., the size of the sample; the size of the observed differences within the sample) exist because samples are based on the principle of random selection and therefore are subject to some degree of *random fluctuation*. That is, for purely random reasons there can be small differences between the sample and the population. Thus, whenever we examine cross-tabulations such as the one shown above, political scientists always must ask whether what they are seeing is a real difference—one that would turn up if the entire population were examined—or only a random fluctuation, which does not reflect a true difference in the population.

The differences observed in the region/ideology table from Germany seem to be legitimate. Women are more likely to identify with the center and are more likely to identify with the right. But how do we know that these results are not merely the result of random fluctuations? Fortunately, there is a simple technique for calculating the odds that a given difference is real or random. This calculation is called a *test of statistical significance*. Differences observed in samples are said to be statistically significant when the odds against random results are high enough. There is no mathematical way to determine just how high is high enough. But, through the years, social scientists have settled on the rule of thumb that they will ignore all differences (or correlation coefficients) unless the odds are at least 20 to 1 against their being random. Put another way, social scientists reject all findings when the probability that they are random is greater than .05, or 5 in 100. What this level of significance means is that if 100 random samples were drawn independently from the same population, a difference this large would not turn up more than 5 times, purely by chance. In fact, many social scientists think this is too lenient a standard, and some even require that the probability that a finding is random be less than .01, or 1 in 100. To apply these rules of thumb, social scientists calculate the level of significance of the differences in question and compare them against these standards.

There are two ways to see what the level of significance is for this table. If you want to know the exact probability of whether the results may be due to random error, you need to switch to the statistics summary view.

Data File:	**WVS02–GERMANY**
Task:	**Cross-tabulation**
Row Variable:	**151) LT-RT-3**
Column Variable:	**304) GENDER**
➤ *View:*	**Statistics (Summary)**

LT-RT-3   by   GENDER

Nominal Statistics

Chi-Square: 17.327	(DF =	2; Prob. = 0.000)	
V:	0.102	C:	0.101
Lambda:	0.036	Lambda:	0.000	Lambda:	0.016
(DV=304)		(DV=151)			

Ordinal Statistics

Gamma:	-0.076	Tau-b:	-0.043	Tau-c:	-0.049
s.error	0.041	s.error	0.023	s.error	0.026
Dyx:	-0.050	Dxy:	-0.038		
s.error	0.027	s.error	0.020	Prob. =	0.063

Ignore everything on this screen except for the first two lines of text under the heading "Nominal Statistics." At the end of the first line you'll see "Prob. = 0.000." This value indicates that the odds these results are simply due to randomness are less than 1 in 1,000 (.000). Because social scientists require only that these odds be 1 in 20 (.05) or 1 in 100 (.01), we can be confident that these gender/ideology differences would be found if we interviewed the entire population of Germany.

There is another number on this screen that you'll find useful. In the second row, locate the value V = 0.102. The V stands for Cramer's V, which is a correlation coefficient developed for cross-tabulations such as this. Cramer's V is similar to Pearson's r in that the measure varies from 0 to 1. If the relationship between these two variables was perfect (that is, if all men were rightists and all women were leftists), then this would be a value of 1. However, unlike Pearson's r, V does not indicate whether the relationship is positive or negative. In addition, V is much less sensitive than r. For example, if V is greater than .10, the relationship is somewhat strong. If V is greater than .20, you've found a very strong relationship. The value of V for this table is somewhat strong (.102). Overall, we can be fairly confident that, in Germany, women are more likely to be centrists. Conversely, we can be confident that men are more likely to be rightists than women.

Whenever you do cross-tabulation analysis, you should always examine three things. First, look at the table to see if the observed differences are worth noting. For example, if the categories you are comparing (e.g., low income/high income) differ by fewer than 5 percentage points, it *might* not be worth pursuing the analysis. Also, if you are testing a hypothesis, you need to be sure that the percentages differ in the predicted direction. For instance, if you predict that men will be more likely to be rightists, then the differences in the table should support this. The second step is to see if the correlation coefficient (V) offers support to the apparent differences. If the percentage differences in your table are worth pursuing, and V offers support for the strength of the relationship, the third step is to determine whether the results are statistically significant. That's when you should apply the probability rules discussed earlier.

ExplorIt makes it easy to go through these steps by placing all the information you need on one screen. Return to the column percentaging view for this cross-tabulation. Notice that the value of V appears on this screen. In addition, you'll see that two asterisks appear after this value. One asterisk indicates that the probability value is between .01 and .05. Two asterisks indicate that the probability value is less than .01. So, to save time, it's not necessary to go to the statistics screen to obtain these results.

Let's return to the issue of ideology. What makes people have the ideological commitments that they have? We already know from our earlier analysis that the nation someone is from seems to have a bearing on one's political outlook. This makes sense because each nation has a distinct history and culture. For example, in Germany, the political ideas were partly shaped by industrialization. For most of the 19th century, only property-owning males could vote, while factory workers were completely without the capacity to participate in politics. Although the political landscape in Germany has changed a great deal since the 19th century, class-based conflict continues to be a defining feature in ideology in this country. In Japan, industrialization happened later than in Germany. Compared to Western societies, conventional wisdom suggests Japanese political culture emphasizes harmony over conflict, but does this affect ideology?

Let's use the WVS02–JAPAN file to find out. We'll also use a variable that measures the class of the person responding to the survey. When a respondent tells the surveyor what his or her class is, it is put on a scale of upper, middle, or working.

➤ *Data File:* **WVS02–JAPAN**
➤ *Task:* **Cross-tabulation**
➤ *Row Variable:* **124) LT-RT-3**
➤ *Column Variable:* **224) CLASS-3**
➤ *View:* **Tables**
➤ *Display:* **Column %**

LT-RT-3   by   CLASS-3
Cramer's V: 0.061

		CLASS-3				
		Up/Up-mid	Middle	Working	Missing	TOTAL
LT-RT-3	Left	38	80	61	16	179
		24.4%	17.3%	19.6%		19.2%
	Center	74	246	177	52	497
		47.4%	53.2%	56.7%		53.4%
	Right	44	136	74	29	254
		28.2%	29.4%	23.7%		27.3%
	Missing	33	141	116	45	335
	TOTAL	156	462	312	142	930
		100.0%	100.0%	100.0%		

Read across the row for those who identify with the political left. Are there clear differences between the class categories? Compare upper-class, middle-class, and working-class leftists to the overall population of leftists in Japan by looking at the last column. Overall, 19.2% of the Japanese population identifies with the political left. Working-class people are only 0.4 percentage points higher than the overall population, middle-income people are only 1.9 percentage points lower, and high-income people are 5.2 percentage points higher than the overall population. To follow our earlier guidelines, only one category of income exceeds 5% in difference compared to the overall population. So, based merely on percentages, about the same percentage of working-, middle-, and upper-class Japanese consider themselves leftists. Now examine the next row. A clear pattern is still not evident. However, if you compare upper-class centrists (47.4%) to the overall Japanese population (53.4%), you do find about a 6.8 percentage-point difference. Only upper-class centrists seem all that different from the overall population. But is this difference statistically significant? As you can see, V is not especially strong (V = 0.061), and it is not significant. If you switch to the statistics summary screen, you'll see that the probability value is 0.136. That means the odds are 136 in 1,000 (or 13.6 in 100) that the results could be due to randomness. From this we can conclude that there is no relationship between class and political ideology in Japan.

Let's switch back to the WVS02–GERMANY file to see if class is related to ideology in Germany.

➤ *Data File:* **WVS02–GERMANY**
➤ *Task:* **Cross-tabulation**
➤ *Row Variable:* **151) LT-RT-3**
➤ *Column Variable:* **324) CLASS-3**
➤ *View:* **Tables**
➤ *Display:* **Column %**

LT-RT-3   by   CLASS-3
Cramer's V: 0.060 *

		CLASS-3				
		Up/Up-mid	Middle	Working	Missing	TOTAL
LT-RT-3	Left	35	260	234	23	529
		26.3%	35.0%	31.7%		32.8%
	Center	52	320	331	28	703
		39.1%	43.1%	44.9%		43.6%
	Right	46	163	173	13	382
		34.6%	21.9%	23.4%		23.7%
	Missing	8	142	195	13	358
	TOTAL	133	743	738	77	1614
		100.0%	100.0%	100.0%		

If we just review the percentages in this table, there does not seem to be much of a relationship between class and ideology. Working- and middle-class people seem to be very similar to the overall population in terms of ideology. However, upper-class people have greater than a 5-percentage-point difference on the left and right. Upper-class people are 6.5 percentage points lower than the population overall in their affiliation with the left, and 10.9 percentage points higher in their affiliation with the ideological right. The relationship is relatively weak (V = 0.060*), but the result is significant. So, in this analysis we would conclude that there is a relationship between ideology and class, but the relationship is quite modest.

In the previous analyses, we used a demographic variable, class, to see whether it was related to citizens' ideology in Germany and Japan. Comparison of the effects of this relationship helps us to determine whether a characteristic like class transcends national differences.

Instead of analyzing the extent to which demographic factors affect differences in ideology, we may want to see whether or not there are important ideological differences between the citizens of nation-states. To answer this type of question, we will use a data set that combines the results of the World Values Survey conducted in eight countries.

➤ *Data File:* **WVS02all**
➤ *Task:* **Cross-tabulation**
➤ *Row Variable:* **5) LT-RT-3**
➤ *Column Variable:* **1) COUNTRY**
➤ *View:* **Tables**
➤ *Display:* **Column %**

LT-RT-3   by   COUNTRY
Cramer's V: 0.159 **

		COUNTRY								
		Germany	USA	Japan	Russia	S Korea	Mexico	Turkey	Nigeria	TOTAL
LT-RT-3	Left	552	196	195	490	385	174	944	656	3592
		32.9%	17.3%	19.0%	31.0%	32.1%	16.3%	22.0%	33.4%	25.8%
	Center	731	579	549	798	453	367	1888	537	5902
		43.6%	51.1%	53.5%	50.5%	37.8%	34.3%	44.0%	27.3%	42.3%
	Right	395	357	283	292	362	528	1460	773	4450
		23.5%	31.5%	27.6%	18.5%	30.2%	49.4%	34.0%	39.3%	31.9%
	Missing	358	68	335	920	0	466	315	56	2518
	TOTAL	1678	1132	1027	1580	1200	1069	4292	1966	13944
		100.0%	100.0%	100.0%	100.0%	100.0%	100.0%	100.0%	100.0%	

This table displays the relationship between the country that a citizen is from and the person's position on the ideological scale. We have seen this table before, but it is important to note that ideology does differ according to one's country of citizenship. You will remember that these eight countries were selected because they represented different nation-state types throughout the world (e.g., liberal democracies, NICs), but you should also note that these data do not represent a sampling of the values of citizens throughout the world. Therefore, you should use the WVS02all file only with reference to the eight countries within the file.

You can do this by using the variable COUNTRY as a column variable (shown above), or you can cross-tabulate two other variables with the variable COUNTRY selected as the control variable. Let's say that you wanted to know whether citizens' views on economic equality were related to ideology in each of the eight countries in the WVS02all data set.

Data File: **WVS02all**
Task: **Cross-tabulation**
➤ *Row Variable:* **6) INCOME EQ2**
➤ *Column Variable:* **5) LT-RT-3**
➤ *Control Variable:* **1) COUNTRY**
➤ *View:* **Tables**
➤ *Display:* **Column %**

INCOME EQ2   by   LT-RT-3
Controls: COUNTRY: USA
Cramer's V: 0.143 **

		LT-RT-3				
		Left	Center	Right	Missing	TOTAL
INCOME EQ2	Income Eq	66	113	54	13	233
		33.8%	19.6%	15.1%		20.6%
	Center	90	330	172	27	592
		46.2%	57.2%	48.2%		52.4%
	Indv Effrt	39	134	131	27	304
		20.0%	23.2%	36.7%		26.9%
	Missing	1	2	0	1	4
	TOTAL	195	577	357	68	1129
		100.0%	100.0%	100.0%		

The option for selecting a control variable is located on the same screen you use to select other variables. For this example, select 1) COUNTRY as a control variable and then click [OK] to continue as usual. Separate tables for each of the countries will now be shown for the 6) INCOME EQ2 and 5) LT-RT-3 cross-tabulation. The survey question was not asked in Germany, so the first table is blank. Click the appropriate button at the bottom of the task bar to look at the second (or "next") country, and so on.

To analyze the relationship between ideology and opinion on income equality in the eight countries in the data file, you need to examine eight different tables. The survey question was not asked in Germany, so the first table is blank. If you click on the button for the second (or "next") country, you should be able to see the table for the USA, then Japan, and so on. One thing you will notice rather quickly is that it is easy to get overwhelmed by the detail of eight tables. One way to simplify this is to compare the Cramer's V coefficients for the eight different tables. You will notice that the Cramer's V for the USA is 0.143**, Japan 0.161**, Russia 0.106**, South Korea 0.148**, Mexico 0.900**, Turkey 0.074**, and Nigeria 0.164**. A comparison of these coefficients indicates that the relationship between views on income equality and ideology is significant in all countries! You are also able to see that the relationship is strongest in Japan, the United States, South Korea, and Nigeria, weakest in Russia, Mexico, and Turkey. Although it is still important to examine the actual percentages in each table to see where the differences between groups actually lie, the examination of correlation coefficients can help you to narrow the number of countries you need to examine.

We covered a lot of ground in this chapter. Admittedly, a lot of this chapter focused on how to properly use the CROSS-TABULATION task and survey data. Survey data is a staple of political research, so it's important that you learn how to analyze it properly. The worksheet section that follows will give you more experience using the CROSS-TABULATION task. You'll also learn a lot more about political ideology.

Terms and Concepts

Survey research	Centrist political culture
Significance	Sample size
Ideology	Test of statistical significance
Social trust	Three questions for cross-tabulation analysis
Laws of probability	Cramer's V
Random techniques	Class

WORKSHEET

NAME:

COURSE:

DATE:

CHAPTER

4

REVIEW QUESTIONS

Based on the first part of this chapter, answer True or False to the following items:

1. People in Brazil are more trusting of fellow citizens than are people in the United States.   T (F)

2. A sample of 1,000 people is more accurate in a small country than it is in a large country.   T (F)

3. In Germany, people from the upper class are more likely to be rightists, and those from the working class are more likely to be leftists.   (T) F

4. Cramer's V is similar to Pearson's r in that both are correlation coefficients.   (T) F

5. If Cramer's V is statistically significant and greater than .10, it usually indicates that some relationship exists.   (T) F

6. Cramer's V does not indicate whether a relationship is positive or negative.   (T) F

7. The two factors that determine the odds that survey results are representative of the entire population are (1) the size of the sample and (2) the size of the observed difference within the sample.   T (F)

EXPLORIT QUESTIONS

Does ideology still matter in the politics of liberal democracies? Conventional wisdom would suggest that ideology still does matter, but it is also possible that globalization, the end of the Cold War, and other factors have moved liberal democracies beyond ideological conflict. We could argue endlessly about this without any analysis to support our claims, or we could test our hypotheses by analyzing survey data from a number of liberal democracies. We can express the two sides of the argument about the relevance of ideology in the form of two hypotheses:

H1: There is a relationship between ideology and political attitudes in liberal democracies.

H0: There is no relationship between ideology and political attitudes in liberal democracies.

A hypothesis is a testable statement of relationship between a dependent variable and an independent variable. The first hypothesis is the argument that "ideology still matters," and the second argues that "ideology no longer matters." *Strictly speaking* we can never really *prove* a hypothesis because it is always possible that something else is responsible for the relationship. But we can reject it. In this example, the second hypothesis (*H0*) is called the null hypothesis. The null hypothesis is really what we will test in this worksheet section. If ideology still matters, we would expect that people on the left, right, and center would have *different* views about a wide range of political issues, and the null hypothesis is invalid. We will analyze four political issues to test our hypotheses: immigration, economic competition, abortion, and homosexuality.

> **If you have any difficulties using the software to obtain the appropriate information, or if you want to learn more about additional features of ExplorIt's CROSS-TABULATION task, refer to the ExplorIt help topics under the Help menu.**

I. As discussed in the preliminary part of this chapter, the advantage to using individual-level data (opposed to country-level data) is that you can examine differences within specific nations. Your task in this first question is to examine the relationship between political ideology and immigration in liberal democracies. In the space below, you will compare attitudes on issues and ideology in the United Kingdom, Germany, Japan, Sweden, and the United States. Unlike in the earlier part of the chapter, the variable numbers are not indicated as they may be different for each country's file. For each country listed below, you will need to open the appropriate data file, conduct the cross-tabulation that is indicated, write down the percentaged results, and indicate if the results are statistically significant for the sample that agrees with the following responses.

We have noted in our discussion of ideology that it can also be an indicator of a citizen's view of social issues. The following two variables examine public opinion toward two social issues that governments can regulate: immigration and assistance to the poor. For each country, fill in the percentaged results for the population of the sample that agrees with the following response:

Place **strict limits** on the number of foreigners who can come here.

To be more specific in the construction of our hypothesis for this question, the hypotheses would be

H1: People on the ideological right are more likely to favor strict limits on the number of foreigners in the country than people on the ideological left.

H0: There is no relationship between ideology and one's attitude toward limits on immigration.

Now let's test the hypothesis.

> *Data Files:* **WVS02–UK**
> **WVS02–GERMANY**
> **WVS02–JAPAN**
> **WVS02–SWEDEN**
> **WVS02–USA**
> *Task:* **Cross-tabulation**
> *Row Variable:* **IMMIGRANTS**
> *Column Variable:* **LT-RT-3**
> *View:* **Tables**
> *Display:* **Column %**

Fill in the table below.

% LIMITS	LEFT	CENTER	RIGHT	VALUE V	SIGNIFICANT?	
UK	42.3 %	47.4%	50.4 %	0.126 ~~3657~~	(YES)	NO
GERMANY	51.4 %	54.0%	62.9 %	0.179	(YES)	NO
JAPAN	36.3 %	36.7%	50.0%	0.122	(YES)	NO
SWEDEN	25.2%	29.5 %	33.0 %	0.056	YES	(NO)
USA	25.9 %	42.6 %	41.4 %	0.093	(YES)	(NO)

8. Which is the best interpretation of the results in the table?

    a. In four out of five countries, people on the right are more likely to favor strict limits on the number of foreigners in the country than people on the left.

    b. In four out of five countries, people on the left are more likely to favor strict limits on the number of foreigners in the country than people on the right.

    c. 42.3% of the people on the left are from the UK.

    d. In the UK, 50.4% of the people on the right favor strict limits on the number of foreigners in the country.

    (e.) both a and d

9. In which countries are the people on the right more likely to favor strict limits on the number of foreigners in the country than people on the left? (circle all that apply)

    a. UK

    (b) Germany

    c. Japan

    d. Sweden

    e. USA

10. In order for us to reject the null hypothesis (H0) for the analysis between ideology and immigration attitudes in a country, which of the following conditions must apply?

    a. The percentage of those favoring strict limits on foreigners must be close to the same for people on the left and right.

    b. The percentage of those favoring strict limits on foreigners must be higher for people on the right than people on the left.

    c. The results must be significant.

    d. both a and c

    (e.) both b and c

11. In which countries would we reject the null hypothesis? (circle all that apply)

    a.   UK

    b.   Germany

    c.   Japan

    d.   Sweden

    (e)   USA

II. Examine the relationship between ideology and citizens' opinions on the value of economic competition. For each country, fill in the percentaged results for the population of the sample that agrees with the following response:

Competition is beneficial. It stimulates people to work hard and develop new ideas.

Using the previous hypothesis as a model, formulate a hypothesis to express your expectation concerning the relationship between ideology and attitudes toward competition.

_____

_____

_____

Now state the null hypothesis for the preceding hypothesis.

_____

_____

Data Files:	**WVS02–UK**
	WVS02–GERMANY
	WVS02–JAPAN
	WVS02–SWEDEN
	WVS02–USA
Task:	**Cross-tabulation**
➤ Row Variable:	**COMPETITN**
➤ Column Variable:	**LT-RT-3**
➤ View:	**Tables**
➤ Display:	**Column %**

Fill in the table below.

% BENEFICIAL	LEFT	CENTER	RIGHT	VALUE V	SIGNIFICANT?
UK	31.9 %	43.0 %	63.2 %	0.142	(YES) NO
GERMANY	47.1 %	50.6 %	64.4 %	0.096	YES (NO)
JAPAN	48.1 %	31.9 %	50.0 %	0.149	(YES) NO

Comparative Politics

% BENEFICIAL	LEFT	CENTER	RIGHT	VALUE V	SIGNIFICANT?
SWEDEN	39.5 %	52.3 %	73.8 %	0.203	(YES) NO
USA	55.6 %	54.5 %	66.9 %	0.091	YES (NO)

12. From this analysis we may conclude that the majority of the population in each country believes in the value of competition.   (T)   F

13. The relationship between ideology and the value of competition is strong and significant in (circle all that apply)
    - (a) UK.
    - (b) Germany.
    - c. Japan.
    - d. Sweden.
    - (e) USA.

14. The relationship between ideology and the value of competition is weak but significant in (circle all that apply)
    - a. UK.
    - (b) Germany.
    - c. Japan.
    - d. Sweden.
    - e. USA.

15. Do these results indicate that you should reject your null hypothesis?   Yes   (No)

16. We can judge the strength of the relationship between two variables by looking at
    - a. the percentage differences that exceed 5% in either direction when we read across the rows.
    - b. the percentage differences that exceed 5% in either direction when we read down the columns.
    - (c) the Cramer's V statistic.
    - d. the probability statistic.

17. In _____ a majority of the population in every ideological category believes that competition is beneficial.
    - a. UK
    - b. Germany
    - c. Japan
    - d. Sweden
    - (e) USA

Chapter 4: Political Culture in Liberal Democracies   79

III. In some nation-states, the issue of abortion has been hotly debated along ideological lines. Let's see if this holds true for all five nation-states, using the survey question "Do you think that abortion can be justified?"

Using the previous hypothesis as a model, formulate a hypothesis to express your expectation concerning the relationship between ideology and attitudes toward abortion.

_____

_____

Now state the null hypothesis for the preceding hypothesis.

_____

_____

Data Files:	**WVS02–UK**
	WVS02–GERMANY
	WVS02–JAPAN
	WVS02–SWEDEN
	WVS02–USA
Task:	**Cross-tabulation**
➤ *Row Variable:*	**ABORT-3**
➤ *Column Variable:*	**LT-RT-3**
➤ *View:*	**Tables**
➤ *Display:*	**Column %**

For the table below, fill in the percentaged results for those who think abortion is NEVER justified.

% NEVER	LEFT	CENTER	RIGHT	VALUE V	SIGNIFICANT?
UK	_____%	_____%	_____%	_____	YES NO
GERMANY	_____%	_____%	_____%	_____	YES NO
JAPAN	_____%	_____%	_____%	_____	YES NO
SWEDEN	_____%	_____%	_____%	_____	YES NO
USA	_____%	_____%	_____%	_____	YES NO

18. The best description of the result for the UK would be:
    a. People on the right are more likely to think that abortion can never be justified than people on the left. The result is significant.
    b. People on the right are more likely to think that abortion can never be justified than people on the left. The result is not significant.
    c. The results of this analysis are not significant, so the percentages don't really matter.
    d. The value of $V = 0.049$ tells us that the relationship is too weak to be significant.

19. The best description of the result for Japan would be:
    a. People on the right are more likely to think that abortion can never be justified than people on the left. The result is significant.
    b. People on the right are more likely to think that abortion can never be justified than people on the left. The result is not significant.
    c. The results of this analysis are not significant, so the percentages don't really matter.
    d. The value of $V = 0.083$ tells us that the relationship is too weak to be significant.

20. Ideology and attitudes on abortion are most strongly correlated in
    a. UK and Germany.
    b. Germany and Japan.
    c. Germany and the United States.
    d. the United States and Sweden.

21. The best description of the result for Sweden would be:
    a. People on the right are more likely to think that abortion can never be justified than people on the left. The result is significant, but the percentage differences are so small that it would be hard to argue that the difference is all that meaningful.
    b. People on the right are more likely to think that abortion can never be justified than people on the left. The result is not significant, and the percentage differences are so small that it would be hard to argue that the difference is all that meaningful.
    c. The results of this analysis are not significant, so the percentages don't really matter.
    d. The value of $V = 0.053$, so the relationship is too weak to be significant.

22. Are there any countries where you would not reject the null hypothesis?   Yes   No

23. If you answered "yes" in the preceding question, in which country (or countries) would you not reject the null hypothesis?

_____

IV. Does ideology play a role in one's belief of whether homosexuality is ever justified?

Using the previous hypothesis as a model, formulate a hypothesis to express your expectation concerning the relationship between ideology and attitudes toward homosexuality.

_____

_____

Now state the null hypothesis for the preceding hypothesis.

_____

_____

Data Files:	**WVS02–UK**
	WVS02–GERMANY
	WVS02–JAPAN
	WVS02–SWEDEN
	WVS02–USA
Task:	**Cross-tabulation**
➤ *Row Variable:*	**HOMOSEX-3**
➤ *Column Variable:*	**LT-RT-3**
➤ *View:*	**Tables**
➤ *Display:*	**Column %**

For the table below, fill in the percentaged results for those people who think homosexuality is NEVER justified.

% NEVER	LEFT	CENTER	RIGHT	VALUE V	SIGNIFICANT?
UK	_____%	_____%	_____%	_____	YES NO
GERMANY	_____%	_____%	_____%	_____	YES NO
JAPAN	_____%	_____%	_____%	_____	YES NO
SWEDEN	_____%	_____%	_____%	_____	YES NO
USA	_____%	_____%	_____%	_____	YES NO

24. In the analysis of attitudes toward homosexuality, political ideology seems to have a strong correlation in (choose all that apply)

    a. UK

    b. Germany

    c. Japan

    d. Sweden

    e. USA

25. In all statistically significant results, people on the right are more likely than people on the left to indicate that homosexuality is never justified. (Ignore the center categories.)   T   F

26. The best interpretation of the analysis of attitudes toward homosexuality and ideology in Japan is:

    a. People on the right are more likely to think that homosexuality can never be justified than people on the left. The result is significant.

    b. People on the right are more likely to think that homosexuality can never be justified than people on the left. The result is not significant.

    c. The results of this analysis are not significant, so the percentages don't really matter.

    d. The percentage difference between left and right is less than 5% so the differences don't really matter.

V. In the table below, place a checkmark (✔) in each column to indicate if the issue is related to political ideology in each country. Then tally the marks and place the total in the column at the right. The first country has already been done for you.

Fill in the table below.

ISSUE/ COUNTRY	IMMIGRANTS	COMPETITION	ABORTION	HOMOSEXUALITY	TOTAL
UK	✔	✔		✔	3
27. GERMANY	_____	_____	_____	_____	_____
28. JAPAN	_____	_____	_____	_____	_____
29. SWEDEN	_____	_____	_____	_____	_____
30. USA	_____	_____	_____	_____	_____

N YOUR OWN WORDS

In your own words, please answer the following questions. Be sure to support your claims with evidence.

1. In a paragraph, respond to the following statement: "Ideology is universal. In every nation, people are divided on issues according to their ideology." Support your statement with specific examples from the analyses you conducted in this chapter.

2. "The left-right ideological spectrum fits best with economic issues, and less well with moral issues." Support or refute this statement on the basis of your analysis.

POLITICAL PARTICIPATION: MAKING DEMOCRACY WORK

Politics ought to be the part-time profession of every citizen.

DWIGHT D. EISENHOWER, 1954

Tasks: Mapping, Scatterplot, ANOVA, Cross-tabulation
Data Files: GLOBAL, WVS02all, WVS02–UK, WVS02–GERMANY, WVS02–JAPAN,
WVS02–SWEDEN, WVS02–USA

I n the previous chapter we examined some of the cultural values that support democratic political participation. But what makes democracy consistently work over time? In this chapter we will examine the relationship between the public and the government in a number of nation-states to better understand some of the answers to this question.

In Chapter 3 we defined the political dimension of liberal democracies as "nation-states with well-defined, predictable democratic political institutions and processes, and a high degree of political legitimacy." Well-defined, predictable, democratic institutions are identifiable in part because they feature strong commitments to political rights and civil liberties enshrined in their constitutional and legal systems. Differences related to ideology and policy are worked out by means of a competitive political process whereby the interests in a country compete for votes and the right to participate in making decisions.

The World Bank measures the level of political competitiveness in a society as it conducts its analysis. Let's see how the competitiveness of liberal democracies compares to the competitiveness of the other types of nation-states.

➤ Data File: **GLOBAL**
➤ Task: **Cross-tabulation**
➤ Row Variable: **304) LEVEL:CMPT**
➤ Column Variable: **130) WORLDS.7**
➤ Graph: **Bar Stack%**

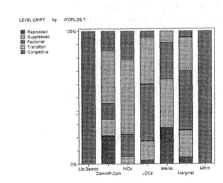

From this analysis we can see that all of the liberal democracies are characterized as competitive, compared to very few to none in any other category. The fact that citizens can count on an open, free marketplace of ideas shapes the ways that individuals choose to participate and their feelings of support for the political system. The competitive nature of liberal democracies leads citizens to have a stronger sense that politics matter, so it is not surprising to see that citizens in liberal democracies generally seem more interested in politics.

➤ Data File: **WVS02all**
➤ Task: **Cross-tabulation**
➤ Row Variable: **15) INTRST POL**
➤ Column Variable: **2) WORLDS7**
➤ View: **Tables**
➤ Display: **Column%**

INTRST POL   by   WORLDS 7

	WORLDS 7					
	Lib Democ	Comm/P-Com	NICs	LDCs	Islamic	TOTAL
Interested	2891	978	1144	1063	1419	7495
	63.3%	39.2%	42.2%	52.6%	41.8%	49.4%
Not intrst	1678	1514	1567	957	1972	7688
	36.7%	60.8%	57.8%	47.4%	58.2%	50.6%
Missing	29	8	24	2	1216	1279
TOTAL	4569	2492	2711	2020	3391	15183
	100.0%	100.0%	100.0%	100.0%	100.0%	

63.3% of the citizens in our three liberal democracies are more interested in politics than any of the other categories. Only the LDCs manage to generate more than a majority of the population that would express some interest in politics. It follows logically that stronger citizen interest in politics would result in greater rates of political participation.

Political participation refers to the actions taken by ordinary citizens in pursuit of their political goals. Most people assume that in democratic societies participation usually takes a number of very conventional forms. For example, voting, signing petitions, or volunteering for political campaigns are all conventional modes of political participation. But we also know that in some countries free elections and the rights associated with political participation are not available to the public. When these basic rights are not guaranteed, we can also assume that participation in more conventional modes of political participation will be much lower.

But we don't need to assume; we can actually test this hypothesis. Let's look at the percentage of the population that has signed a petition.

➤ Data File: **GLOBAL**
➤ Task: **Mapping**
➤ Variable 1: **470) PETITION**
➤ View: **List: Rank**

PETITION: Percent who have signed a political petition. (WVS, 2002)

RANK	CASE NAME	VALUE
1	New Zealand	90.6
2	Sweden	87.3
3	United States	81.3
4	United Kingdom	80.7
5	Australia	78.9
6	Canada	74.1
7	Belgium	71.8
8	Switzerland	68.0
8	France	68.0
10	Norway	64.7

Notice that all of the top ten countries happen to be advanced industrial democracies. In fact, you don't find a country that is not a liberal democracy in the top thirteen! And you do not find a single liberal democracy in the bottom forty. This would indeed support the notion that conventional participation is associated with a high level of democratic development.

What about unconventional forms of participation, like sit-ins where citizens occupy buildings or factories? If our hypothesis is accurate, then we should expect that these actions would be lower in countries where a full range of participatory options is available (liberal democracies) and higher where these options are not as readily available.

SIT-IN: Percentage of the population that has occupied buildings or factories. (WVS, 2002)

Data File: **GLOBAL**
Task: **Mapping**
➤ Variable 1: **471) SIT-IN**
➤ View: **List: Rank**

RANK	CASE NAME	VALUE
1	Greece	27.4
2	Uganda	9.9
3	France	9.3
4	Nigeria	9.1
5	Italy	8.0
6	Belgium	5.9
7	Netherlands	5.4
8	Dominican Republic	4.6
9	India	4.5
10	Chile	4.2

The first thing you should notice is that the percentage of the population that has engaged in this kind of participation is low for every country. However, you will also notice that five of the top ten countries are not liberal democracies. What about other forms of unconventional participation like illegal or unauthorized strikes?

STRIKE: Percentage of the population that has taken part in an unofficial strike. (WVS, 2002)

Data File: **GLOBAL**
Task: **Mapping**
➤ Variable 1: **474) STRIKE**
➤ View: **List: Rank**

RANK	CASE NAME	VALUE
1	Denmark	22.2
2	Armenia	15.0
3	Moldova	12.9
4	France	12.7
5	Uruguay	10.7
6	Czech Republic	10.4
7	India	9.9
8	Greece	9.8
8	Georgia	9.8
10	Korea, South	9.5

Not all strikes are illegal in most countries, but most countries do have laws that govern the conditions under which workers can go on strike. In countries without competitive political systems, strikes can serve to put pressure on political leaders, so we would expect to see more strikes where citizens have more limited recourse to influence politics. The preceding ranking of the percentage of the population that has participated in unauthorized strikes indicates that eight of the top ten countries are not liberal democracies.

From this preliminary examination of conventional and unconventional forms of political participation, it seems that those countries with established protections of civil liberties tend to have the highest percentage of the population engaging in conventional forms of participation (such as petitioning). Those with a weaker tradition of protecting these freedoms tend to have a higher percentage of the population engaged in unconventional forms of participation (like sit-ins or unauthorized strikes).

To better understand the relationship between participation and the type of state, we could rank each participation variable and then try to identify the number of countries in the top ten and bottom ten in each category, but there is actually a better way to do this.

Let's examine the relationship between political participation and the type of nation-state using the WORLDS.7 variable. Our hypothesis will be that "conventional forms of political participation are higher in developed democracies than in those that are less developed." One of the most conventional forms of participation is voter turnout, which is a percentage that compares the number of people that voted in an election to the population of eligible voters. What we want to do is look at the relationship between the percentage of the population that turns out to vote in an election and the WORLDS.7 variable. Before we continue, though, the introduction of one last lesson in research methodology is in order. Conduct the following analysis and then I'll explain why the results aren't useful to us.

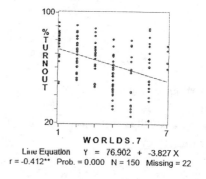

Data File:	**GLOBAL**
➤ *Task:*	**Scatterplot**
➤ *Dependent Variable:*	**475) %TURNOUT**
➤ *Independent Variable:*	**130) WORLDS.7**
➤ *View:*	**Reg. Line**

Line Equation   Y = 76.902 + -3.827 X
r = -0.412** Prob. = 0.000   N = 150   Missing = 22

Carefully examine the regression line and think about how you might summarize the relationship between these two variables. In scatterplot analysis (or any type of correlation analysis), you want to be able to say that as the values for one variable increase, the values for the other variable increase (a positive correlation) or decrease (a negative correlation). However, in order to make such an interpretation, the category values for both variables must have some type of natural or intrinsic meaning. That is, a category of 2 (Communist/Postcommunist) must have more of whatever the variable is measuring than a category coded 1 (Liberal Democracy). A category of 3 (New Industrializing Country) must have more of whatever is being measured than a category coded 2 (Communist/Postcommunist), and so forth. But as you examine the WORLDS.7 variable, you quickly notice that the categories 1 through 7 do not have an intrinsic order. For example, it wouldn't make any sense to say that as the type of state *increases*, the voter turnout *decreases*. Nor would it make any sense to say that a liberal democratic state is less of a state than a newly industrialized country (NIC). With the WORLDS.7 variable, the values 1 through 7 are used strictly to represent different groupings of countries. The category numbers have no other meaning. Hence, this variable cannot be used in correlation or scatterplot analysis.

You might be thinking, "Why don't we use the CROSS-TABULATION task?" Good question. The WORLDS.7 variable can be used in cross-tabulations. The problem is with the other variable, %TURNOUT. The voter turnout variable is a decimal variable that has over 100 different category values ranging from 21.7% to 92.5%. Cross-tabulations work best when both variables have predetermined or grouped categories (e.g., First World, Second World, Third World; Yes, No). If you try to create a cross-tabulation using WORLDS.7 and %TURNOUT, your table will have 3 columns and about 100 rows! Such a table would be useless. (In fact, ExplorIt won't even let you create a table that has more than 100 categories.)

So, what do you do when one variable has a limited set of categories (e.g., WORLDS.7) and the other variable has a wide range of values that go from low to high? If the independent variable (i.e., the variable causing the effect in the other variable) is the one that has a limited set of categories, you can use ExplorIt's Analysis Of Variance task. Return to the main menu and select ANOVA (the acronym for ANalysis Of VAriance).

Data File: **GLOBAL**
➤ Task: **ANOVA**
➤ Dependent Variable: **475) %TURNOUT**
➤ Independent Variable: **130) WORLDS.7**
➤ View: **Graph**

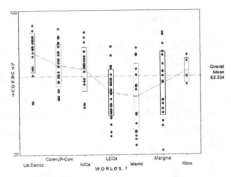

To reproduce this graphic, select the ANOVA task, and select 475) %TURNOUT as the dependent variable and 130) WORLDS.7 as the dependent variable. The first view shown is the Graph view.

What does this graph tell us? To begin with, just like a scatterplot, each nation is represented by one of the dots on the graph. The location of a nation on the graph is based on the percentage of voter turnout in the nation's national election and its category in the Seven Worlds classification. First the dot is placed horizontally according to its category. You will notice that on the bottom of the graph, each category in the Seven Worlds classification is represented. For example, the country of Italy would be placed in the Liberal Democracy category. Then Italy is placed vertically according to its voter turnout in the last election (approximately 92.5%), which is scaled on the left side of the graph.

The rectangle shown for each category of the independent variable (WORLDS.7) indicates the high and low range in which most countries in that category are located. While some countries will be located outside of this range, the majority (around 70%) will be found within the range of this rectangle.

When you read an ANOVA graphic, focus on the mean in this graphic (i.e., the average voter turnout) for each category of the independent variable (WORLDS.7). The location of the mean is shown with a flat line in the center of each rectangle. Your task, then, is to compare the mean for one category against the means for the other categories. It's fairly easy to see whether a mean for one category is higher or lower than a mean for another category because there is a line that connects each of these mean points. The flatter the lines between the means, the less difference there is between the categories. For example, there is a very substantial difference in average voter turnout between NICs and Islamic countries, but very little difference between Islamic countries and less developed countries (LDCs).

We can now easily compare different types of nation-states. In the next graph you can see that liberal democracies have the highest levels of voter turnout. The average voter turnout in communist/post-communist systems is lower than it is in liberal democracies. Islamic countries and marginal states have the lowest levels of voter turnout. You can also look at the average turnout values themselves in the form of a table.

Means, Standard Deviations and Number of Cases of
Dependent Var: %TURNOUT
by Categories of Independent Var: WORLDS.7
Difference of means across groups is statistically significant
(Prob. = 0.000)

	N	Mean	Std.Dev.
Lib Democ	24	77.054	11.187
Comm/P-Com	28	69.882	11.780
NICs	21	67.552	12.488
LDCs	34	54.291	12.990
Islamic	18	52.039	18.756
Marginal	20	59.475	17.976
Micro	5	66.680	6.895

If you are continuing from the previous example, select the [Means] button.

This table shows the actual average level of voter turnout within each category of the independent variable (WORLDS.7). As we can see, liberal democratic systems have the highest average level of voter turnout (77.1%). Communist/postcommunist states have lower average turnout (69.9%), and NICs (67.6) are at almost the same level as communist/postcommunist states. LDCs (54.3%) and Islamic states (52%) also have very similar voter turnout rates. Interestingly enough, marginal states (states in the midst of civil wars) have relatively high voter turnout rates (59.5%). Microstates (66.7%), with very small populations, tend to have turnout rates similar to NICs.

The ANOVA task is pretty easy to use. The initial graphic generally provides a clear picture of whether the pattern supports your initial hypothesis. If it does, then go to the screen with the means to view the actual numbers behind the table. There is one more issue: statistical significance. How do you know if the differences between the means are due to chance or if you can consider the results statistically significant? Simple. As in our earlier analyses with Cramer's V, there is a probability value shown directly above the table containing the means. If the difference is statistically significant, there is a sentence that states that the "difference of means across groups is statistically significant." This can be verified by examining the probability value. If it is between .000 and .05, we can feel confident that the differences between the means are not random findings. If the value is over .05, there is a chance that our findings are due to randomness. In this case, since the probability value is 0.000, we know that these results are statistically significant. If the significance is greater than .05, then we cannot say that there is a relationship between the two variables in our analysis.

The results indicate that we may not need to reject the hypothesis that states, "Conventional forms of participation are higher in developed democracies than in those that are less developed." Voter turnout (a conventional form of political participation) is the highest in the liberal democracies category.

In the worksheet section that follows, we'll refine our hypotheses about political participation so that we might better understand the factors that make democracy work.

Terms and Concepts

Competitive political systems

Conventional political participation

Unconventional political participation

Sit-ins

Petition

Voter turnout

Mean

Analysis of Variance (ANOVA)

WORKSHEET

NAME: _____

COURSE: _____

DATE: _____

CHAPTER

5

REVIEW QUESTIONS

Based on the first part of this chapter, answer True or False to the following items:

1. Signing a petition and voting are conventional forms of political participation.   T   F

2. Liberal democracies tend to have higher levels of voter turnout and petitioning than LDCs.   T   F

3. People in liberal democracies are more likely to be interested in politics than citizens of other types of countries.   T   F

4. Scatterplots are not that useful when you are using a variable that has a few categories without any meaning to their order.   T   F

5. When your independent variable has a specific set of categories (e.g., Yes, No; Free, Not Free) and the dependent variable has a wide range of values that go from 0 to 100, it is more appropriate to use the ANOVA task than the CROSS-TABULATION or SCATTERPLOT tasks.   T   F

6. The ANOVA task is different from the CROSS-TABULATION or SCATTERPLOT task in that it does not require you to determine statistical significance.   T   F

7. The differences in voter turnout across different types of nation-states are statistically significant.   T   F

EXPLORIT QUESTIONS

If you have any difficulties using the software to obtain the appropriate information, or if you want to learn more about additional features of Explorit's ANOVA task, refer to the Explorit help topics under the Help menu.

I. In the preliminary part of this chapter, you analyzed political interest and the type of nation-state for eight countries using the WVS02all file. Now let's look at the same variables with a larger set of countries using ANOVA. Gabriel Almond and Sidney Verba have argued that citizens in liberal democracies will have a higher level of interest in politics. Thus, we might hypothesize:

H1: Citizens in liberal democracies will be more likely to take an interest in politics than those in less democratic countries.

H2: Citizens in liberal democracies will be more likely to discuss politics with others than those in less democratic countries.

Chapter 5: Political Participation: Making Democracy Work

91

State the null hypothesis for H1 (refer back to Worksheet 4 for a model null hypothesis):

_____

_____

Now let's test this hypothesis.

> *Data File:* **GLOBAL**
> *Task:* **ANOVA**
> *Dependent Variable:* **476) POL INTRST**
> *Independent Variable:* **130) WORLDS.7**
> *View:* **Means**

> You may need to use both the Graph view and the Means view to answer the following questions.

8.   The graph indicates that citizens in liberal democracies have a higher interest in politics than do citizens in other types of nation-states.   T   F

9.   What is the mean level of political interest for citizens in liberal democracies?   _____

10. What is the mean level of political interest for citizens in Islamic countries?   _____

11. Is the difference in political interest between these types of countries significant?   Yes   No

12. What is the probability?   _____

13. Do these results indicate that you should reject the null hypothesis associated with H1?   Yes   No

Now let's analyze the willingness to discuss politics, which is the second part of Almond and Verba's hypothesis.

State the null hypothesis for H2:

_____

_____

> *Data File:* **GLOBAL**
> *Task:* **ANOVA**
> *Dependent Variable:* **477) TALK POL**
> *Independent Variable:* **130) WORLDS.7**
> *View:* **Means**

> You may need to use both the Graph view and the Means view to answer the following questions.

In the space provided, write the mean percentage of the population who often discuss politics with friends.

14. Lib Democ.   _____

15. Comm/P-Com   _____

16. NICs   _____

17. LDCs   _____

18. Islamic   _____

19. Are the differences between these types of countries significant?   Yes   No

20. What is the probability?   _____

21. As predicted, citizens in liberal democracies discuss politics more than citizens in any other type of nation-state.   T   F

22. From these results, we can support a new hypothesis: Citizens in communist and postcommunist societies discuss politics more than citizens in liberal democracies.   T   F

23. Do these results indicate that you should reject the null hypothesis associated with H2?   Yes   No

II. Let's return to the issue with which we started this chapter: political participation in liberal democracies. Is there a certain characteristic that liberal democracies have, but other types of states don't have? In the analysis below, examine each of the dependent variables provided in relation to the independent variable WORLDS.7.

>   Data File: **GLOBAL**
>   Task: **ANOVA**
> ➤ Dependent Variables: **470) PETITION**
>   **472) BOYCOTT**
>   **473) DEMONSTR**
>   **471) SIT-IN**
> ➤ Independent Variable: **130) WORLDS.7**
>   ➤ View: **Means**

In the space provided, write down the mean percentage for the four types of states (ignore the categories for Islamic, marginal, and microstates) and the significance for each variable.

STATE TYPE	PETITION	BOYCOTT	DEMON- STRATION	SIT-IN
LIBERAL DEMOC.	_____	_____	_____	_____
COMM/P-COM	_____	_____	_____	_____
NICs	_____	_____	_____	_____
LDCs	_____	_____	_____	_____
SIGNIFICANT?	Y N	Y N	Y N	Y N

24. Citizens in liberal democracies are more accustomed to signing petitions and boycotting products than citizens in other types of states.   T   F

25. The percentage of citizens who participate in demonstrations is likely to be higher in countries with underdeveloped democratic systems.   T   F

26. We cannot draw conclusions about the relationship between the level of participation in demonstrations and the type of state because the relationship is not significant.   T   F

27. Citizens are more likely to have occupied buildings or factories (SIT-IN) in liberal democracies than in NICs.   T   F

III. So far we have examined participation at the nation-state level, but in reality, political participation has more to do with individual decisions as they relate to the political process. To better understand individual political participation, we need to use individual-level data.

What factors make people more likely to sign petitions? What factors influence people to participate in demonstrations? Let's explore these questions using the CROSS-TABULATION task. As in the worksheet section for Chapter 4, the variable numbers are not indicated as they may be different for each country's file. We'll use the World Values Survey (WVS) question that asks respondents whether they have ever signed a petition. For each country listed below, you will need to open the appropriate data file, conduct the cross-tabulation that is indicated, write down the percentaged results for the first row of the table (i.e., % Have done), write down the value for V, and then indicate whether the results are statistically significant.

> **If you have not used the CROSS-TABULATION task with survey data, you may wish to review Chapter 4.**

➤ *Data Files:* **WVS02–UK**
                       WVS02–GERMANY
                       WVS02–JAPAN
                       WVS02–SWEDEN
                       WVS02–USA
➤ *Task:* **Cross-tabulation**
➤ *Row Variables:* **SIGN PETN**
                       DEMONSTR
➤ *Column Variables:* **CLASS-3**
                       GENDER
➤ *View:* **Tables**
➤ *Display:* **Column %**

Fill in the tables below with the percentage that have signed petitions and then answer the "In Your Own Words" questions at the end of this chapter. [Hint: Complete all analyses for one country and then continue to the next.]

SIGN PETN by CLASS-3

% HAVE DONE	UPPER	MIDDLE	WORKING	VALUE V	SIGNIFICANT?	
UK	_____%	_____%	_____%	_____	YES	NO
GERMANY	_____%	_____%	_____%	_____	YES	NO
JAPAN	_____%	_____%	_____%	_____	YES	NO
SWEDEN	_____%	_____%	_____%	_____	YES	NO
USA	_____%	_____%	_____%	_____	YES	NO

SIGN PETN by GENDER

% HAVE DONE	MALE	FEMALE	VALUE V	SIGNIFICANT?	
UK	_____%	_____%	_____	YES	NO
GERMANY	_____%	_____%	_____	YES	NO
JAPAN	_____%	_____%	_____	YES	NO
SWEDEN	_____%	_____%	_____	YES	NO
USA	_____%	_____%	_____	YES	NO

Fill in the tables below with the percentage that have participated in demonstrations and then answer the "In Your Own Words" questions.

DEMONSTR by CLASS-3

% HAVE DONE	UPPER	MIDDLE	WORKING	VALUE V	SIGNIFICANT?	
UK	_____%	_____%	_____%	_____	YES	NO
GERMANY	_____%	_____%	_____%	_____	YES	NO
JAPAN	_____%	_____%	_____%	_____	YES	NO
SWEDEN	_____%	_____%	_____%	_____	YES	NO
USA	_____%	_____%	_____%	_____	YES	NO

DEMONSTR by GENDER

% HAVE DONE	MALE	FEMALE	VALUE V	SIGNIFICANT?	
UK	_____%	_____%	_____	YES	NO
GERMANY	_____%	_____%	_____	YES	NO
JAPAN	_____%	_____%	_____	YES	NO
SWEDEN	_____%	_____%	_____	YES	NO
USA	_____%	_____%	_____	YES	NO

IN YOUR OWN WORDS

In your own words, please answer the following questions.

1. What is the nature of the relationship between political participation (measured by signing petitions and participating in demonstrations) and social class? In which countries is class strongly related to political participation? Where is it weakest? Be sure to support your generalizations with evidence from your analysis.

2. Do women have higher or lower rates of political participation? What is the nature of the relationship between political participation and gender? In which countries is gender strongly related to political participation? Where is it weakest? Be sure to support your generalizations with evidence from your analysis.

Europe

CHAPTER 6

ELECTORAL SYSTEMS AND POLITICAL PARTIES IN LIBERAL DEMOCRACIES

*Democracy is still upon its trial. The civic genius of
our people is its only bulwark.*

WILLIAM JAMES, 1897

*Party-spirit . . . at best is but the madness of many for
the gain of a few.*

ALEXANDER POPE, 1714

Tasks: Mapping, Univariate, ANOVA, Cross-tabulation, Historical Trends
Data Files: GLOBAL, EUROPE, HISTORY, CSES-GERMANY02, CSES-UK05

ELECTORAL SYSTEMS

With so many new democratic governments across the world, it seems necessary to examine the different types of electoral systems that are currently in place. Elections are one of the ways that citizens attempt to influence the politics in their country. In a sense, elections translate the sentiments of citizens into a formal government. Most democracies hold elections every three to five years so citizens can express their political, economic, and even social preferences. These expressions often change the composition of the leadership that governs each democratic nation-state.

Most people who are unfamiliar with comparative politics are surprised when they learn of the many different types of electoral systems. The Institute for Democracy and Electoral Assistance (IDEA) has classified the world's electoral systems into nine different types.

> ➤ *Data File:* **GLOBAL**
> ➤ *Task:* **Univariate**
> ➤ *Primary Variable:* **448) ELECT04**
> ➤ *View:* **Bar - Freq.**

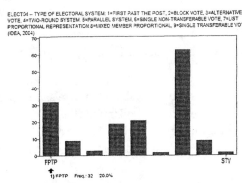

ELECT04 -- TYPE OF ELECTORAL SYSTEM: 1=FIRST PAST THE POST, 2=BLOCK VOTE, 3=ALTERNATIVE VOTE, 4=TWO-ROUND SYSTEM, 5=PARALLEL SYSTEM, 6=SINGLE NON-TRANSFERABLE VOTE, 7=LIST PROPORTIONAL REPRESENTATION 8=MIXED MEMBER PROPORTIONAL, 9=SINGLE TRANSFERABLE VOTE (IDEA, 2004)

1) FPTP   Freq.: 32   20.0%

Make sure you select the [Bar - Freq.] option. Move the right or left arrows on your keyboard to see the frequency percentage of each electoral system type.

We don't have time to go into the differences between these electoral systems, but this graph does give you a sense of the variation that exists. As shown below, each of these systems can be reduced to three categories: plurality-majoritarian electoral systems, proportional electoral systems, and semi-proportional electoral systems.

Plurality-majoritarian	**Semi-proportional**	**Proportional**
First Past the Post	Parallel System	List Proportional Representation
Block Voting	Single-Nontransferable Vote	Mixed Member Proportional
Alternative Vote		Single Transferable Vote
Two Round System		

Plurality-majoritarian electoral systems (or simply, majoritarian electoral systems) favor majorities or large parties and limit the number of parties in the system. For the most part, legislators in these systems are elected by a majority (50% + 1) of votes in a district or by the plurality of the votes cast (i.e., he/she who has the most votes wins). **Proportional** electoral systems seek to translate the percentage of votes for a given party directly to the number of seats that will be in a legislature. **Semi-proportional** electoral systems fall in between these two extremes and mix the use of majoritarian and proportional methods of election. As such, these electoral systems can be placed along a spectrum, with majoritarian systems on one end and proportional systems on the other end.

| **Majoritarian** | **Semi-proportional** | **Proportional** |

Let's look at the percentage of the world's electoral systems that fall into these three "families" of electoral systems.

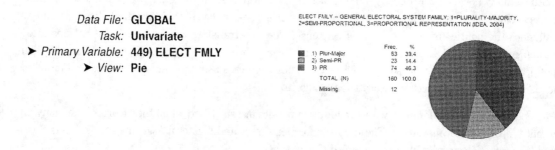

Data File: **GLOBAL**
Task: **Univariate**
➤ Primary Variable: **449) ELECT FMLY**
➤ View: **Pie**

ELECT FMLY – GENERAL ELECTORAL SYSTEM FAMILY: 1=PLURALITY-MAJORITY, 2=SEMI-PROPORTIONAL, 3=PROPORTIONAL REPRESENTATION (IDEA, 2004)

		Freq.	%
	1) Plur-Major	53	39.4
	2) Semi-PR	23	14.4
	3) PR	74	46.3
	TOTAL (N)	160	100.0
	Missing	12	

More than one-third (39.4%) of the world's countries use some kind of majority system, about half (46.3%) use proportional representation, and around 14% use a semi-proportional system. Because of the prevalence of majoritarian and proportional systems, our analysis below will concentrate primarily on them.

Majoritarian systems tend to eliminate small parties and strengthen large parties. This is the type of system that exists in the United States and the United Kingdom. Most majoritarian (or modified majoritarian) systems divide the nation into relatively similar-sized districts. When elections occur, several parties run against each other for each seat that is available. The majoritarian system favors the winning party by overrepresenting it in the legislature. The advantage of this type of electoral system is that it creates a strong majority and often a strong minority to govern the country. To illustrate a majoritarian system, examine Table 6.1 for the United Kingdom election of 2005. The first column of numbers shows the percentage of vote that each party obtained, the second column shows the percentage of seats the party actually won, and the last column indicates the percentage of over- or underrepresentation of each party in the United Kingdom's Parliament.

Table 6.1. UK Election and Party Representation, 2005 Results

Party	% of Total Vote	% Seats in Parliament	Over/Under Represented
Labour	35.3	55.1	+19.8
Liberal Democrats	22.1	9.6	–12.5
Conservatives	32.3	30.1	–2.2
Other	10.3	4.6	–5.7

The Labour Party won only 35.3% of the vote, but it wields a strong-majority (55.1%) in Parliament thanks to the majoritarian electoral system. At the expense of the liberal democrats, the conservatives, and the other small parties, the Labour Party is overrepresented in Parliament by 19.8 percentage points! The liberal democrats, which obtained 22.1% of the votes and received only 9.6% of the seats, are underrepresented by 12.5 percentage points. Other parties without a plurality of votes also suffer the same fate.

Proportional electoral systems are at the other end of the spectrum. Instead of trying to ensure a majority in Parliament, these systems seek to ensure fair representation of voter preference. Sweden is a good example of a country that uses a proportional electoral system. As shown in Table 6.2, the Social Democratic Party received the greatest percentage of votes in the 2002 election (39.8%), and it ended up obtaining 41.2% of the seats in the Swedish Riksdag (Parliament). The Swedish voting rules specify that seats in the legislature must be allocated in proportion to the percentage of the vote that each party received in the election. As you look down the list, you'll see that all parties are within 1.4 percentage point of this desired goal. Parties that receive less than 4% of the popular vote are not represented in Parliament.

Table 6.2 Swedish Election and Party Representation, 2002 Results

Party	% of Total Vote	% Seats in Parliament	Over/Under Represented
Social Democrats	39.8	41.2	+1.4
Left Party	8.3	8.6	+0.3
Greens	4.6	4.9	+0.3
Conservatives	15.2	15.8	+0.6
Liberals	13.3	13.8	+0.5
Christian Democrats	9.1	9.5	+0.4
Center	6.1	6.3	+0.2
Other Parties	3.0	0.0	–3.0

As indicated above, the great advantage of a proportional electoral system is that it fairly represents the voters' preferences. The disadvantage is that no single party has a majority of the seats in the legislature. In order to govern in this type of system, parties must cooperate with one another and form coalitions. This makes the task of governing more challenging.

From this example it is clear that electoral systems can influence the composition of power among the leadership. But do electoral systems shape other features of politics, government, and policy? Let's examine the effect of the electoral system on the representation of women in parliament to better understand this issue. The following variable measures the percentage of members who are elected to that nation's parliament (or legislature).

          Data File: **GLOBAL**
          ➤ *Task:* **Mapping**
      ➤ *Variable 1:* **347) %FEM.LEGIS**
          ➤ *View:* **Map**
        ➤ *Display:* **Legend**

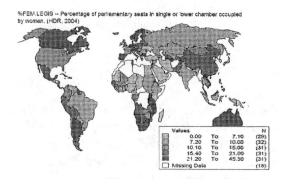

Click on the nation of Sweden to see where it ranks. The percentage of women in parliament and Sweden's rank will appear at the bottom of the graphic. Now click on the United States.

As you can see, the representation of women varies widely. It also seems as though there are some regional patterns in the map. Clearly, most of the countries with high representation of women in parliament are located in Europe. But there are also some exceptions to this pattern. Women seem well represented in Argentina, Costa Rica, South Africa, Namibia, Mozambique, and Tanzania. What causes women to be better represented in some countries and not so well represented in others?

Let's examine this relationship to see if the electoral system that a nation-state uses is associated with the representation of women. What we want to do is look at the relationship between the representation of women in the legislature and the ELECT FMLY variable. (If you have not used the ANOVA task before now, you may want to review this task as it is introduced in Chapter 5.)

          Data File: **GLOBAL**
          ➤ *Task:* **ANOVA**
   ➤ *Dependent Variable:* **347) %FEM.LEGIS**
  ➤ *Independent Variable:* **449) ELECT FMLY**
          ➤ *View:* **Graph**

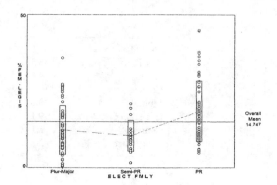

                                              Comparative Politics

What does this graph tell us? We can now easily compare different types of electoral systems. In this graph you can see that the first category, plurality-majoritarian systems, has the second lowest level of female representation in the legislature. The average score of semi-proportional systems is just lower than that of plurality-majoritarian systems. The third category (PR systems) has substantially higher average levels of female representation than the other two electoral systems. You can also look at these mean values themselves in the form of a table.

Data File: **GLOBAL**
Task: **ANOVA**
Dependent Variable: **347) %FEM.LEGIS**
Independent Variable: **449) ELECT FMLY**
➤ View: **Means**

Means, Standard Deviations and Number of Cases of
Dependent Var: %FEM.LEGIS
by Categories of Independent Var: ELECT FMLY
Difference of means across groups is statistically significant
(Prob. = 0.000)

	N	Mean	Std.Dev.
Plur-Major	56	12.011	8.147
Semi-PR	21	10.138	5.161
PR	70	18.319	10.112

If you are continuing from the previous example, select the [Means] button.

As you learned in Chapter 5, this table shows the actual average level of women's representation within each category of the independent variable (ELECT FMLY). As we can see, PR systems have the highest average level of women's representation in the legislature (18.3%). The semi-PR systems have the lowest average level of women's representation (10.1%). The plurality-majoritarian systems are far below the PR systems, with a mean level of representation at 12.0%, but they are higher than the semi-PR systems.

It is one thing to note that women's representation is higher in PR systems and quite another to understand why this is the case. In plurality-majoritaraian systems, voters generally elect a single representative. Often each candidate represents a single party and voters face choosing one or another candidate. Imagine that you prefer to elect women to office because they are underrepresented in the United States. You are faced with electing a female candidate from the Democratic Party or a male from the Republican Party. This puts the voter on the horns of a dilemma. Generally speaking, for most people ideology is more important than the gender of a candidate. If you are like those who care more about ideology than gender, you would probably vote for the Republican male candidate.

There are a wide variety of PR systems, but in most PR-list systems, voters do not have to choose between the gender of a candidate and the party of their choice. If you live in Sweden and prefer women in leadership, you can actualize both of these preferences at the polls. In its simplest form, List PR involves each party presenting a list of candidates to the electorate, voters voting for a party, and parties receiving seats in proportion to their overall share of the national vote. Winning candidates are taken from the lists in order of their position on the lists. So, when a voter enters the voting booth in Sweden, she selects one party's list of candidates. In many countries she can also vote for candidates who are lower on the list so that they are moved up the list. For example, she may want to promote more women candidates in her chosen party, so she would give a vote to a candidate on her list. In PR-list systems, voters can choose a party and influence the representation of the types of candidates that they prefer at the same time.

In the worksheet section at the end of the chapter, you'll examine how election models have an impact on factors such as election turnouts and the number of parties that participate in the election process.

POLITICAL PARTIES

While candidates compete for votes during elections, it is also the case that almost every election system features a system of political parties. These party systems differ throughout the world, but have the greatest coherence in the liberal democracies of Europe.

One way to think comparatively about European political parties is to divide them into "families" of parties that are ideologically similar. Since the end of World War II there have been about 12 main party families in Europe. Not every family is in every country. In fact, a country like the United Kingdom will have only four of the twelve party families represented here. But organizing political parties does help us to simplify the study of political parties so that we can compare one nation with another (see Table 6.3).

Table 6.3 Party Families in Europe

Extreme Left	Left	Center	Right	Extreme Right	Other
Communist	Social Dem.	Liberal	Christian Dem.	Nationalist	Regionalist
Socialist	Labour	Agrarian	Conservative		
Former Communist	Greens				

The extreme left consists of those parties that are more radical in their orientation to democratic politics. In a few countries they are still called communist parties, but many of them have changed their names to something that sounds a bit more up to date. In most European countries these parties support the democratic process but are also willing to use strikes, demonstrations, and the nationalization of industry to achieve their goals. Communists usually have strong ties to labor unions in their respective countries. Open the EUROPE data file and rank the percentage of the vote obtained by extreme left parties in recent elections.

➤ Data File: **EUROPE**
➤ Task: **Mapping**
➤ Variable 1: **31) %EXT.LEFT**
➤ View:` **List: Rank**

%EXT.LEFT: Percentage of electoral support for parties of the extreme left (including communist and former communist). (P&E 2006)

RANK	CASE NAME	VALUE
1	Moldova	51.0
2	Bulgaria	31.0
3	Russia	21.6
4	Czech Republic	12.8
5	Italy	8.1
6	Portugal	6.5
7	Greece	5.9
8	France	4.8
9	Slovak Republic	3.9
10	Latvia	3.8

As you can see from the ranking, the extreme left is popular only in a few countries in Eastern and Southern Europe. An analysis of the support for communism over time in Germany, Sweden, and France also reveals some interesting patterns.

> ➤ *Data File:* **HISTORY**
>   ➤ *Task:* **Historical Trends**
> ➤ *Variables:* **4) %COMMGM**
>   **5) %COMMFR**
>   **6) %COMMSW**

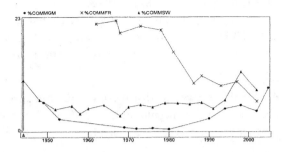

Electoral support for communists in Germany, France, and Sweden

In Sweden (red) and Germany (blue), electoral support for communist parties has been relatively low compared to France (green). In France, support for communist parties was highest during the 1960s and 70s when around 20% of the vote went to the Communist Party. Since 1980, the French Communist Party has fallen on hard times.

> *Data File:* **HISTORY**
>   *Task:* **Historical Trends**
> ➤ *Variables:* **7) %SOCIALFR**
>   **5) %COMMFR**

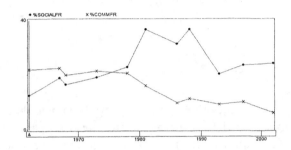

Electoral support for the socialist and communist parties in France

This graph again shows the communist vote in France over the last three decades, but this time it's contrasted with the trend line for the French Socialist Party (shown in blue). Scroll through the events until you get to the 1981 election of socialist François Mitterrand as president of the French Republic. You will also notice that since this time, the socialists have dominated the political left of French politics consistently outpacing the communists at every election.

Let's take a look at the Socialist Party across all of Europe.

> ➤ *Data File:* **EUROPE**
>   ➤ *Task:* **Mapping**
> ➤ *Variable 1:* **33) %SOCIALIST**
>   ➤ *View:* **Map**
>   ➤ *Display:* **Legend**

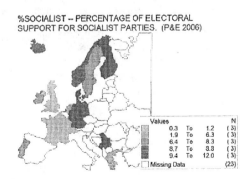

Although socialist parties are categorized on the extreme left, they are generally more moderate than their communist counterparts. A key factor that sets socialists apart from social democrats (categorized as "left") is that the former are more prone to advocate state ownership of industry. More recently, former communists and other extreme leftists have become the leading opponents of globalization on the left.

As this map shows, socialist parties have been fairly popular in Scandinavia and Southern Europe and continue to be quite popular in Eastern Europe as well. If you look at the ranked list for this variable, you see that Yugoslavia (12.0%), Finland (9.9%), and Denmark (9.4%) are strongholds for the socialist parties.

Let's look at the map for social democrats.

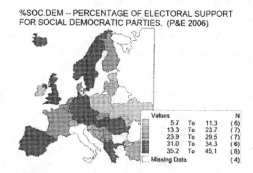

Data File: **EUROPE**

Task: **Mapping**

➤ Variable 1: **35) %SOC.DEM**

➤ View: **Map**

➤ Display: **Legend**

Historically, social democrats have been avid defenders of democracy, but they have also actively promoted the construction of an extensive welfare state in the European nations where they reside. Innovations such as old-age pensions, universal health care, and child care have been the policies championed by the social democrats.

Social democrats have been among the largest parties on the left in Europe. If you look at the ranked list for social democrats, you see that in recent elections between 40% and 50% of the vote in Hungary, Portugal, Greece, and Spain went to social democrats. This party has obtained 20% of the vote in 25 European nations. Historically speaking, social democrats have been significant actors in the party politics of Europe. Their influence in countries like Germany, Sweden, and the United Kingdom has profoundly shaped the policies of these nations.

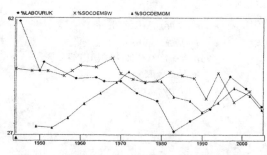

➤ Data File: **HISTORY**

➤ Task: **Historical Trends**

➤ Variables: **8) %LABOURUK**

9) %SOCDEMSW

10) %SOCDEMGM

Electoral support for social democratic parties in UK, Sweden, and Germany

This graphic shows the electoral fortunes of social democratic parties in the United Kingdom (called the Labour Party), Sweden, and Germany. Notice that with the exception of the Labour Party's strong showing in the 1945 election, social democratic strength in the three countries was at its highest in the late 1960s and early 70s. All three of the parties declined with the economic crises of the 1970s and early 80s. Interestingly enough, following the end of the Cold War, most of these parties started to bounce back, but they have faded a bit in recent elections.

The Green Party is a recent upstart that is also categorized as a party on the left. It emphasizes local control of the government and environmental concerns. It's not exactly clear where a party like this should be placed on the political spectrum, but because of its emphasis on political equality and, sometimes, radical change, the Green Party is placed on the left side of the political spectrum. Let's see how it has fared over the last couple of decades in France, Sweden, and Germany.

> Data File: **HISTORY**
> Task: **Historical Trends**
> ➤ Variables: **11) %GREENFR**
> **12) %GREENSW**
> **13) %GREENGM**

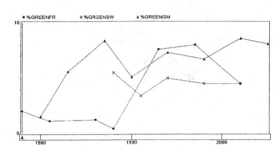

Electoral support for green parties in France, Sweden, and Germany

The Green Party in France received around 1% of the vote in the 1980s, but by the mid-1990s this grew to 8% of the vote. Across all three countries, though, the Green Party has never obtained as much as 10% of the vote.

Here are two ranked lists for all European countries that have a green party. The top list shows the percentage of vote for green parties in the most recent election. The bottom list shows the actual percentage of parliamentary seats that were allocated to the green parties as a result of these elections.

> ➤ Data File: **EUROPE**
> ➤ Task: **Mapping**
> ➤ Variable 1: **37) %GREEN**
> ➤ Variable 2: **38) STS.GREEN**
> ➤ Views: **List: Rank**

%GREEN: Percentage of electoral support for green parties

RANK	CASE NAME	VALUE
1	Luxembourg	11.6
2	Austria	9.5
3	Germany	8.1
4	Finland	8.0
5	Switzerland	7.9

STS.GREEN: Percentage of parliamentary seats allocated to green parties

RANK	CASE NAME	VALUE
1	Luxembourg	11.7
2	Austria	9.3
3	Germany	8.3
4	Switzerland	7.0
5	Finland	7.0

You can see from the rank list for the map that only 15 of the 38 nations in Europe have green parties that have made a political showing in a recent election. They retain parliamentary seats in almost all of the countries where they have won a measurable percentage of the vote. Issues such as the war in Iraq, nuclear power, and environmental conservation tend to be important to the Greens.

Liberal parties tend to be at the center of the political spectrum. These parties were the first "reforming" parties in Europe. Originally, they sought to make the political processes more democratic, advocated voting rights for women and workers, and have also been strong advocates of free-market economics.

Data File: **EUROPE**
Task: **Mapping**
➤ Variable 1: **39) %LIBERAL**
➤ View: **Map**
➤ Display: **Legend**

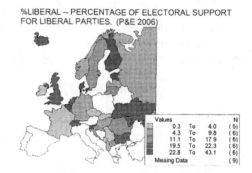

The pattern of this map isn't especially clear. If you look at the ranked list, you'll see that many of the Eastern European nations have high percentages of votes going to liberal parties, such as Estonia (43.1%), Slovenia (22.8%), and Ukraine (22.3%). Perhaps the democratic and free-market ideas espoused by the liberal parties have more salience in countries where democracy and market economies are only now emerging.

Once again, let's see how the liberal democratic parties have fared over the last several decades. We'll pick Sweden, the United Kingdom, and the free democrats of Germany as illustrations.

➤ Data File: **HISTORY**
➤ Task: **Historical Trends**
➤ Variables: **14) %FREEDEMGM**
15) %LIBRLSW
16) %LIBDEMUK

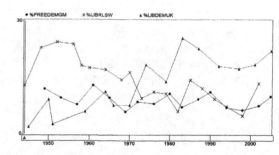

Electoral support for liberal parties in UK, Sweden, and Germany

Since World War II, liberal democratic parties have generally been too small to govern on their own or to lead coalitions in any parliament, but they have often served as effective partners to parties of both the left and the right. As a result of this pattern of partnership, these parties have remained relatively vital, albeit small. In Germany, the free democrats have fluctuated around the same rate of support (around 10%) for 50 years. In Sweden, the liberals were once fairly strong, but their influence has waned until it re-emerged in 2002. In the United Kingdom, the liberals have suffered several divisions but have recently reconstituted themselves to become a force for the other parties to reckon with.

Comparative Politics

Let's shift to the right side of the political spectrum and look at Christian democratic parties and conservative parties.

➤ *Data File:* **EUROPE**
  ➤ *Task:* **Mapping**
➤ *Variable 1:* **43) %CH.DEM**
    ➤ *View:* **Map**
  ➤ *Display:* **Legend**

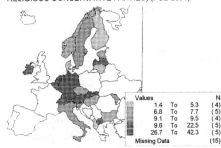

If the social democrats have been the dominant party on the left in postwar Europe, then either Christian democratic parties or secular conservative parties have been the dominant parties on the political right. Some scholars describe Christian democracy as having three distinct strands.[1] The predominately Catholic version of the party was founded in many Catholic countries (Austria, Belgium, Italy, Luxembourg, and Switzerland) to advance the interests of the Catholic Church as governments became more secular during the 19th century. In Germany, Christian democrats draw support from Catholics and Protestants. And in Northern Europe (Denmark, Norway, Sweden, Netherlands), there are very small Protestant evangelical Christian democratic parties. These parties have usually been advocates for a more "socially conservative" agenda, meaning that the defense of traditional morality has been important. Unlike American religious conservatives, the Christian democrats have also usually been moderate advocates for social benefits such as pensions and worker rights, and they exhibit a reluctance to pursue policies that result in class conflict.

➤ *Data File:* **HISTORY**
  ➤ *Task:* **Historical Trends**
➤ *Variables:* **20) %CHDEMSW**
               21) %CHDEMGM

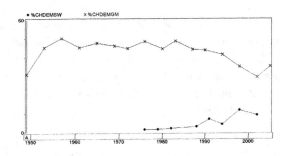

Support for Christian democrats in Sweden and Germany

One can see from the analysis of historical trends that the inclusion of Protestants and Catholics has served the German party well (shown in green). The German party has consistently dominated the center-right of German politics since the end of War World II. The Swedish party has been represented only since the 1970s, but has actually performed better in recent times. In 1991 the Christian democrats in Sweden even served as a partner in the government with a coalition of center-right political parties.

The conservative party, operating from a secular platform, is also on the right side of the political spectrum. Let's start by looking at trend lines for the conservative parties in France, Sweden, and the United Kingdom.

---

[1] This characterization of Christian democratic parties is drawn from Michael Gallagher, Michael Laver, and Peter Mair, Representative Government in Modern Europe (New York: McGraw-Hill, 1995), pp. 192–194.

Data File: **HISTORY**

Task: **Historical Trends**

➤ Variables: **22) %CONSERVFR**

       23) %CONSERVSW

       24) %CONSERVUK

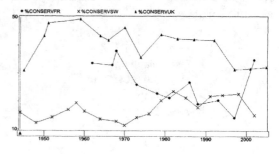

Support for conservatives in France, Sweden, and the UK

Historically speaking, secular conservatives peaked in Britain and France during the 1950s and 60s respectively. In both countries the party experienced a resurgence in the 1980s, but its support then dropped off until a recent resurgence by conservatives in France in 2002. In Sweden, secular conservatives have been the largest party on the right, but they have lost ground to the more centrist liberals. What is the pattern of conservative support across Europe?

➤ Data File: **EUROPE**

➤ Task: **Mapping**

➤ Variable 1: **45) %CONSERVAT**

➤ View: **Map**

➤ Display: **Legend**

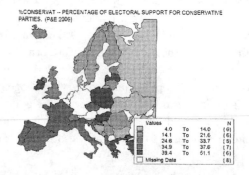

As is evident from the map legend, 18 European nations have 24.6% or more of their votes going to secular conservative parties. If you look at the list of nations, you see that Poland tops the list with 51.1%, followed by Turkey (49%) and Greece (45.4%). In general, secular conservative parties are most popular in the southern and eastern parts of Europe. Secular conservatives are usually placed farther on the right because of their more strident opposition to socialism and social democracy, their free-market libertarianism, and a strong emphasis on patriotism and the promotion of "national interests."

In contrast to secular conservatives, the extreme right is a very difficult group to categorize. Generally these types of parties have strong nationalist tendencies and very high levels of antipathy toward foreigners, whether they are immigrants or citizens of neighboring countries.

Data File: **EUROPE**

Task: **Mapping**

➤ Variable 1: **47) %EXT.RIGHT**

➤ View: **Map**

➤ Display: **Legend**

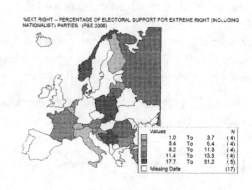

Recently the extreme right has had some success in elections in the Northern European countries of Norway (22.1%) and Denmark (13.3%). But these types of parties have also been fairly popular in Eastern European countries like Yugoslavia (17.7%), the Slovak Republic (20.5%), and most notably, Bosnia (51.2%).

> ➤ *Data File:* **HISTORY**
> ➤ *Task:* **Historical Trends**
> ➤ *Variables:* **25) %EXRIGHTFR**
> **26) %EXRIGHTGM**

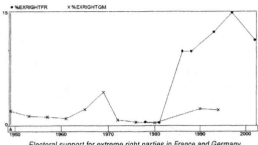

Electoral support for extreme right parties in France and Germany

Of recent concern to a number of political observers has been the popularity of extreme right movements in southern Europe. France, in particular, is growing increasingly wary of the success of the far-right National Front, which polled more than 10% in the last two elections.

The final group of parties is also hard to classify because it is neither right nor left. The parties in this group are usually organized around a specific ethnic identity that exists under the sovereignty of a larger, dominant nation. For example, Scottish people have organized the Scottish National Party to press for the interests of Scots in the English-dominated nation of Great Britain.

> ➤ *Data File:* **EUROPE**
> ➤ *Task:* **Mapping**
> ➤ *Variable 1:* **49) %REGIONAL**
> ➤ *View:* **Map**
> ➤ *Display:* **Legend**

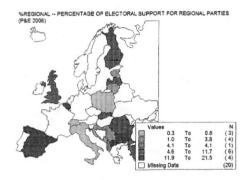

Eighteen European countries have regionalist parties that obtained at least some percentage of the vote in the most recent elections. Here, Macedonia (21.5%) leads the pack, followed by Belgium (18.7%), Bulgaria (12.7%), and Spain (11.9%).

Now that we have covered the basics of parties and elections in Europe, you are on your own.

Terms and Concepts

Plurality-majoritarian
Semi-proportional
Proportional
Consequences of plurality-majoritarian elections
Consequences of proportional elections
Party families:
    Communist
    Socialist

Social Democratic Parties
Liberal
Green
Christian Democratic
Conservative
Extreme right
Regional

WORKSHEET

CHAPTER

6

NAME: Ramona Khan

COURSE:

DATE: 2/26/07

Workbook exercises and software are copyrighted. Copying is prohibited by law.

REVIEW QUESTIONS

Based on the first part of this chapter, answer True or False to the following items:

1. Majoritarian electoral systems encourage coalition building in the legislature to achieve majorities.   T (F)

2. Proportional electoral systems seek to ensure fair representation in the legislature by allocating seats according to the percentage of votes each party obtained.   (T) F

3. Majoritarian systems of representation tend to overrepresent larger parties.   (T) F

4. Most countries use a semi-proportional electoral system for electing their leaders, rather than one that is majoritarian or proportional.   T (F)

5. The differences in the representation of women across the various types of electoral systems are statistically significant.   (T) F

6. Over the last couple of decades, the Communist Party in France has lost ground to less radical parties, such as the Socialist Party.   (T) F

7. When a Socialist Party receives a high percentage of the vote in a country, the Social Democratic Party also tends to do well.   (T) F

8. Liberal parties in Europe are similar to liberal parties in the United States in that they are all located on the left side of the ideological spectrum.   (T) F

9. The Christian Democratic Party is considered to be a radical party because of its religious ideology.   T (F)

10. Green parties tend to be stronger in Western Europe than in Eastern Europe.   T (F)

EXPLORIT QUESTIONS

I. In the first section of this chapter, you compared electoral systems and outcomes in political systems around the world. Now let's look at election systems in Europe. The variable 15) GOVERNMEN2 in the EUROPE data file, divides the European countries into those with new political systems since 1989 and those with democratic political systems in existence prior to 1989. Countries with established democracies prior to 1989 are called "old" democracies, and countries that have established democracies since 1989 are called "transition states." The variable 28) ELECT FMLY identifies each country's electoral system family in 2004, while the variable 26) ELECT96 identifies each country's electoral system family in 1996. Generally speaking, is there a prominent type of electoral system in Europe? Has the type of system changed over time? Using these three variables, generate two tables, print each of them out, and answer the questions that follow.

➤ *Data Files:*   **EUROPE**
      ➤ *Task:*   **Cross-Tabulation**
➤ *Row Variables:*   **28) ELECT FMLY**
                   26) ELECT96
➤ *Column Variable:*   **15) GOVERNMEN2**
       ➤ *View:*   **Tables**
     ➤ *Display:*   **Column%**

11. In 2004, more than three-quarters of older democracies in Europe had proportional electoral systems.   (T)   F

12. In 1996, more than half of the 17 transitional countries in Europe had majoritarian or semi-proportional types of electoral systems.   (T)   F

13. From 1996 to 2004, electoral systems in the transition states did not change very much.   T   (F)

II.   Do new democracies in Europe have higher levels of voter turnout than old democracies? We might hypothesize that there will be higher rates of voter turnout in transitional European governments because democratic elections give these citizens rights they didn't previously have.

        Data Files: **EUROPE**
           ➤ *Task:*   **ANOVA**
➤ *Dependent Variable:*   **29) %TURNOUT**
➤ *Independent Variable:*   **15) GOVERNMEN2**
            ➤ *View:*   **Means**

     You may need to use both the Graph view and the Means view to answer the following questions.

14. The graph indicates that old democracies have higher voter turnout than transitional countries.   (T)   F

15. What is the mean voter turnout for old democracies?   36.5 %

16. What is the mean voter turnout for transitional governments?   36.5 %

17. Is the difference in turnout between old democracies and transitional governments significant?   Yes   (No)

18. What is the probability?   _____

19. As predicted, transitional nations in Europe have higher rates of voter turnout than do older democratic nations.   (T)   F

Let's look at this same hypothesis (that transitional nations will have higher voter turnout rates than established democracies) using the entire GLOBAL data file. The GOVERNMENT variable in the GLOBAL data file is the same as the GOVERNMEN2 variable in the EUROPE file. However, because we are talking about nation-states around the world, there is greater variety for this variable in the GLOBAL file. Write the entire variable description for 450) GOVERNMENT in the space provided below.

The Nature of Government And Politics 1= Established Multiparty Democracy 2 = recently established Multiparty Democracy in Transition; 3= One party regime; 4= Autocratic regime; 5= Disordered state/civil war (Kidron & Segal 1995) Range. 1 to 5
(1) old Demos (2) Transition (3) one party (4) Autocratic (5) civil war

Given this variable description, you may wonder why we would study voter turnout in countries where one-party rule, autocracy, or civil war makes elections less relevant. The fact is that many of these kinds of nation-states still convene elections or elect members of parliament. While these states still hold elections, we might hypothesize that citizens in these countries know that elections don't mean much, so they are less inclined to turn out to vote. Let's check this out.

➤ *Data Files:* **GLOBAL**
➤ *Task:* **ANOVA**
➤ *Dependent Variable:* **475) %TURNOUT**
➤ *Independent Variable:* **450) GOVERNMENT**
➤ *View:* **Means**

You may need to use both the Graph view and the Means view to answer the following questions.

In the space provided, write down the mean voter turnout for each government system.

20. Old Democracy *65.47*
21. Transitional *63.55*
22. One Party *52.02*
23. Autocratic *57.18*
24. Civil War *70.07*

25. Is the difference in turnout between old democracies and transitional governments significant? Yes (No)

26. What is the probability? *0.032*

27. Transitional nation-states are more likely than older democracies to have higher voter turnouts. T (F)

28. One-party governments have the highest voter-turnout rates.   T   (F)

29. Nation-states experiencing civil war have the lowest voter-turnout rates because the government is not stable.   (T)   (F)

30. In terms of voter turnout, the analysis containing all transitional nation-states differs substantially from the analysis that includes only European countries.   T   (F)

III. Now let's look at the effect that the electoral system has on voter turnout. Is voter turnout higher among PR systems or majoritarian systems? How does the analysis of global turnout compare to the analysis of European turnout?

>   *Data Files:* **GLOBAL**
>   *Task:* **ANOVA**
> ➤ *Dependent Variable:* **475) %TURNOUT**
> ➤ *Independent Variable:* **449) ELECT FMLY**
>   ➤ *View:* **Means**

In the space provided, write down the mean voter turnout for each election system.

31. Plurality-Majoritarian   58.62

32. Semi-PR   56.80

33. PR   68.87

34. Is the difference in turnout between the three electoral systems significant?   Yes   (No)

35. What is the probability?   0.000

36. Proportional systems tend to have higher voter turnout than the plurality-majoritarian systems or semi-PR systems.   T   (F)

Now analyze voter turnout for the European systems using the EUROPE data file. Be sure to write down the mean voter turnout for each electoral system using 28) ELECT FMLY and 29) %TURNOUT.

37. Plurality-Majoritarian   68.40

38. Semi-PR   60.40   *this file is not working: it says it has a decimal point.*

39. PR   75.713

40. Is the difference in turnout between the three electoral systems significant?   (Yes)   No

41. What is the probability?   0.093

42. In Europe, proportional systems tend to have higher voter turnout than the plurality-majoritarian systems or semi-PR systems.   (T)   F

EXPLORIT QUESTIONS

In the chapter you had a broad overview of the political party families. Now let's take a look at how people voted in actual elections. In the Comparative Study of Electoral Systems survey, citizens from a number of countries around the world were asked to name the party that they voted for in the last election. Open the CSES–GERMANY02 file and try to guess who won the 2002 election:

> *Data File:* **CSES–GERMANY02**
> *Task:* **Univariate**
> *Primary Variable:* **1) PTY VOTE**
> *View:* **Pie**

43. Based on the pie chart, which party most likely won the 2002 election in Germany?

    a. Party of Democratic Socialism (PDS)

    (b.) Social Democratic Party (SPD)

    c. Greens

    d. Liberal democrats (FDP)

    e. Christian Democrats (CDU/CSU)

Now let's check out the same study for the 2005 election in the United Kingdom.

> *Data File:* **CSES–UK 05**
> *Task:* **Univariate**
> *Primary Variable:* **1) PTY VOTE**
> *View:* **Pie**

44. Based on the pie chart, which party most likely won the 2005 election in the UK?

    (a.) Labour

    b. Liberal

    c. Conservative (Tory)

In this part of this worksheet section, you'll look at how supporters of these parties differ in terms of gender, education, religion, and socioeconomic status.

IV. Use the CSES–GERMANY02 data file and then the CSES–UK05 file to perform the series of cross-tabulations indicated. For each result, you need to fill in the percentaged results for the row that is specified in the table below. Also indicate whether the results are statistically significant (circle Y for Yes, N for No).

GERMANY SURVEY

> *Data File:* **CSES–GERMANY02**
> *Task:* **Cross-tabulation**
> *Row Variables:* **2) LT-RT-3**
> **3) GENDER**
> **4) EDUCATION**
> **5) RELIGION**
> **8) UNION?**
> *Column Variable:* **1) PTY VOTE**
> *View:* **Tables**
> *Display:* **Column %**

Fill in the table below.

	PDS	SPD	GREEN	FDP	CDU/CSU	V =	SIGNIFI-CANT?
2) LT-RT-3 % Right	11.9 %	8.7 %	32.9%	1.6 %	34.5%	___	Ⓨ N
3) GENDER % Female	43.0 %	51.6%	50.5 %	56.8 %	47.9%	___	Y Ⓝ
4) EDUCATION % University	13.1 %	16.2%	8.9 %	31.3 %	19.3 %	___	Ⓨ N
5) RELIGION % Catholic	34.0%	26.0 %	65.7 %	27.6 %	42.5%	___	Ⓨ N
8) UNION? % Yes	14.6 %	21.3 %	8.3 %	18.5 %	9.3 %	___	Ⓨ N

Print the table that analyzes the relationship between religion and party preference and attach it to your assignment. *See attachment*

45. What is the best interpretation of the table that analyzes ideology and party vote in Germany?

   a. There is no relationship between ideology and party vote in Germany.

   b. 32.9% of Green voters placed themselves on the political right.

   c. 34.5% of CDU/CSU supporters placed themselves on the political right.

   d. 8.7% of those on the political right support the SPD.

   e. both b and c

46. What is the best interpretation of the table that analyzes religious preference and party vote in Germany?

   a.   There is no relationship between religious preference and party vote in Germany.

   b.   42.5% of CDU/CSU supporters are Catholic, and this result is significant.

   c.   65.7% of Green supporters are Catholic, and this result is significant.

   d.   7.6% of PDS voters express none as their religious preference.

   e.   all of the above

   (f.) both b and c

47. From the table using column percentages that analyzes religious preference and party vote in Germany, we can understand

   a.   the percentage of Catholics that voted for the Christian Democrats.

   b.   the percentage of Christian Democrats who are Catholic.

   (c.) neither of the above

   d.   both a and b

UNITED KINGDOM SURVEY

> ➤ *Data File:* **CSES–UK05**
> ➤ *Task:* **Cross-tabulation**
> ➤ *Row Variables:* **2) LT-RT-3**
> **3) GENDER**
> **4) EDUCATION**
> **5) RELIGION**
> **8) UNION?**
> ➤ *Column Variable:* **1) PTY VOTE**
> ➤ *View:* **Tables**
> ➤ *Display:* **Column %**

Fill in the table below.

	LABOUR	LIBERAL	TORY	V =	SIGNIFICANT?
2) LT-RT-3 % Right	8.4 %	10.3%	56.6%	___	(Y) N
3) GENDER % Female	51.8 %	50.6%	47.3%	___	Y (N)
4) EDUCATION % University	27.1%	37.3 %	33.3%	___	Y (N)

Chapter 6: Electoral Systems and Political Parties in Liberal Democracies

5) RELIGION
% Anglican   **39.7** %   **37.7**%   **51.6** %   ____   (Y) N

8) UNION?
% Yes   **23.9** %   **18.7** %   **12.7**%   ____   Y (N)

48. Which of the following is the best interpretation of the relationship between 1)PTY VOTE and 3) GENDER in the United Kingdom?

    a. Males are more likely to support the Conservative Party (Tories) than females.

    b. Tories are more likely to be female than male.

    (c.) The results are not statistically significant, so no conclusions can be drawn about this relationship.

49. In both Germany and the United Kingdom, the parties with the highest percentage of the population with university education tend to be

    a. parties of the right like the Tories and the CDU/CSU.

    b. parties of the center like the Liberals and the Free Democrats.

    (c.) parties of the left like Labour and the SPD.

    d. irrelevant because the results of the relationship between 1) PTY VOTE and 4) EDUCATION are not significant.

50. The best interpretation of the relationship between union membership and party vote is:

    a. The relationship between these two variables is not significant. Unions don't seem to matter any more in Germany or the UK.

    (b.) The relationship between these two variables is significant in the UK, but not in Germany.

    c. Supporters of parties on the right tend to have a higher percentage of union member support than do parties on the left in both the UK and Germany. The relationship between union membership and party choice is still relatively strong and significant.

    d. Supporters of parties on the left tend to have a higher percentage of union member support than do parties on the right in both the UK and Germany. The relationship between union membership and party choice is still relatively strong and significant.

Now, print the table that you created that analyzes the relationship between religion and party preference in the United Kingdom and attach it to your assignment. Next create a table that selects 5) RELIGION as the column variable and 1) PTY VOTE as the row variable. Use the column percentages and print out the table.

51. Which of the two tables that you just printed tells you the percentage of Labour voters who are Catholic?

    a. The table with 1) PTY VOTE selected as the column variable.

    (b.) The table with 5) RELIGION selected as the column variable.

    c. Both of them can tell us this information.

52. What is the best interpretation of the table that analyzes 5) RELIGION (column variable) and 1) PTY VOTE (row variable)?

    a. Catholics vote for the Labour Party more than any other party.

    b. Every religious group tends to support Labour more than the Tory Party.

    c. A majority of every religious grouping supports the Labour Party.

    d. both a and b

Now let's look at some issues that might have been relevant for the 2002 election in Germany and the 2005 election in the UK. In both instances, parties of the left (SPD in Germany and Labour in the UK) held power leading up to the elections. Let's see how citizens' vote choices are related to opinions on government performance, voter efficacy (the sentiment that one's vote matters), attitudes toward democracy and perceptions of corruption in both of these countries. For each result below, fill in the percentage results for the row that is specified in the table. Also, indicate the strength of relationship (V) and whether the results are statistically significant.

GERMANY SURVEY

> ➤ *Data File:* **CSES–GERMANY02**
> ➤ *Task:* **Cross-tabulation**
> ➤ *Row Variables:* **10) GOV PERF**
>   **12) VOTE.DIFF**
>   **13) DEMOCRACY**
> ➤ *Column Variable:* **1) PTY VOTE**
> ➤ *View:* **Tables**
> ➤ *Display:* **Column %**

Fill in the table below.

	PDS	SPD	GREENS	FDP	CDU/CSU	V =	SIGNIFI-CANT?
10) GOV PERF % Bad/VB	81.0%	21.8%	87.2%	26.8%	88.5%	___	Y̶ N
12) VOTE.DIFF % Yes	26.6%	22.3%	4.7%	19.0%	10.5%	___	Y̶ N
13) DEMOCRACY % Agree	94.4%	94.8%	94.8%	94.9%	91.2%	___	Y N̶

UNITED KINGDOM SURVEY

➤ *Data File:* **CSES–UK05**
➤ *Task:* **Cross-tabulation**
➤ *Row Variables:* **10) GOV PERF**
12) VOTE.DIFF
13) DEMOCRACY
➤ *Column Variable:* **1) PTY VOTE**
➤ *View:* **Tables**
➤ *Display:* **Column %**

Fill in the table below.

	LABOUR	LIBERAL	TORY	V =	SIGNIFI-CANT?
10) GOV PERF % Bad/VB	7.7 %	50.3 %	88.0 %	___	(Y) N
12) VOTE.DIFF % Yes	12.8 %	23.4 %	14.9 %	___	Y (N)
13) DEMOCRACY % Agree	96.3 %	92.3 %	94.6 %	___	Y (N)

53. In the UK and Germany, voters who voted against Labour or the SPD respectively tended to rate government performance as "bad." (T) F

54. Which of the following offers the best interpretation of the table that analyzes the relationship between efficacy (i.e., the belief that one's vote makes a difference) and party vote in Germany?

    a. There is no relationship between efficacy and party vote in Germany.

    b. CDU/CSU supporters have a stronger sense of political efficacy than supporters of most other parties.

    c. FDP supporters have a stronger sense of political efficacy than supporters of most other parties.

    d. PDS supporters have a stronger sense of political efficacy than supporters of most other parties.

    e. Green supporters have the weakest sense of political efficacy.

    (f.) both d and e

55. Which of the following offers the best interpretation of the table that analyzes the relationship between efficacy (i.e., the belief that one's vote makes a difference) and party vote in the UK?

    a. There is no relationship between efficacy and party vote in the UK.

b. Tory supporters have a stronger sense of political efficacy than supporters of most other parties.

c. Liberal supporters have a stronger sense of political efficacy than supporters of most other parties.

d. Labour supporters have a weaker sense of political efficacy than supporters of most other parties.

e. both c and d

IN YOUR OWN WORDS

Open the GLOBAL file, select the ANOVA task and use 449) ELECT FMLY as the independent variable and 312) POL RIGT04, 305) CIV LIBS04, and 457) NO CORRUPT as dependent variables. Then answer the following questions.

1. Based on the analysis of the relationship between 449) ELECT FMLY and 312) POL RIGT04, 305) CIV LIBS04, and 457) NO CORRUPT, indicate whether or not there seems to be a relationship between the type of election system that a nation chooses and its level of political freedom. Support your conclusions with evidence.

2. Based on the analyses in Part I of this worksheet section, write a paragraph that summarizes the similarities and differences of those who are most likely to prefer parties of the left in the United Kingdom (Labour) or in Germany (Social Democrats and Greens).

Part III

COMMUNIST AND POSTCOMMUNIST SOCIETIES

CHAPTER 7

AFTER COMMUNISM

Under capitalism, man exploits man. Under
communism, it's just the opposite.

JOHN KENNETH GALBRAITH

Communism doesn't work 'cause people like to
own stuff.

FRANK ZAPPA

Tasks: Mapping, Historical Trends, Univariate, Cross-tabulation, ANOVA
Data Files: GLOBAL, EUROPE, ASIA, HISTORY, PEW GLOBAL02, WVS02–RUSSIA,
WVS02–POLAND

The Cold War ended with the fall of the Berlin Wall in 1989, but politics across the Eurasian continent is still mostly characterized by the differences that resulted from divisions between East and West for more than 40 years.

> ➤ *Data File:* **GLOBAL**
> ➤ *Task:* **Mapping**
> ➤ *Variable 1:* **451) COMMUNIST**
> ➤ *View:* **Map**
> ➤ *Display:* **Legend**

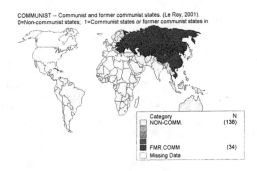

COMMUNIST -- Communist and former communist states. (Le Roy, 2001).
0=Non-communist states; 1=Communist states or former communist states in

You can see from this map that Europe was roughly divided between East and West.

> ➤ *Data File:* **EUROPE**
> ➤ *Task:* **Mapping**
> ➤ *Variable 1:* **20) COLD WAR**
> ➤ *View:* **Map**
> ➤ *Display:* **Legend**

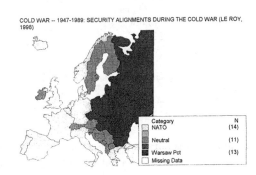

COLD WAR -- 1947-1989: SECURITY ALIGNMENTS DURING THE COLD WAR (LE ROY, 1998)

As the legend indicates, the countries highlighted in yellow belonged to the Western bloc of countries associated with a military alliance called the North Atlantic Treaty Organization (NATO), which also included the United States and Canada (not shown on this map). With a few exceptions during this period (i.e., Turkey, Greece, Portugal, and Spain), these nations were democratic and capitalist. The Eastern bloc of countries, shown in the darkest color, were associated with the Soviet Union and were members of an alliance called the Warsaw Pact. These nations were organized along the lines of a centrally planned economy and a communist political system. There were also a few neutral countries between the two blocs. Switzerland, Austria, Ireland, Finland, and Sweden were neutral, but democratic and capitalist. Albania and Yugoslavia were communist but did not affiliate with the Warsaw Pact.

In the first chapter of this workbook, you examined the independence dates of nation-states. Let's revisit the graph that shows the number of countries that became independent during each decade between the late 1700s and early 2000s.

➤ *Data File:* **HISTORY**
➤ *Task:* **Historical Trends**
➤ *Variables:* **3) IND/DECADE**

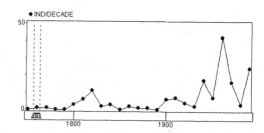

The number of independent countries per decade

From the graph you can see that the 1990s saw the proliferation of independent countries. In 1989, communism collapsed due to revolutions in much of Eastern Europe. Since 1991 the Soviet Union, Czechoslovakia, and Yugoslavia have broken into smaller, independent nation-states (see Table 8.1).

Table 7.1 Breakup of European Nation-States in the 1990s

Soviet Union	Yugoslavia	Czechoslovakia
Armenia	Bosnia-Herzegovina	Czech Republic
Azerbaijan	Croatia	Slovakia
Belarus	Macedonia	
Estonia	Slovenia	
Georgia	Yugoslavia	
Kazakhstan		
Kyrgyzstan		
Latvia		
Lithuania		
Moldova		
Russia		
Tajikistan		
Turkmenistan		
Ukraine		
Uzbekistan		

The collapse of communism has had a profound effect on Europe. With a few exceptions, European nation-states are now oriented more toward cooperation than conflict with one another. The North

Atlantic Treaty Organization (NATO) also experienced a radical transformation during the 1990s. Prior to 1989, NATO allies and Warsaw Pact countries had amassed troops and weapons all along the iron curtain that separated East and West, but by 1994 most of these same nations had established working partnerships, an agreement called "The Partnership for Peace," to resolve disputes peacefully. In 1999 former Warsaw Pact members Poland, Hungary, and the Czech Republic joined NATO as full members. This is what the map of NATO looks like today:

➤ *Data File:* **EUROPE**
➤ *Task:* **Mapping**
➤ *Variable 1:* **21) NATO**
➤ *View:* **Map**
➤ *Display:* **Legend**

In addition to Europe, the rise and fall of communism has also had a profound effect on the geopolitical situation in South and Central Asia. Many states that were formerly part of the Soviet Union are now independent and consider themselves to be part of the Asian continent.

➤ *Data File:* **ASIA**
➤ *Task:* **Mapping**
➤ *Variable 1:* **34) COMMUNIST**
➤ *View:* **Map**
➤ *Display:* **Legend**

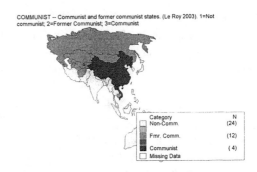

Notice that 12 new nation-states in Asia are former communist regimes and that four nation-states (China, Laos, North Korea, and Vietnam) are still self-proclaimed "People's Republics" or communist states.

Perhaps the greatest contrasts between East and West are now economic. Following World War II, the nations of Western Europe began to cooperate with one another on a host of economic, social, and political issues. While communism was in its final stages of collapse in 1992, the nations of Western Europe established the European Union to promote their common economic agenda. Recently, 11 of the 15 members committed themselves to a common currency. Under the common currency arrangement, the national currencies of countries such as Germany and France have been replaced with a single European currency. We can see by a comparison of maps below that there is a strong overlap between those nations that were in the democratic-capitalist West during the Cold War and those nations that are now members of the European Union.

➤ *Data File:* **EUROPE**
　➤ *Task:* **Mapping**
➤ *Variable 1:* **20) COLD WAR**
➤ *Variable 2:* **22) EUROPE**
　➤ *Views:* **Map**
　➤ *Display:* **Legend**

COLD WAR -- 1947-1989: SECURITY ALIGNMENTS DURING THE COLD WAR (LE ROY, 1998)

Category	N
NATO	(14)
Neutral	(11)
Warsaw Pct	(13)
Missing Data	

$r = 0.536**$

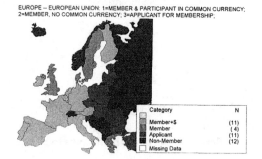

EUROPE -- EUROPEAN UNION: 1=MEMBER & PARTICIPANT IN COMMON CURRENCY; 2=MEMBER, NO COMMON CURRENCY; 3=APPLICANT FOR MEMBERSHIP;

Category	N
Member+$	(11)
Member	(4)
Applicant	(11)
Non-Member	(12)
Missing Data	

As this analysis shows, we can see that 42 years of Cold War between East and West had an effect on the contemporary shape of membership in the European Union. But the differences between East and West go beyond just organizational membership issues. The divisions between the two blocs are now mostly associated with strong cross-national differences in wealth.

Data File: **EUROPE**
　➤ *Task:* **ANOVA**
➤ *Dependent Variable:* **11) GDPCAP PPP**
➤ *Independent Variable:* **20) COLD WAR**
　➤ *View:* **Means**

Means, Standard Deviations and Number of Cases of Dependent Var: GDPCAP PPP by Categories of Independent Var: COLD WAR
Difference of means across groups is statistically significant (Prob. = 0.000)

	N	Mean	Std.Dev.
NATO	14	26535.035	11372.497
Neutral	10	18686.764	11477.646
Warsaw Pct	13	8829.908	3863.163

From this analysis we can see that the average GDP per capita of NATO countries is $26,535 compared to the GDP per capita of former Warsaw Pact countries, which is only $8,829.

Seventeen years after the end of the Cold War it may be appropriate to try to use variables besides those that identify nations as former Warsaw Pact members or NATO members in order to explain or analyze the differences in the countries of Europe. In the mid-1990s it was common to refer to post-communist states as states in transition compared to the established liberal democracies of Europe. In 1995 we used the following variable to differentiate the traditional liberal democracies from the transitional.

> ➤ *Data File:* **GLOBAL**
> ➤ *Task:* **Mapping**
> ➤ *Variable 1:* **450) GOVERNMENT**
> ➤ *Display:* **Legend**

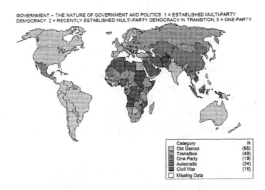

GOVERNMENT – THE NATURE OF GOVERNMENT AND POLITICS. 1 = ESTABLISHED MULTI-PARTY DEMOCRACY. 2 = RECENTLY ESTABLISHED MULTI-PARTY DEMOCRACY IN TRANSITION; 3 = ONE-PARTY

Category	N
Old Demos	(65)
Transition	(49)
One Party	(19)
Autocratic	(24)
Civil War	(16)
Missing Data	

Let's analyze the issue of government censorship and press freedom using the government variable in the EUROPE file.

The changes throughout Eastern Europe extend beyond economic and military factors. The laws and practices in the former communist states reflect a rather wide variation in the level of commitment to democratic norms. For example, the variable PRESS.FREE refers to a state's infringement on the freedom of the media.

> ➤ *Data File:* **EUROPE**
> ➤ *Task:* **ANOVA**
> ➤ *Dependent Variable:* **23) PRESS.FREE**
> ➤ *Independent Variable:* **15) GOVERNMEN2**
> ➤ *View:* **Means**

Means, Standard Deviations and Number of Cases of Dependent Var: PRESS.FREE by Categories of Independent Var: GOVERNMEN2
Difference of means across groups is statistically significant (Prob. = 0.000)

	N	Mean	Std.Dev.
Old Demos	20	17.350	10.017
Transition	17	39.647	21.178

The results of this analysis are significant and they tell us that the transition states still do not recognize press freedom to the same extent as established democracies. The average world press freedom rating for established democracies is 17.35 whereas transitions states average 39.65.

Do transition states differ in their use of capital punishment?[1]

> *Data File:* **EUROPE**
> *Task:* **Cross-tabulation**
> ➤ *Row Variable:* **25) CAP PUN 95**
> ➤ *Column Variable:* **15) GOVERNMEN2**
> ➤ *View:* **Tables**
> ➤ *Display:* **Column %**

CAP PUN 95   by   GOVERNMEN2
Cramer's V: 0.706**

		GOVERNMEN2			
		Old Demos	Transition	Missing	TOTAL
CAP PUN 95	Abolished	14	5	0	19
		70.0%	29.4%		51.4%
	Abol Ord	3	0	0	3
		15.0%	0.0%		8.1%
	No Recent	2	0	0	2
		10.0%	0.0%		5.4%
	Retained	1	12	1	13
		5.0%	70.6%		35.1%
	TOTAL	20	17	1	37
		100.0%	100.0%		

---

[1] There are some instances in this chapter (and in the worksheet section that follows) where the cross-tabulation results using this file produce the statement "Warning: Potential significance problem. This is to alert you that the statistical significance value may not be reliable due to the small number of nations used in the analysis. This is not a problem for the type of analysis that we are currently conducting. For our purposes in this chapter, we will often ignore this warning.

Most people in the United States are surprised to find that, by 1995, established democracies in Europe had abolished capital punishment. As this table shows, only 1 of the 20 established democracies in Europe used capital punishment in 1995. However, 12 of the 17 transition states retained capital punishment for ordinary crimes (e.g., murder). Throughout Europe and the rest of the world, the longer a nation has been a democracy, the less likely it is to use capital punishment.

Let's see if this holds true 11 years later. Do these transitional states come to adopt a different stance on capital punishment with the passage of time?

	Data File:	**EUROPE**
	Task:	**Cross-Tabulation**
➤	Row Variable:	**24) CAP PUN 06**
➤	Column Variable:	**15) GOVERNMEN2**
➤	View:	**Tables**
➤	Display:	**Column %**

CAP PUN 06   by   GOVERNMEN2
Cramer's V: 0.378**

		GOVERNMEN2			
		Old Demos	Transition	Missing	TOTAL
CAP PUN 06	Abolished	20	13	1	33
		100.0%	76.5%		89.2%
	Abol Ord	0	2	0	2
		0.0%	11.8%		5.4%
	Retained	0	2	0	2
		0.0%	11.8%		5.4%
	TOTAL	20	17	1	37
		100.0%	100.0%		

As you can see, the so-called transition states have made significant modifications in their laws and practices surrounding capital punishment! A full 13 transition states have now abolished the death penalty for all crimes and only 2 states retain this in law and practice. Significant change is occurring among these nation-states, so it is probably no longer adequate to simply refer to these states as post–Warsaw Pact states.

What was once a single world living behind an iron curtain is now a tremendously diverse set of nations. In fact, it would be a mistake to simply analyze these countries as though they are the same. But how do we begin thinking about these new nation-states in some coherent way? How do we understand the differences and similarities in this group that contains states that have embraced capitalism and democracy as well as those states that hang on to the authoritarian political traditions of the Soviet Union? In the worksheet section that follows, it will be your turn to deepen your understanding of these nation-states as you engage in comparative analysis.

Terms and Concepts

NATO
Warsaw Pact
Press freedom

WORSHEET

NAME: _____

COURSE: _____

DATE: _____

CHAPTER

7

REVIEW QUESTIONS

Based on the first part of this chapter, answer True or False to the following items:

1. During the Cold War, all European nations were divided between NATO
    and the Warsaw Pact.   T   F

2. The decade of the 1990s saw a large increase in the number of nation-states
    that became independent because of the breakup of the Soviet Union,
    Yugoslavia, and Czechoslovakia.   T   F

3. The Cold War division of Europe did not appear to have any effect on
    communist countries' capacity to accumulate wealth.   T   F

4. There is no significant difference in press freedom between established democracies
    and transition states.   T   F

5. Established democracies are more likely to retain capital punishment laws
    than transition states.   T   F

EXPLORIT QUESTIONS

I. In the wake of the collapse of communism, new independent and former communist states have
    taken a wide variety of forms. In fact, it would be a mistake to see them as though they are uniform
    countries with the same kinds of problems. On the other hand, we know that there are different
    types of nation-states that share some attributes. Someone who teaches and conducts research on
    this region has to think more systematically about how we can organize communist and postcommu-
    nist states. In the worksheet that follows, you will learn how political scientists go about developing
    categories (like the Seven Worlds variable) to organize a diverse set of countries.

    Political scientists usually start by thinking about variables that make sense in the kinds of analysis
    we use. You may remember that our analysis of the Seven Worlds was based on political factors
    (such as the degree of freedom in society), economic factors (such as development), and social
    factors (like religion and other social values). So we might want to do something similar here.
    Let's start with political factors like political rights and civil liberties. The variable 303) FREEDOM in
    the GLOBAL file is a good variable for our purposes because it is a combined measure of the variables
    305) CIV LIBS04 and 312) POL RIGT04. Let's look at this variable, but we'll limit our analysis to those
    countries that are in the communist/postcommunist category.

▷ *Data File:* **GLOBAL**
▷ *Task:* **Univariate**
▷ *Primary Variable:* **303) FREEDOM**
▷ *Subset Variable:* **451) COMMUNIST**
▷ *Subset Category:* **Include: 1) FMR. COMM**
▷ *View:* **Pie**

Because we want to look only at states that were communist prior to 1989, we will need to use a subset variable, 451) COMMUNIST, and select category 1) FMR. COMM for inclusion in the analysis.

Fill in the table below.

303) FREEDOM	Freq.	%
1) MOST FREE	_____	_____
2) PART FREE	_____	_____
3) NOT FREE	_____	_____

If we are going to sort countries into different categories, we should be sure that there is real variation for a variable. That is, there should be plenty of countries in each category. A good rule of thumb for us to judge whether or not we have enough countries will be a minimum of 10% of the countries for each category.

5. According to our rule of thumb, are there enough countries in each of the three FREEDOM categories?   Yes   No

The UNIVARIATE task is a useful method to find out how much variation there is in a variable like 303) FREEDOM, but it doesn't help us to see which countries fit into each category. To do this, we will need to use the MAPPING task.

Data File: **GLOBAL**
▷ *Task:* **Mapping**
▷ *Variable 1:* **303) FREEDOM**
▷ *Subset Variable:* **451) COMMUNIST**
▷ *Subset Category:* **Include: 1) FMR. COMM**
▷ *View:* **List: Rank**

This ranking should allow you to see which countries fit into each category. Put each communist country listed in your ranking into the appropriate category listed below. (Hint: The number of countries in each column should be the same as what you found in your univariate table above.)

FREE (DEMOCRATIC)	PART FREE (AUTHORITARIAN)	NOT FREE (TOTALITARIAN)
_____	_____	_____
_____	_____	_____
_____	_____	_____
_____	_____	_____
_____	_____	_____
_____	_____	_____
_____	_____	_____
_____	_____	_____
_____	_____	_____
_____	_____	_____
_____	_____	_____
_____	_____	_____

Now you have sorted the countries into three political types: democratic nation-states, authoritarian nation-states, and totalitarian nation-states. It is important to be sure that you understand the definition of each category that you create. So, we'll say that *democratic* nation-states have a set of laws and practices that help to protect political rights and civil liberties of citizens. On the other extreme, the *totalitarian* states regulate every aspect of political and social life, and do not recognize civil liberties or the political rights of citizens. In the middle, *authoritarian* nation-states may recognize some civil liberties and political rights, but often ignore others. For example, an authoritarian state may allow freedom of speech, but may ban some political parties.

Well, we've analyzed countries according to some political characteristics, but let's look at the economies of these nation-states. The variable 478) ECON.FREE2 is a measure of level of economic freedom found in the economy. The Wall Street Journal and the Heritage Foundation have developed the regulation variable to indicate the level of government intervention or freedom in an economic system.

Data File: **GLOBAL**
➤ Task: **Univariate**
➤ Primary Variable: **478) ECON.FREE2**
➤ Subset Variable: **451) COMMUNIST**
➤ Subset Category: **Include: 1) FMR. COMM**
➤ View: **Pie**

6. According to our rule of thumb, are there enough countries in each of the three ECON.FREE2 categories?   Yes   No

Now rank the variable 478) ECON.FREE2, the same way you ranked the previous FREEDOM variable.

This ranking should allow you to see which countries fit into each category. Put each communist country listed in your ranking into the appropriate category listed below.

CAPITALIST	REGULATED	STATIST
_____	_____	_____
_____	_____	_____
_____	_____	_____
_____	_____	_____
_____	_____	_____
_____	_____	_____
_____	_____	_____
_____	_____	_____
_____	_____	_____
_____	_____	_____
_____	_____	_____
_____	_____	_____
_____	_____	_____
_____	_____	_____
_____	_____	_____

Now you have sorted the same group of countries into three economic types. *Capitalist* economies are relatively free of government regulation and intervention. *Regulated* economies are more likely to have stronger government intervention in the economies (like government ownership of some firms). *Statist* economies are economic systems where governments still own most of the productive assets.

Next, we can combine both of the variables in the form of a table that allows you to place each country according to two variables. All that you need to do is look at where each country falls on each list you have made and put it in the proper place in the table (Estonia has been done for you).

	DEMOCRATIC	AUTHORITARIAN	TOTALITARIAN
CAPITALIST	ESTONIA		
REGULATED			
STATIST			

Now let's check your work. If you did this correctly, the number of countries in your table should correspond to the number of countries in each cell in the cross-tabulation.

Data File: **GLOBAL**
➤ Task: **Cross-tabulation**
➤ Row Variable: **478) ECON.FREE2**
➤ Column Variable: **303) FREEDOM**
➤ Subset Variable: **451) COMMUNIST**
➤ Subset Category: **Include: 1) FMR.COMM**

From the table that you made, you can see that there are basically six types of communist/postcommunist regimes: democratic-capitalist, democratic-regulatory, authoritarian-regulatory, authoritarian-statist, totalitarian-regulatory, and totalitarian-statist. The other types (e.g., democratic-statist) have no cases in them, so we will not use them. What you have just done is to create *operational definitions* of each of the six types of nation-states. Operational definitions specify how a concept is measured and refer to the variables used to measure the concept.

So an operational definition of a democratic-capitalist state is *a former communist nation that now is considered "free" in the ratings of political rights and civil liberties, and has a low degree of government intervention in the economy.*

Now write an operational definition of the other five types of nation-states:

Democratic-Regulatory

_____

_____

_____

Authoritarian-Regulatory

_____

_____

_____

Authoritarian-Statist

_____

_____

_____

Totalitarian-Regulatory

_____

_____

_____

Totalitarian-Statist

_____

_____

_____

You can see each of the regime types in the following map.

Data File: **GLOBAL**
➤ Task: **Mapping**
➤ Variable 1: **479) COMMTYPE06**
➤ View: **Map**
➤ Display: **Legend**

II.   We have operationally defined each of these regime types and suggested that they have widely varying approaches to politics and economics. Now we need to test the typology and see if it really helps us to explain the political, economic, and social realities of these nation-states. If it explains these realities, then we can say we have probably come up with a *valid* definition of the concept. So let's test a few hypotheses. (If you need to review what you learned about hypothesis testing, refer back to Chapter 5.)

H0: There is no relationship between the press freedom rating of a nation-state and the type of nation-state.

H1: Nation-states with free politics and free markets will tend to have better press freedom ratings than nation-states with totalitarian politics and statist markets.

Let's use ANOVA to test this hypothesis.

Data File: **GLOBAL**
➤ Task: **ANOVA**
➤ Dependent Variable: **300) PRESS.FREE**
➤ Independent Variable: **479) COMMTYPE06**
➤ View: **Summary**

Use the Summary and Means views to answer the following questions.

   7.   What is the mean press freedom rating for each regime type?

REGIME TYPE	MEAN PRESS FREEDOM RATING
Democratic-Capitalist	_____
Democratic-Regulatory	_____

REGIME TYPE	MEAN PRESS FREEDOM RATING
Authoritarian-Regulatory	_____
Authoritarian-Statist	_____
Totalitarian-Regulatory	_____
Totalitarian-Statist	_____

8. Are these results statistically significant?   Yes   No

9. On the basis of these results, we should (circle all that apply)

   a. reject H1 because totalitarian-statist regimes have about the same press freedom as democratic-capitalist regimes.

   b. reject H1 because the results are not significant.

   c. reject H0 because the democratic-capitalist and democratic-regulatory regimes have lower press freedom ratings than totalitarian-regulatory and totalitarian-statist regimes.

   d. reject H0 because the result of the analysis is significant.

Now let's see if there is a difference in the level of wealth between the different regimes.

H0: There is no relationship between the level of wealth per capita in a nation-state and the type of nation-state.

H1: Nation-states with free politics and free markets will tend to have higher levels of wealth per capita than nation-states with totalitarian politics and statist markets.

Analyze the relationship between 133) GDPCAP PPP (dependent variable) and 479) COMMTYPE06 (independent variable) using ANOVA. Print the graph and attach it to this assignment.

10. Are these results statistically significant?   Yes   No

11. On the basis of these results, we should (circle all that apply)

   a. reject H1 because totalitarian-statist regimes have about the same level of wealth as democratic-capitalist regimes.

   b. reject H1 because the results are not significant.

   c. reject H0 because the democratic-capitalist and democratic-regulatory regimes have higher levels of wealth than totalitarian-regulatory and totalitarian-statist regimes.

   d. reject H0 because the result of the analysis is significant.

III. Corruption and the lack of respect for the rule of law is said to be one of the leading challenges associated with democratic transition and economic development in former communist countries. Prior to the fall of communism, bureaucratic authorities and political elites dominated individual and collective decision making in these countries. Now, in an environment of increasing freedom and declining state capacity to enforce laws, corruption is said to be rampant in the former communist countries. But is it any more "rampant" in former communist states than in any other types of states?

12. Look at the variable description for 301) INDX:CORPT. A score of 9.7 on this variable means that the nation-state is

   a. very corrupt.

   b. somewhat corrupt (about in the middle).

   c. hardly corrupt.

Now let's analyze corruption using the WORLDS.7 variable to see if corruption is any worse in former communist states than in other states.

> *Data File:* **GLOBAL**
> *Task:* **ANOVA**
> ➤ *Dependent Variable:* **301) INDX:CORPT**
> ➤ *Independent Variable:* **130) WORLDS.7**
> ➤ *View:* **Means**

> **You may need to use both the Graph view and the Means view to answer the following questions.**

13. Levels of corruption in communist and postcommunist societies are most similar to levels of corruption in NICs.   T   F

14. Based on the graph alone, list the type of country that has the most corruption. _____

15. Now list the three types of countries that are the most corrupt and their mean corruption scores.

COUNTRY TYPE	MEAN CORRUPTION SCORE
_____	_____
_____	_____
_____	_____

16. Are the differences between types of nations and the levels of corruption statistically significant?   Yes   No

Sometimes researchers conduct analysis with definite ideas about likely outcomes. For example, we hypothesized that freer societies would have better press freedom ratings than societies that were not free. This makes sense. However, sometimes researchers can guess only that there will be some kind of relationship between two variables, but they may not know the direction. This is the case with corruption. On the one hand, a case could be made that corruption is more likely in freer societies in which the government has less control. On the other hand, it could also be argued that societies with totalitarian control are more susceptible to corruption because individuals must "pay off" political bosses to get things done. For this reason we will test the following hypothesis:

H0: There is no relationship between the level of corruption in a nation-state and the type of former communist nation-state.

H1: There is a relationship between the level of corruption in a nation-state and the type of former communist nation-state.

Notice that the hypothesis is making rather modest claims—only that there is a relationship between the two variables—and it does not specify the direction (e.g., that democratic-capitalist nations are more or less corrupt). Now let's test these hypotheses.

Data File:	**GLOBAL**
Task:	**ANOVA**
Dependent Variable:	**301) INDX:CORPT**
➤ *Independent Variable:*	**479) COMMTYPE06**
➤ *View:*	**Means**

You may need to use both the Graph view and the Means view to answer the following questions.

17. Based on the ANOVA graph alone, the types of countries in the transition states typology do not differ in their levels of corruption.   T   F

18. Based on the graph alone, list the type of country that is the least corrupt.   _____

19. Print the means table of your analysis of the relationship between 301) INDX:CORPT and 479) COMMTYPE06.

20. On the basis of these results, do you reject the null hypothesis?   Yes   No

21. Based on these results, one might conclude that (circle one of the following)

    a. economic liberalization appears to be more important than democratization in determining the level of corruption in a country.

    b. democratization appears to be more important than economic liberalization in determining the level of corruption in a country.

    c. both democratization and economic liberalization seem to have an impact on the level of corruption in a country.

IV. Now that you have analyzed what businesspeople and investors think about corruption in communist and former communist societies, what do the actual people who live in these countries think about corruption?

➤ *Data File:* **PEW GLOBAL02**
➤ *Task:* **Cross-tabulation**
➤ *Row Variable:* **3) CORRUPTLDR**
➤ *Column Variable:* **2) WORLDS.7**
➤ *View:* **Tables**
➤ *Display:* **Column %**

22. What percentage of citizens in liberal democracies believe that corrupt political leaders are a very big problem? _____%

23. What percentage of Comm/P-Comm citizens believe that corrupt political leaders are a very big problem? _____%

IN YOUR OWN WORDS

In your own words, please answer the following questions.

1. Are the perceptions of businesspeople and analysts who created the INDX:CORPT variable and characterize postcommunist states as corrupt similar to the perceptions of the citizens of postcommunist states? Answer this question and explain your answer on the basis of evidence.

2. Is there a difference in the attitudes that citizens have toward the democratization process depending on whether they were part of the Soviet Union or a satellite? Open the WVS02–RUSSIA data file and look at the variables PRE REGIME and NOW REGIME using the UNIVARIATE task. Now do the same thing with the WVS02–POLAND file. Do the results surprise you? If so, why? If not, why not? As always, base your written response on evidence.

RUSSIA, POLAND, AND DEMOCRATIC TRANSITION

I cannot forecast to you the action of Russia. It is a riddle, wrapped in a mystery, inside an enigma....

SIR WINSTON CHURCHILL, 1939

Tasks: Mapping, Scatterplot, Historical Trends, Univariate, Auto-Analyzer, Cross-tabulation
Data Files: GLOBAL, EUROPE, HISTORY, WVS02–RUSSIA, WVS02–POLAND, WVS02–USA, WVS02–ANALYZER

W hat Winston Churchill perceived in 1939 is still true in the new millennium. Most of the problems that interest researchers in comparative politics today—democratic transition, political economy, nationalism, religious and ethnic conflict—are all present in the study of the politics of Russia. These issues are also present in the study of the former Soviet satellites, but you will see that they exist to a much lesser degree. In this chapter we will examine the political culture, behavior, and attitudes of citizens in Russia and Poland. You will recall that in Chapter 7 we determined there is a wide variety of regimes in states that were formerly communist.

> ➤ *Data File:* **GLOBAL**
> ➤ *Task:* **Mapping**
> ➤ *Variable 1:* **452) COMM TYPE00**
> ➤ *Variable 2:* **479) COMM TYPE06**
> ➤ *View:* **Map**
> ➤ *Display:* **Find Case: Russia**

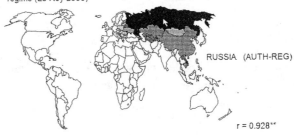

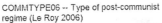

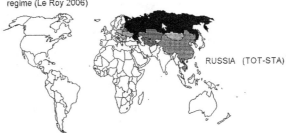

Select Russia to highlight the communist types for Russia in 2000 and 2006.

You will remember that in Chapter 7 we classified Russia as a totalitarian-statist regime, but in an earlier edition of this text we would have classified Russia as an authoritarian-regulatory regime. This may be a bit baffling given that Russia still convenes regular elections and has a competitive party system. In terms of political rights and civil liberties, Russia seems to have slipped back into patterns of stronger state control.

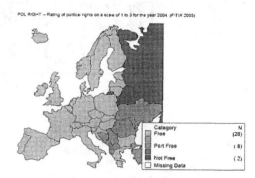

> *Data File:* **EUROPE**
> *Task:* **Mapping**
> *Variable 1:* **59) POL RIGT**
> *View:* **Map**
> *Display:* **Legend**

According to Freedom House, which is the source of the data, political rights in Russia are still somewhat limited. By comparison, Poland emerges with a relatively strong rating. According to Freedom House, the political rights measure is based on a number of factors:

> *Free and fair elections, competitive parties or other political groupings, and the opposition plays an important role and has actual power. Citizens enjoy self-determination or an extremely high degree of autonomy (in the case of territories), and minority groups have reasonable self-government or can participate in the government through informal consensus.*

According to Freedom House, Russia's political rights ratings are relatively low due to significant allegations of corruption at the last election, President Vladimir Putin's tendency toward the concentration of power in the hands of former military and security officers, the repression of the media, and the activities of the military in the civil war in Chechnya.[1]

By comparison, Poland's new democratic system is relatively strong, elections are fair, and the leadership is adhering to constitutional norms.

Civil liberties are another measure of a nation's commitment to democratic norms and values. How well does a nation protect free expression, a free press, freedom of association, minority opinions, and the right to worship?

---

[1] *Freedom in the World*, 2000–2005.

Data File: **EUROPE**
Task: **Mapping**
➤ Variable 1: **58) CIV LIBS**
➤ View: **Map**
➤ Display: **Legend**

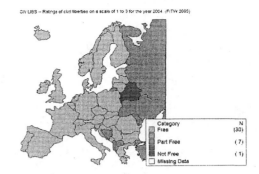

According to this map, Poland is more free than Russia in the area of civil liberties. In Freedom House's report on Poland, the only problem cited is the considerable backlog of criminal cases in the Polish legal system. These cases may actually serve to deny due process of law to Polish defendants, so Poland is cited for improvement in this area.

Russia, on the other hand, has considerable problems in the area of civil liberties. A Freedom House survey of the press in Russia reports that Russian police have engaged in persistent harassment of media outlets that report on corruption or criticize the government for its war in Chechnya. Reporters and editors have been harassed, beaten, and detained without charge for their press activities. Freedom House also reports that "uneven respect for religious freedom characterizes the local authorities' relationship to religious organizations." Under a 1997 law, churches must be registered with the government and prove that they have been in existence for more than 15 years. The reports also cite problems in union representation and organization and the lack of an independent judiciary.

Despite these problems, concern for the economy in Poland and Russia overwhelmed most other issues in the 1990s. Open the HISTORY file so that you can see the annual growth in GDP since 1990.

➤ Data File: **HISTORY**
➤ Task: **Historical Trends**
➤ Variables: **48) GR:RUSSIA**
          49) GR:POLAND

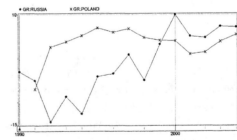

Annual GDP growth in Russia and Poland, 1990 - 2004

As you can see, the collapse of communism and the Soviet Union has actually been beneficial for economic growth in Poland. In Russia this was not the situation until the year 2000. Russia's economy declined in almost every year between 1990 and 1999. Only in 2000 did the Russian economy begin to experience positive growth, and since 2000 Russia's economic performance has accelerated.

Was this divergent pattern of growth the norm everywhere else? Were all the economies within the former Soviet Union hurt by the transition that occurred between 1989 and 1991? The following variable measures the average annual rate of economic growth from 1990 to 1999.

> Data File: **EUROPE**
> Task: **Mapping**
> Variable 1: **12) GROW 90–99**
> View: **Map**
> Display: **Legend**

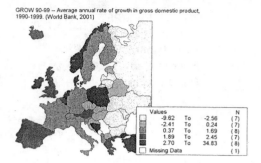

GROW 90-99 -- Average annual rate of growth in gross domestic product, 1990-1999. (World Bank, 2001)

Values			N
-9.62	To	-2.56	(7)
-2.41	To	0.24	(7)
0.37	To	1.69	(8)
1.89	To	2.45	(7)
2.70	To	34.83	(8)
Missing Data			(1)

From this map it appears that almost all of the former communist nations of Europe grew at an average annual rate that is either negative or near zero during the period 1990–99. Poland is one of a few exceptions to this rule. Poland grew at a remarkable rate of 3.7% per year, whereas Russia's economy declined at a rate of 5.22% per year. This means that Poland's economy increased by more than 30% during this period while Russia's economy decreased by 50%!

Why is this the case? Some analysts would argue that it has to do with the level of government intervention in the economy. The Wall Street Journal and the Heritage Foundation have co-published a rating system that assesses economic freedom in a country.

Data File: **EUROPE**
Task: **Mapping**
> Variable 1: **55) ECON.FREE**
> View: **Map**
> Display: **Legend**

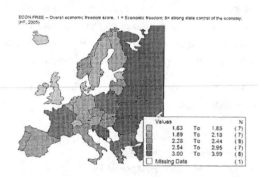

ECON.FREE -- Overall economic freedom score. 1 = Economic freedom; 5= strong state control of the economy. (HF, 2005)

Values			N
1.63	To	1.85	(7)
1.89	To	2.13	(7)
2.38	To	2.44	(8)
2.54	To	2.95	(7)
3.00	To	3.99	(8)
Missing Data			(1)

A low number in this ranking indicates a low level of government intervention in the economy, whereas a high number indicates a high level of government intervention in the economy. As you can see, Russia has the fourth highest level of government intervention in the economies of Europe. If you look at the rankings for this variable [List: Rank], the only nations with more government intervention are Ukraine, Bosnia, and Belarus. In the worksheet section that follows, you will begin to explore the relationship between government intervention in the economy and economic growth, but first let's turn to the people of Russia and Poland. How do these citizens view the economic changes in their society?

> Data File: **WVS02–RUSSIA**
> Task: **Univariate**
> Primary Variable: **155) BUS OWNSHP**
> View: **Pie**

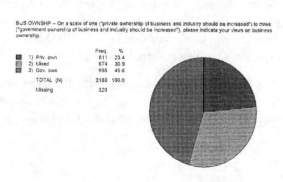

BUS OWNSHP -- On a scale of one ("private ownership of business and industry should be increased") to three ("government ownership of business and industry should be increased"), please indicate your views on business ownership.

	Freq.	%
1) Priv. own	511	23.4
2) Mixed	674	30.9
3) Gov. own	995	45.6
TOTAL (N)	2180	100.0
Missing	320	

Only 23.4% of the population in Russia seems to favor more private ownership of business and industry, while 45.6% of the population favors more government ownership of business. How is the same issue viewed in Poland?

> ➤ *Data File:* **WVS02–POLAND**
> ➤ *Task:* **Univariate**
> ➤ *Primary Variable:* **148) BUS OWNSHP**
> ➤ *View:* **Pie**

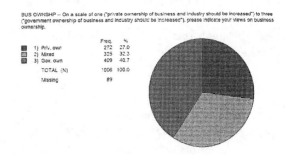

BUS OWNSHP -- On a scale of one ("private ownership of business and industry should be increased") to three ("government ownership of business and industry should be increased"), please indicate your views on business ownership.

	Freq.	%
1) Priv. own	272	27.0
2) Mixed	325	32.3
3) Gov. own	409	40.7
TOTAL (N)	1006	100.0
Missing	89	

Polish citizens are still somewhat skeptical about private ownership, but they are not as hesitant as Russians. While 27.0% of the population favors increased privatization, 40.7% favors increased government intervention. 32.3% of the Polish population favors a more mixed perspective. Poland does seem slightly more receptive to private ownership of industry, and a little more hesitant to want to return to the days of government ownership, than does Russia. Compare these results in Russia and Poland to the same question asked of the U.S. population.

> ➤ *Data File:* **WVS02–USA**
> ➤ *Task:* **Univariate**
> ➤ *Primary Variable:* **138) BUS OWNSHP**
> ➤ *View:* **Pie**

BUS OWNSHP -- BUS OWNSHP -- On a scale of one ("private ownership of business and industry should be increased") to three ("government ownership of business and industry should be increased"), please indicate your views on business ownership.

	Freq.	%
1) Priv. own	815	68.3
2) Mixed	257	21.5
3) Gov. own	121	10.1
TOTAL (N)	1193	100.0
Missing	7	

The overwhelming majority of the U.S. population surveyed favors increased private ownership in the United States. While a belief in private or public ownership does not make an economy run, a population in favor of private enterprise will make the transition to capitalism much easier.

Some scholars have suggested that the simultaneous introduction of democracy and free markets to countries like Russia and Poland is unfortunate. Analysts fear that as the Russian economy deteriorate in the 1990s, the population blamed democracy for their economic woes. The World Values Survey asks a question to try to understand this sentiment. It asked respondents to agree or disagree with the statement "In democracy, the economic system runs badly."

> ➤ *Data File:* **WVS02–ANALYZER**
> ➤ *Task:* **Auto-Analyzer**
> ➤ *Primary Variable:* **6) DEM:ECONOM**
> ➤ *View:* **Country**

DEM:ECONOM -- In democracy, the economic system runs badly.

	Germany	USA	Japan	Russia	S Korea	Mexico	Turkey	Nigeria
S. Agree	1.9%	3.7%	0.9%	10.6%	2.3%	11.2%	6.4%	12.2%
Agree	14.1%	19.2%	19.7%	45.4%	15.8%	42.2%	24.7%	24.7%
Disagree	54.7%	63.1%	68.7%	39.8%	69.4%	33.0%	54.2%	47.2%
S.Disagree	29.3%	13.9%	10.7%	4.2%	12.5%	13.7%	14.7%	15.9%
Number of cases	1747	1156	878	2016	973	1198	4107	1958

Russians are most likely (45.4%) to agree with this statement and Germans (14.1%) are least likely. The difference is statistically significant.

Evidence from this table clearly indicates that Russian citizens have had a very strong negative reaction to transition. So much so, a majority of the citizens surveyed believe that democracy is associated with the nation's economic hardship. Fifty-six percent of Russians agree or strongly agree with the idea that in democracy, the economic system runs badly, and they may have a point. If you recall our earlier examination of economic growth over time, you will remember that the Russian economy has suffered when it first introduced democratic political reforms. But what about Poland? We would guess that its better economic performance might actually lead its citizens to have a more positive attitude about democracy.

➤ *Data File:* **WVS02–POLAND**
➤ *Task:* **Univariate**
➤ *Primary Variable:* **175) DEM:ECONOM**
➤ *View:* **Pie**

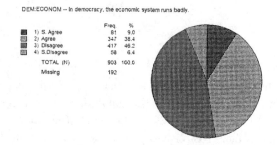

DEM:ECONOM -- In democracy, the economic system runs badly.

	Freq.	%
1) S. Agree	81	9.0
2) Agree	347	38.4
3) Disagree	417	46.2
4) S.Disagree	58	6.4
TOTAL (N)	903	100.0
Missing	192	

In Poland, the majority of the population (52.6%) tends to disagree with the assertion that "in democracy, the economic system runs badly." However, this response is also consistent with the more positive Polish experiences during the 1990s.

There are likely to be other factors that are responsible for this low opinion of democracy. In the previous chapter, you explored the relationship between age and one's attitude toward the current regime in Russia. Now it's your turn to do more comparative politics.

Terms and Concepts

Characteristics of Russia and Poland
    Civil liberties
    Political rights
    GDP per capita
    GDP growth
    Democratic attitudes

WORKSHEET

NAME: _____

COURSE: _____

DATE: _____

REVIEW QUESTIONS

Based on the first part of this chapter, answer True or False to the following items:

1. Russia has changed its classification from authoritarian-regulatory to totalitarian-statist because of its weak protection of civil liberties and political rights.　　T　　F

2. The Russian government protects civil liberties better than the Polish government.　　T　　F

3. Free and fair elections, competitive party systems, and minority participation are all examples of civil liberties.　　T　　F

4. The GDP of Russia grew at a negative rate in the 1990s.　　T　　F

5. During the 1990s, Poland's economy suffered significant negative growth.　　T　　F

6. Compared to other European nation-states, the Russian government is not very involved in the regulation of the economy.　　T　　F

7. Russians are generally more inclined than Poles to believe that "in democracy, the economic system runs badly."　　T　　F

8. In the World Values Survey, Russians are the most inclined to believe that "in democracy, the economic system runs badly."　　T　　F

EXPLORIT QUESTIONS

I. Do economies that are more highly regulated have higher rates of economic growth than those that are less regulated? Analyze the relationship between ECON.FREE and GROW 90–99 in the GLOBAL file and then the EUROPE file and answer the questions that follow.

> ➤ *Data File:* **GLOBAL**
> ➤ *Task:* **Scatterplot**
> ➤ *Dependent Variable:* **138) GROW 90–99**
> ➤ *Independent Variable:* **266) ECON.FREE**
> ➤ *View:* **Reg. Line**

9. What is the value of r?　　　　r = _____

10. Is the result statistically significant?   Yes   No

Now remove three outliers from the analysis by clicking on the [Outlier] button and then clicking on [Remove] for each case that appears. You should remove Turkmenistan, Equatorial Guinea, and Bosnia and Herzegovina. The scatterplot will rescale.

11. After you have removed the outliers, what is the value of r?   r = _____

12. Is the relationship significant?   Yes   No

Now conduct the same analysis with the nations of Europe.

> *Data File:* **EUROPE**
> *Task:* **Scatterplot**
> *Dependent Variable:* **12) GROW 90–99**
> *Independent Variable:* **55) ECON.FREE**
> *View:* **Reg. Line**

13. What is the value of r?   r = _____

14. Is the result statistically significant?   Yes   No

Now remove one outlier from the analysis by clicking on the [Outlier] button and then clicking on [Remove]. The scatterplot will rescale.

15. Which case did you remove?   _____

16. After you have removed the outlier, what is the value of r?   r = _____

17. Is the relationship significant?   Yes   No

On the basis of this analysis, answer Question 1 in the "In Your Own Words" section at the end of this chapter.

II. Has a democratic culture taken root in Poland and Russia? In spite of increased freedoms, many Poles and Russians do not see the contemporary political and social situations in their countries in a positive light. In fact, in our analysis of attitudes toward the pre-1989 communist regimes in Chapter 7 we saw that there are still many people who see that era in a positive light. Have these individuals come to value democracy? Is there a significant difference in democratic values between those who liked the previous political regime and those who did not? Complete the table below for Russia and Poland and then answer the questions that follow. For each country listed below, you will need to open the appropriate data file, conduct the cross-tabulation that is indicated, write down the percentaged results for the first row of the table (e.g., Good, Bad), write down the value for V, and then indicate whether the results are statistically significant.

> *Data Files:* **WVS02–RUSSIA**
>   **WVS02–POLAND**
> ➤ *Task:* **Cross-tabulation**
> ➤ *Row Variables:* **CONF:EURO**
>   **DEM:BETTER**
>   **DEMOCRACY**
> ➤ *Column Variable:* **PRE REGIME**
>   ➤ *View:* **Tables**
>   ➤ *Display:* **Column %**

Fill in the table below.

RUSSIA

	BAD	SAME	GOOD	VALUE V	SIGNIFICANT?
175) CONF:EURO % High Confidence	_____%	_____%	_____%	_____	Y N
188) DEM:BETTER % Agree	_____%	_____%	_____%	_____	Y N
183) DEMOCRACY % Good	_____%	_____%	_____%	_____	Y N

18. What is the best interpretation of the analysis of one's view of the previous regime and one's confidence in the European Union?

 a. People who think that the previous regime was good tend to have more confidence in the European Union than people who think that the previous regime was bad.

 b. People who think that the previous regime was bad tend to have more confidence in the European Union than people who think that the previous regime was good.

 c. People who have confidence in the European Union are more likely to think that the previous regime was bad.

 d. People who have confidence in the European Union are more likely to think that the previous regime was good.

 e. None of the above. The results were not significant.

19. Which group of Russians is more likely to believe that "democracy may have its problems, but it is better than all other forms of government"?

 a. Those who believe that the former communist regime was bad.

 b. Those who believe that the former communist regime was about the same.

 c. Those who believe that the former communist regime was good.

 d. None of the above. The results were not significant.

20. What is the best interpretation of the analysis of relationship between one's view of the previous regime and one's view of a democratic political system?

     a.   42.4% of the people who think that democracy is good thought that the previous regime was good, and the result is significant.

     b.   20.7% of the people who think that democracy is bad thought that the previous regime was bad, and the result is significant.

     c.   The majority of the people who thought that the previous regime was bad believe that the development of democracy is good. These results are significant.

     d.   Both a and b.

Fill in the table below.

POLAND

	BAD	SAME	GOOD	VALUE V	SIGNIFICANT?
165) CONF:EURO % High Confidence	_____%	_____%	_____%	_____	Y N
178) DEM:BETTER % Agree	_____%	_____%	_____%	_____	Y N
173) DEMOCRACY % Good	_____%	_____%	_____%	_____	Y N

21. Are Poles who think that the communist regime was bad more confident in the European Union than those who think it was good?   Yes   No

22. Which group of Poles is more likely to believe that "democracy may have its problems, but it is better than all other forms of government"?

     a.   Those who believe that the former communist regime was bad.

     b.   Those who believe that the former communist regime was about the same.

     c.   Those who believe that the former communist regime was good.

     d.   None of the above. All groups felt generally the same way about democracy.

23. In the analysis of Poland, what is the best interpretation of the relationship between one's view of the communist regime and the question of whether the development of democracy is good?

    a. People who believe that the previous regime was bad are more likely to believe that the development of democracy is good.

    b. People who believe that the previous regime was bad are less likely to believe that the development of democracy is good.

    c. Neither. The results are not significant.

24. In general, people in Russia are more likely than people in Poland to believe that the development of democracy is good.   T   F

III. One of the attributes of Russian and Polish political culture is a very large, conservative peasant-farmer class. Historically, this group is associated with political submissiveness and resistance to change. One way that we can measure this is to see whether or not people who live in small towns have different attitudes toward democracy and their relationship to the European Union than those who live in larger cities. City sizes have been divided into towns or villages of fewer than 10,000 people, cities from 10,000 to 100,000, and "big cities" with more than 100,000 people. Complete the table below for Russia and Poland and then answer the questions that follow.

> ➤ *Data Files:* **WVS02–RUSSIA**
> **WVS02–POLAND**
> ➤ *Task:* **Cross-tabulation**
> ➤ *Row Variables:* **CONF:EURO**
> **DEM:BETTER**
> **DEMOCRACY**
> ➤ *Column Variable:* **TOWN SIZE**
> ➤ *View:* **Tables**
> ➤ *Display:* **Column %**

Fill in the table below.

RUSSIA

	TOWN	CITY	BIG CITY	VALUE V	SIGNIFICANT?
175) CONF:EURO % High Confidence	_____%	_____%	_____%	_____	Y N
188) DEM:BETTER % Agree	_____%	_____%	_____%	_____	Y N
183) DEMOCRACY % Good	_____%	_____%	_____%	_____	Y N

Chapter 8: Russia, Poland, and Democratic Transition

25. In terms of Russians' confidence in the European Union, do people from towns feel less confident in the EU than those from big cities?   Yes   No

26. In which town size are people least likely to agree with the statement that "democracy may have its problems, but it is better than all other forms of government"?

    _____

27. Are people from big cities more likely to favor the development of democracy than people from small towns?   Yes   No

Fill in the table below.

POLAND

	TOWN	CITY	BIG CITY	VALUE V	SIGNIFICANT?
165) CONF:EURO % High Confidence	_____%	_____%	_____%	_____	Y N
178) DEM:BETTER % Agree	_____%	_____%	_____%	_____	Y N
173) DEMOCRACY % Good	_____%	_____%	_____%	_____	Y N

28. In terms of Poles' confidence in the European Union, do people from towns feel less confident in the EU than those from big cities?   Yes   No

29. In which town size are people less likely to agree with the statement that "democracy may have its problems, but it is better than all other forms of government"?

    a. town
    b. city
    c. big city
    d. none, the result is not significant

30. Because the relationship between TOWN SIZE and DEMOCRACY is not significant, we can't draw conclusions about this relationship.   T   F

IN YOUR OWN WORDS

In your own words, please answer the following questions.

1. In the analysis of the relationship between economic growth and economic regulation in the GLOBAL file, the relationship was extremely weak. But in the EUROPE file, once the outlier was removed the relationship was very strong. Why would this relationship be weak in the analysis of countries around the world, but strong among European countries? Also, how can we justify the removal of an outlier like Bosnia?

2. Based on all of your analysis in this chapter, which country (Poland or Russia) is more likely to have a backlash against democratic reform? Which is less likely? Why?

Part IV

NEWLY INDUSTRIALIZING COUNTRIES

Central and South America

Asia

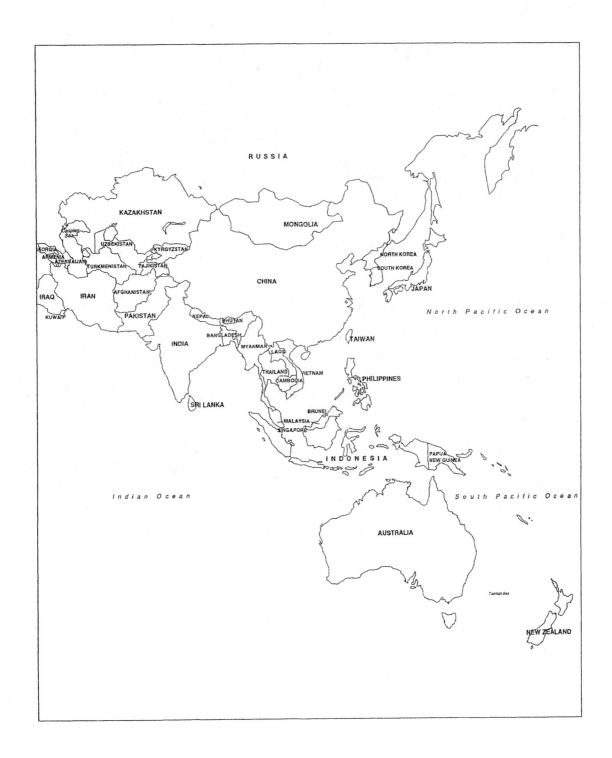

CHAPTER **9**

NEWLY INDUSTRIALIZING
COUNTRIES

*Before, we fought the war for independence, for
freedom, for the unification of the country. Now our
battle is for the development of our country. . . .*

NGUYEN XUAN PHONG,
FOREIGN MINISTER, VIETNAM, 1993

Tasks: Mapping, Univariate, Scatterplot, Historical Trends, ANOVA, Cross-tabulation
Data Files: GLOBAL, LATIN, ASIA, HISTORY, WVS02all, WVS02–BRAZIL, WVS02–MEXICO

The end of the Cold War may have brought the collapse of communism, but it also revealed the extent to which another group of countries, the newly industrializing countries (NICs), had separated themselves from the pack that was known as the Third World. Before 1990 it was easier to lump Third World countries into a category of nation-states associated with poverty, corrupt government, and authoritarian politics. Now, we will see, it is clearly not so easy to assume this about NICs. Before we get involved in analysis, let's open the GLOBAL data file and figure out where the NICs are located.

➤ *Data File:* **GLOBAL**
➤ *Task:* **Mapping**
➤ *Variable 1:* **130) WORLDS.7**
➤ *Subset Variable:* **130) WORLDS.7**
➤ *Category:* **Include: 3) NICs**
➤ *View:* **Map**

WORLDS.7 -- CLASSIFICATION OF COUNTRIES INTO "SEVEN WORLDS" OR
CATEGORIES: 1 = LIBERAL DEMOCRACY, 2 = COMMUNIST/POST-COMMUNIST, 3 =

[Subset]

**Because we want to see only the NICs appear in the map, select 130) WORLDS.7 as the
subset variable and check the box for category 3) NICs.**

You will remember that most of the communist and postcommunist countries were located in Europe and Asia, but most NICs are located in Asia and Latin America. While they may not have a lot in common from the standpoint of geography, the NICs have had a common experience of emerging democracy in recent years. To begin our analysis of the NICs, let's compare the overall freedom in the world rating using the ANOVA task. This rating is an average of the political rights and civil liberties ratings so it ranges from 1 to 7, where 1 is the most free and 7 is the least free.

163

Data File: **GLOBAL**
➤ Task: **ANOVA**
➤ Dependent Variable: **480) FREEDOM2**
➤ Independent Variable: **130) WORLDS.7**
➤ View: **Summary**

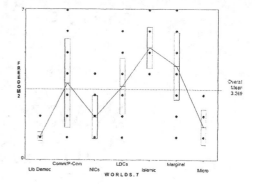

You will notice from the graph that the liberal democracies, microstates, and NICs have the lowest or "most free" ratings of the seven types of nation-states in our study. If you switch to the Means table, you will see that the NICs have an average rating of 1.952, which is more than a full point lower than LDCs (3.417), communist/postcommunist states (3.559), marginal states (4.360), or Islamic states (5.240). While the NICs still are almost a full point higher than liberal democracies (1.042), the NICs that are emerging democracies clearly stand apart from other groups that were once part of the bloc called the "Third World."

The pattern of emerging democracy among the NICs during the past 25 years can be seen up close if we examine the region of Latin America that includes Mexico and the Caribbean, as well as Central and South America.

➤ Data File: **LATIN**
➤ Task: **Mapping**
➤ Variable 1: **34) WORLDS.7**
➤ View: **Map**
➤ Display: **Legend**

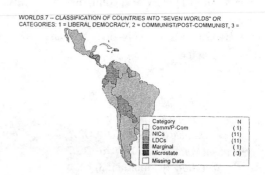

If you display the legend, you will see that Latin America has a mixture of different types of states that range from NICs like the major states of Mexico and Brazil to LDCs like Bolivia and Paraguay.

Political development, measured in terms of the expansion of political rights and the recognition of civil liberties, has improved in recent years but these improvements have not come easy to this region. The Americas were the first region to be colonized by Europeans.

Data File: **LATIN**
Task: **Mapping**
➤ Variable 1: **19) COLONIZE**
➤ View: **Map**
➤ Display: **Legend**

COLONIZE – EUROPEAN COLONIZER (LE ROY 1998)

Category	N
Spain	(20)
Portugal	(1)
Britain	(3)
France	(2)
Netherland	(1)
Missing Data	

Beginning in the 15th century, the Spanish and Portuguese kingdoms competed fiercely to secure the most land in the New World. Before all of the land had even been fully explored, the pope managed to prod the Portuguese and the Spanish into a treaty dividing up "all heathen lands 500 miles to the west of the Azores islands." This left Spain with most of the land in the Americas and Portugal with the region that is present-day Brazil. The British laid claim to North America. In 1519, Hernando Cortes arrived in Mexico from Cuba and began the brutal conquest of the Aztec empire. Farther south, Francisco Pizarro conquered Peru for Spain in 1531. Both efforts at conquest took years, and the native peoples lost hundreds of thousands of lives during the violent wars and counter-rebellions. Spain and Portugal dominated the Southwestern Hemisphere through the beginning of the 19th century. Between 1800 and 1825, the world witnessed the first collapse of a global empire. During this remarkable period of time, the empires of Spain, Britain, and Portugal all lost hold of most of their New World possessions.

Data File: **LATIN**
Task: **Mapping**
➤ Variable 1: **17) IND DATE**
➤ View: **List: Rank**

IND DATE: Year of independence

RANK	CASE NAME	VALUE
1	Belize	1981
2	Suriname	1975
3	Bahamas	1973
4	Barbados	1966
4	Guyana	1966
6	Trinidad & Tobago	1962
6	Jamaica	1962
8	Panama	1903
9	Cuba	1902
10	Dominican Republic	1844

As you can see from the ranking, all but a few of the major countries in South America were "liberated" between 1810 and 1828. This 18-year period also corresponds to the demise of the Spanish empire, which began more than 100 years earlier with the defeat of the Spanish fleet in 1688. Caribbean island possessions of Spain, such as Cuba, were retained much longer because they were easier to hold than the vast land masses of South and Central America. Six of the 27 countries in the southern part of the Americas—Suriname, Dominican Republic, Haiti, Jamaica, Guyana, and Belize—were colonized by Britain, France, and the Netherlands. These colonies were held until after World War II in a pattern similar to what was experienced in Africa and Asia. Knowledge of this pattern of independence helps us to understand the historical trend of independence.

> *Data File:* **HISTORY**
> > *Task:* **Historical Trends**
> *Variables:* **3) IND/DECADE**

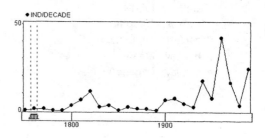

Number of independent nations each decade

If you scroll through the events below the timeline, you will notice that the Latin American wars of independence correspond to a sharp rise in the number of countries that became independent in the early 1820s.

The colonial legacy of imperial domination and the wars of liberation left these new nations with a strong political tradition of authoritarian government that persisted through the 1970s. In 1978, most of the governments of Latin America were still characterized by military dictatorships or one-party dominant regimes that allowed little dissent.

> *Data File:* **LATIN**
> > *Task:* **Mapping**
> *Variable 1:* **31) GOVT 1978**
> > *View:* **Map**
> > *Display:* **Legend**

You will notice that in 1978, 16 of the 27 states in Latin America were dominated by dictators in places like Chile, Nicaragua, and Paraguay or by one-party political machines like Mexico's ruling PRI party. The heavy hand of authoritarian government in many of these non-democratic regimes was confronted by a number of political insurgencies, or civil wars, that challenged the legitimacy of these governments.

> *Data File:* **LATIN**
> > *Task:* **Mapping**
> *Variable 1:* **23) INSURGENCY**
> > *View:* **Map**
> > *Display:* **Legend**

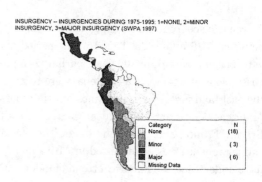

In Nicaragua, civil war led to revolution and the overthrow of the regime of Anastasio Somoza, while the citizens of Guatemala, El Salvador, and Peru suffered decades of civil warfare in the countryside.

Most countries with insurgency movements within them also had repressive political regimes in the 1970s. This violent—and, in some countries, often highly ideological—conflict resulted in serious abuses of human rights that continue to this day despite the fact that most of these countries have now embraced democracy. The HUMAN RTS variable indicates the type of human-rights abuses perpetrated by governments in Latin America.

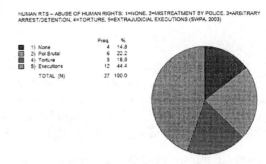

Data File: **LATIN**
➤ Task: **Univariate**
➤ Primary Variable: **24) HUMAN RTS**
➤ View: **Pie**

HUMAN RTS – ABUSE OF HUMAN RIGHTS: 1=NONE, 2=MISTREATMENT BY POLICE, 3=ARBITRARY ARREST/DETENTION, 4=TORTURE, 5=EXTRAJUDICIAL EXECUTIONS (SWPA. 2003)

	Freq.	%
1) None	4	14.8
2) Pol Brutal	6	22.2
4) Torture	5	18.5
5) Executions	12	44.4
TOTAL (N)	27	100.0

As you can see, the legacy of authoritarianism and violent conflict in South American countries has persisted beyond the 1970s. Only 20% of countries in South America do not have complaints of some sort against their government. Fifty-two percent of all governments in the 1990s continue to use extra-judicial executions, which are executions without a trial. These same governments often use torture, arbitrary arrest, and harassment to silence their political opponents.

Despite these difficulties, the overwhelming trend is toward multiparty democracy and away from authoritarian forms of political organization.

Data File: **LATIN**
➤ Task: **Mapping**
➤ Variable 1: **36) GOVERNMENT**
➤ View: **Map**

GOVERNMENT – GOVERNMENT: THE NATURE OF GOVERNMENT AND POLITICS (Le Roy. 2006)

The map of Latin America now looks remarkably free compared to the picture of politics in 1978. Remember that in 1978, 16 of the 27 nation-states in Latin America were directly controlled by the military or one-party states, now only Cuba fits that description. This is not to say that many of these new democracies don't also struggle in their efforts to become more democratic, but it is astonishing to see so much political change between 1978 and the present.

The trend of emerging democracy is mirrored for NICs in other parts of the world. The 1980s and 90s witnessed the scuttling of repressive regimes in NICs like South Africa, or gradual transition from authoritarianism in countries like the Phillipines, Thailand, and Taiwan.

A second characteristic that distinguishes NICs from other nation-states is the pattern of economic growth and development experienced by these nations. For the past 20 years, NICs have experienced profound economic, political, and social transformation as a result of industrialization. Let's compare the average GDP per capita for each type of country using the WORLDS.7 variable.

> *Data File:* **GLOBAL**
> *Task:* **ANOVA**
> *Dependent Variable:* **133) GDPCAP PPP**
> *Independent Variable:* **130) WORLDS.7**
> *View:* **Means**

Means, Standard Deviations and Number of Cases of Dependent Var: GDPCAP PPP by Categories of Independent Var: WORLDS.7
Difference of means across groups is statistically significant (Prob. = 0.000)

	N	Mean	Std.Dev.
Lib Democ	24	27710.982	8023.393
Comm/P-Com	31	6224.717	4503.199
NICs	19	9210.532	5065.291
LDCs	35	3025.699	2131.618
Islamic	18	5632.952	5103.788
Marginal	19	1554.439	1288.400
Micro	6	8137.019	5696.064

Compared to other nation-states that used to be in the Third World category, the NICs are a group of countries that now stand apart. Notice that the average GDP per capita in newly industrializing countries is $9,211. This exceeds former communist countries ($6,225), LDCs ($3,026), and the oil-producing Islamic states ($5,633) by quite a bit. All groups of countries are far below the super-rich liberal democracies ($27,711), but when we analyze GDP per capita, the NICs are clearly separating from other nation-states.

But how did this happen? One of the factors responsible for the economic growth experienced by the NICs is that much of the wealth of these nations is attributed to growth in industrial production.

> *Data File:* **GLOBAL**
> *Task:* **ANOVA**
> *Dependent Variable:* **208) % INDUS $**
> *Independent Variable:* **130) WORLDS.7**
> *View:* **Summary**

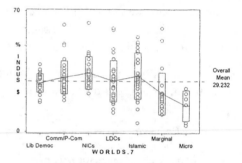

From this graph you can see that NICs now lead the world in the percentage of their economies' wealth that is derived from industrial production. If you think about it, this makes sense. Most of the clothes that you wear and goods that you buy (like DVD players and other electronics) are made in newly industrializing countries like Mexico, Malaysia, and Taiwan. This highlights another interesting fact about the NIC economies: that their recent growth is attributed not only to industrial production, but to the export of manufactured goods and technology as well. The variable 159) MFG_EXP is a measure of the manufactured goods that are exported as a percentage of all exports.

> *Data File:* **GLOBAL**
> *Task:* **ANOVA**
> *Dependent Variable:* **159) MFG EXP**
> *Independent Variable:* **130) WORLDS.7**
> *View:* **Summary**

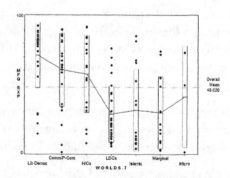

While NICs aren't the leading exporter of manufactured goods, they are not far behind communist/postcommunist countries, or liberal democracies, and they are clearly ahead of all other country groups. If you switch to the Means table, you will see that an average of 57.6% of NIC exports are manufactured goods.

Comparative Politics

What about DVD players or the computer that you are using right now? The next variable measures the exports of high technology as a percentage of overall exports.

Data File: **GLOBAL**

Task: **ANOVA**

➤ Dependent Variable: **157) TECH_EXP**

➤ Independent Variable: **130) WORLDS.7**

➤ View: **Means**

Means, Standard Deviations and Number of Cases of Dependent Var: TECH_EXP by Categories of Independent Var: WORLDS.7
Difference of means across groups is statistically significant (Prob. = 0.000)

	N	Mean	Std.Dev.
Lib Democ	24	18.365	8.884
Comm/P-Com	23	6.830	6.695
NICs	17	20.509	23.512
LDCs	27	5.194	6.703
Islamic	14	2.401	3.216
Marginal	12	3.289	6.070
Micro	3	5.230	8.927

From this analysis of the average technical exports, you can see that NICs now lead the world in the export of high-technology products (expressed as a percentage of all exports). This means that these economies are more dependent on the production and export of high-technology goods than any other economies in the world.

The Asian region has seen more export-led gains in the past 30 years than any other region in the world. And these advances show in the trend analysis of economic growth patterns during this time.

The following variables indicate the five-year average of economic growth rates between 1975 and the mid-1990s in each region of the world. For our purposes here, East Asia is defined as those nations which border the Pacific Ocean and South Asia is defined as those nations that border the Indian Ocean.

➤ Data File: **HISTORY**

➤ Task: **Historical Trends**

➤ Variables: **42) GROW.WORLD**
41) GROW.EASIA
43) GROW.SASIA

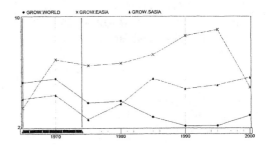

Average annual GDP growth in five-year periods: World, East Asia/Pacific, and South Asia

You can see from the analysis that East Asia and South Asia have grown at faster rates than the world average since 1980. As you'll see in the next analysis, countries in East Asia and South Asia have grown at faster rates since 1980 than the regions of Africa and Latin America.

Data File: **HISTORY**

Task: **Historical Trends**

➤ Variables: **41) GROW.EASIA**
43) GROW.SASIA
44) GROW.AFRIC
46) GROW.LATIN

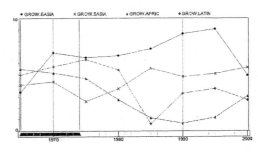

Average annual GDP growth in five-year periods: East Asia/Pacific, South Asia, sub-Saharan Africa, and Latin America/Caribbean

Africa has the slowest growth rate for the 1980s and 90s, with Latin America at only a slightly higher rate of growth. East Asia and South Asia have clearly grown the fastest in the developing world during this period. To see the economic growth rates for individual countries, return to the GLOBAL file.

> ➤ *Data File:* **GLOBAL**
> ➤ *Task:* **Mapping**
> ➤ *Variable 1:* **138) GROW 90–99**
> ➤ *View:* **Map**
> ➤ *Display:* **Legend**

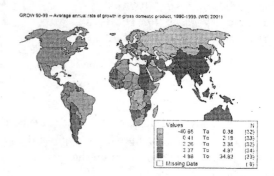

The darker colors on this map (which indicate the highest growth rates) are clearly concentrated in East and South Asia for the 1990s. Let's take a closer look at the growth rates in the countries in these regions.

> *Data File:* **GLOBAL**
> *Task:* **Mapping**
> *Variable 1:* **138) GROW 90–99**
> ➤ *View:* **List: Rank**

GROW 90–99: Average annual rate of growth in gross domestic product, 1990–1999

RANK	CASE NAME	VALUE
1	Bosnia and Herzegovina	34.83
2	Equatorial Guinea	17.58
3	Lebanon	11.53
4	Kuwait	10.05
5	China	9.76
6	Maldives	7.73
7	Singapore	7.65
8	Vietnam	7.43
9	Malaysia	7.21
10	Georgia	6.88

The countries in Asia dominate this list—5 of the 10 countries with the highest annual growth rates in 1990–99 were from Asia. China led the list of Asian nations with an annual GDP growth rate of 9.76%. If you calculate this growth rate across 10 years, you realize that China's GDP grew by 104% during that period! Again, this makes you realize that countries that are experiencing massive economic growth have different challenges from those that are growing at very slow rates or have declining GDPs.

If you scroll to the bottom of this list, you see that 27 countries had *declining* GDPs over this same 10-year period. Seven countries averaged more than a 5% decline. That means their annual GDPs were sliced to one-third of what they had been just 10 years earlier! This gives you a perspective of how impressive the growth rates in many Asian countries have been—and how devastating that sustained negative economic growth can be.

As we saw earlier, there are many sectors that contribute to a nation's economic growth, including industry, the service sector, and the information/technology sectors. Let's look at how growth in the industrial sector during the 1990s contributes to the growth or decline of GDP worldwide.

Comparative Politics

Data File: **GLOBAL**
➤ Task: **Scatterplot**
➤ Dependent Variable: **138) GROW 90–99**
➤ Independent Variable: **481) IND GROWTH**
➤ View: **Reg. Line**

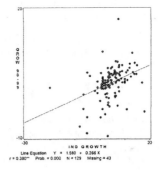

You will notice that there is a strong relationship between the industrial production growth rate and overall economic growth (r = 0.380**).

The puzzle as to why the economies of the Asia-Pacific region have grown at such a rapid rate between 1975 and through the 1990s is very complex, but we can understand some elements of it. One of the most significant factors has been the fact that private corporations have invested huge sums of money in developing the industrial capacity of the Asia-Pacific region. Let's look at the ASIA file to see this up close.

➤ Data File: **ASIA**
➤ Task: **Scatterplot**
➤ Dependent Variable: **13) GROW 90–99**
➤ Independent Variable: **14) INDUS GROW**
➤ View: **Reg. Line**

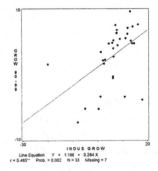

As this scatterplot shows, the relationship in Asia between industrial production growth and growth in GDP is much stronger (r = 0.485**) than found with the GLOBAL file. Notice that the graph includes countries that have experienced negative growth (i.e., those countries whose economies and industrial sectors have shrunk over the past year). When you see a scatterplot with a relationship this strong where most cases are clustered together, sometimes it's worth investigating those cases not located with the rest of the bunch. Click on the cases that have the greatest negative GDP growth rates. You should immediately notice that nearly all of these countries are from the former Soviet Union and are now in the process of making a transition to a market economy. All of them experienced negative economic and industrial growth during the period that these data were collected. Thus, we can see that political factors, such as the collapse of communism, have a direct influence on the economic patterns we witness. Now look at the cluster of dots at the top right corner of the scatterplot. Most of these countries are relatively small and have been dubbed "the Asian tigers" because of their astonishing growth rates between the late 1970s and 1990s. Ironically, in the late 1990s, these countries were also the victims of severe economic turmoil. In Indonesia, this turmoil even resulted in a popular uprising and a change in leadership.

Another factor in the astonishing growth rates of the Asia-Pacific region has been the role of government. Initially it was thought that these countries succeeded because of their relatively low level of economic regulation. Economic regulation is the degree to which the government allows an economy to be managed by the government. On one end of the spectrum of this variable (1) are the countries that have relatively free markets. On the other end of the spectrum (3) are governments that have economies that are completely managed and regulated by the government. Do the data support the idea that unregulated markets had the highest growth rates in Asia during the period 1990–99?

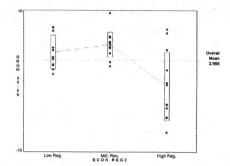

Data File: **ASIA**
➤ Task: **ANOVA**
➤ Dependent Variable: **13) GROW 90–99**
➤ Independent Variable: **29) ECON REG2**
➤ View: **Graph**

The evidence does support the hypothesis. If we look more closely at the data, our analysis does raise some questions. If you examine the cases in the High Reg. category, you will notice that they consist of countries that were in the former Soviet Union. If you exclude these countries, the relationship between economic growth and economic regulation in Asia becomes fuzzy.

One theory for this relationship is that many of the nations experiencing strong economic growth also have government policies designed to protect the domestic economy. These regulations make consumer products very expensive; thus, people are much more likely to save their money than to buy these over-priced items. Let's investigate the savings levels in Asia a bit further.

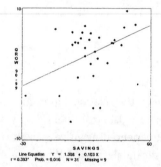

Data File: **ASIA**
➤ Task: **Scatterplot**
➤ Dependent Variable: **13) GROW 90–99**
➤ Independent Variable: **16) SAVINGS**
➤ View: **Reg. Line**

The moderately strong relationship between a high savings rate and high levels of growth (r = 0.393*) suggests that government policy may have something to do with high growth rates in Asia. High levels of savings by citizens allow for a large pool of capital that business can invest in the domestic economy.

So far we've analyzed a few factors that explain the distinctives of newly industrialized countries. In the worksheet section that follows, you will examine a few more.

Terms and Concepts

NIC
Military dictatorship in Latin America
Factors influencing economic growth
Exports

WORKSHEET

Workbook exercises and software are copyrighted. Copying is prohibited by law.

NAME:

COURSE:

DATE:

CHAPTER

9

REVIEW QUESTIONS

Based on the first part of this chapter, answer True or False to the following items:

1. Newly industrializing countries are found only in Asia.   T   F

2. The liberation of Latin America occurred at the same time as the American Revolution.   T   F

3. There are more military dictatorships in Latin America today than there were in the 1970s.   T   F

4. After liberal democracies, NICs are the second most "free" group of nation-states in the world.   T   F

5. Throughout the 1980s, East Asia had a faster growth rate than South Asia and the rest of the world.   T   F

6. Much of the rapid growth in Asia is attributed to the export of high-technology and manufactured goods.   T   F

7. The Asian countries that were previously part of the Soviet Union have seen rapid economic growth since their independence.   T   F

8. There is a moderately strong, positive correlation between the savings rate in Asian countries and economic growth.   T   F

EXPLORIT QUESTIONS

I. So far we have analyzed the political and economic development of NICs, but what about social development? Factors such as the birth rate, life expectancy, and infant mortality should increase with stable politics and growing economies. Earlier in this book we used the GLOBAL file to determine that GDP per capita was inversely related to birth rates—countries with higher birth rates had lower GDP per capita. Let's see whether this holds true when we include only the NICs in our analysis.

> *Data File:* **GLOBAL**
> *Task:* **Scatterplot**
> *Dependent Variable:* **28) BIRTHRATE**
> *Independent Variable:* **133) GDPCAP PPP**
> *Subset Variable:* **130) WORLDS.7**
> *Subset Category:* **Include: 3) NICs**
> *View:* **Reg. Line**

9. What is the correlation coefficient?   r = _____

10. Are these results statistically significant?   Yes   No

11. In the NICs, as birth rates increase, the GDP per capita decreases.   T   F

12. If NICs want to increase their rates of GDP per capita, they need to increase their population base.   T   F

II. Now let's analyze some other dimensions of social development. First, we will analyze the mortality rate of children under the age of five, life expectancy, and finally, the education levels of citizens in NICs compared to those in other countries. Compare the NICs to other countries that used to be in the broad Third World category (LDCs, Islamic states, and marginal states) using the ANOVA task. Analyze each of the relationships and fill in the table below.

> *Data File:* **GLOBAL**
> *Task:* **ANOVA**
> *Dependent Variables:* **32) MORTAL<5**
> **40) LIFE EXPCT**
> **339) EDUC INDEX**
> *Independent Variable:* **130) WORLDS.7**

	NICS	LDCS	ISLAMIC	MARGINAL	SIGNIFICANT?
MORTAL<5	_____	_____	_____	_____	Y N
LIFE EXPCT	_____	_____	_____	_____	Y N
EDUC INDEX	_____	_____	_____	_____	Y N

13. If we assume that our measures of the mortality of children under age five, life expectancy, and the education index are accurate measures of social development, then we can say

   a. NICs have about the same level of social development as LDCs.

   b. NICs have a higher level of social development than LDCs, Islamic states, or marginal states, but the results of this analysis are not significant.

   c. NICs have a higher level of social development than LDCs, Islamic states, or marginal states, and the results of this analysis are significant.

   d. none of the above

III. Now let's look at the politics of a couple of emerging democracies. One of the challenges of democratic transition is that the population often has more confidence in authoritarian rule than they have in democratic institutions. Let's see if this is the case in a Latin American democracy.

> ➤ *Data Files:* **WVS02all**
>> ➤ *Task:* **Cross-Tabulation**
> ➤ *Row Variable:* **16) JUNTA**
> ➤ *Column Variable:* **1) COUNTRY**
>> ➤ *View:* **Tables**
>> ➤ *Display:* **Column%**

14. Which country has the highest percentage of its population endorsing the notion that
    military rule would be a "good thing?"   _____

    While it is not true that even a majority in any one country identifies rule by the army as a desirable end, it is the case that a significant percentage of the population in several countries sees army rule as desirable.

    You have been hired as a consultant to help the president of Brazil avert what seems to be an impending coup. She urgently needs to reduce corruption and improve the image of government agencies. The Brazilian president would like to target the government agencies that seem most corrupt to the overall population, especially those that are in favor of military rule (a junta). The four areas to be examined are the military, the police force, the legislature, and the legal system. The survey you administered in Brazil includes a series of questions that assess the confidence rates for the various government agencies. Use these data to determine the agencies in which people have a great deal of confidence and no confidence. Also examine which agencies the supporters of military rule have the most confidence in and the least confidence in.

    You will need to use the WVS02–BRAZIL file and the CROSS-TABULATION task to complete this series of analyses. The variable 144) JUNTA will be the independent variable (the column variable) in each analysis. The dependent variables (row variables) are listed below. For each result, fill in the percentages (use column percentaging) for the row that is specified in the table below. Note that you are also asked to fill in the "total percent" for that row (which indicates the overall percentage of respondents who gave that answer to the survey question). Finally, indicate whether the results are statistically significant (circle Y for Yes, N for No).

    > ➤ *Row Variables:* **124) CONF:ARMY**
    >> **127) CONF:COPS**
    >> **128) CONF:PARL**
    >> **136) CONF:LEGAL**

    Fill in the table below.

	GOOD	BAD	TOTAL	V =	SIGNIFI-CANT?
124) CONF:ARMY					
% Great Deal	____%	____%	____%	_____	Y N
% None	____%	____%	____%		

	GOOD	BAD	TOTAL	V =	SIGNIFI-CANT?
127) CONF:COPS					
% Great Deal	_____%	_____%	_____%	_____	Y N
% None	_____%	_____%	_____%		
128) CONF:PARL					
% Great Deal	_____%	_____%	_____%	_____	Y N
% None	_____%	_____%	_____%		
136) CONF:LEGAL					
% Great Deal	_____%	_____%	_____%	_____	Y N
% None	_____%	_____%	_____%		

15. Overall, in which two agencies do people in Brazil have the lowest level of confidence (none)?

_____

_____

16. Overall, in which of the four agencies do people have a great deal of confidence?   _____

17. In which two agencies do supporters of military government in Brazil have the least confidence?

_____

_____

18. In which agency do supporters of military government in Brazil have the most confidence?   _____

19. In which agency do opponents of military government in Brazil have the most confidence?   _____

20. For all four institutions, Brazilian opinion on military rule makes a difference in terms of perceived confidence. Each result is statistically significant.   T   F

21. In terms of support for military government, the area having the greatest differences in confidence levels is the police.   T   F

IV. Your consultant work for Brazil was so well received that the president of Mexico hired you to do the same work in his country. Follow the instructions provided in the previous question using the WVS02–MEXICO file, but keep in mind that the Mexican president is interested in leading a program of military reform. He is most interested in appealing to his constituents who have deep suspicions about the military. [Use 167) JUNTA as the column variable.]

Fill in the table below.

	GOOD	BAD	TOTAL	V =	SIGNIFI-CANT?
149) CONF:ARMY					
% Great Deal	____%	____%	____%	____	Y N
% None	____%	____%	____%		
152) CONF:COPS					
% Great Deal	____%	____%	____%	____	Y N
% None	____%	____%	____%		
153) CONF:PARL					
% Great Deal	____%	____%	____%	____	Y N
% None	____%	____%	____%		
148) CONF:CHRCH					
% Great Deal	____%	____%	____%	____	Y N
% None	____%	____%	____%		

22. Overall, in which two agencies do people in Mexico have the lowest level of confidence (i.e., none)? _____

_____

23. Overall, in which of the four agencies are people most likely to say that they have a great deal of confidence (i.e., a great deal)? _____

24. In which two agencies do supporters of military government in Mexico have the least confidence? _____

_____

25. In which agency do supporters of military government in Mexico have the most confidence? _____

26. In which agency do opponents of military government in Mexico have the most confidence? _____

27. In all four areas, Mexican opinion on military rule makes a difference in terms of perceived confidence. Each result is statistically significant. T   F

28. In terms of support for military government, the area having the greatest
differences in confidence levels is the parliament.   T   F

IN YOUR OWN WORDS

In your own words, please answer the following questions.

1. If the Brazilian president had to pick one agency to improve in order to avert a military coup, which
one should she pick? Why? What should be her second choice? Be sure to support your answers
with evidence.

2. If the president of Mexico were to draw on one institution to help him in his reform of the military,
which one should he draw on? Why? What should be his second choice? Be sure to support your
answers with evidence.

CHAPTER 10

POLITICAL CULTURE IN SOUTH KOREA AND INDIA

We must ask ourselves if "Asian values" can assist us in the years of economic and socio-political uncertainty ahead. If they are relevant, they should be able to withstand the stress-test of an economic down-turn.

-YB DATO' HISHAMUDDIN HUSSEIN, MALAYSIAN GOVERNMENT MINISTER

Tasks: Cross-tabulation, Mapping, Univariate, Historical Trends
Data Files: GLOBAL, ASIA, HISTORY, WVS02all, PEW GLOBAL02, WVS02–SOUTH KOREA, WVS02–INDIA, WVS02–JAPAN, WVS02–ANALYZER

In our initial study of newly industrializing countries (NICs), we learned that these nations are characterized by emerging democratic systems and rapidly growing economies. We also learned that NICs exist in a wide variety of regions, but that most are concentrated in Asia and the Western Hemisphere.

➤ *Data File:* **GLOBAL**
➤ *Task:* **Cross-tabulation**
➤ *Row Variable:* **464) REGION2**
➤ *Column Variable:* **130) WORLDS.7**
➤ *View:* **Graph**
➤ *Display:* **Bar Stack**

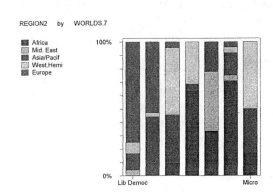

The table associated with this graph indicates that 36.4% of the newly industrializing countries are in the Asian and Pacific regions, while 50.0% of NICs are located in the Western Hemisphere. As political scientists have tried to understand the successful stories of development for NICs, some research has focused on the hypothesis that so-called Asian values are responsible for the rapid economic growth that NICs have experienced in the East Asian region.

Researchers claim that Asian values, rooted in the traditions and values of the philosopher Confucius, have supported economic growth and development in the East Asian NICs where these values dominate. The values include a preference for cooperation over conflict, social conservatism, respect for authority, and the priority of family. More recently, researchers have also observed that many Asian cultures also express a great deal more optimism about the future than their Western counterparts.

In the worksheet section of this chapter, we will explore the "Asian values" hypothesis to see if there is any merit to the argument that there is such a thing as distinctively Asian values that have enabled NICs to experience rapid development. Before we do that, we need to get acquainted with the two NICs that we will examine in our study—South Korea and India.

SOUTH KOREA

South Korea has remained relatively independent of foreign powers for much of its history. Japan and China have always had a strong influence on the Korean peninsula, but it was not until the 20th century that Japanese domination over Korea was solidified in the brutal 40-year occupation that began in 1905 and ended with the defeat of Japan in World War II. Eight days before the surrender of the Japanese in WWII, the Soviet Union entered the war on the side of the Allied forces. At the end of the war, the United States agreed to partition Korea into North and South for occupation purposes. The territory north of the 38th parallel would be occupied by the USSR, and the south would be occupied by the United States. As tensions between the Soviet Union and the United States increased in the late 1940s, it became apparent that Korea would be partitioned in the same way that Germany was divided. This division put considerable stress on the economy. The northern part of the country was the primary industrial center whereas the south was the primary source of food for the country. Civil unrest occurred on both sides of the border. The North embraced a Stalinist model of political leadership under Kim Jong Il, and the South reverted to authoritarian government under Syngman Rhee. The tensions between the two countries resulted in war from 1949 to 1953. The United States and a United Nations force intervened on the side of the South, while newly communist China intervened on the side of the North. The tension between the two countries has not yet subsided, and the war has never officially ended. The result of this has been that both countries continue, especially North Korea, to maintain huge armies relative to the size of their population.

➤ Data File: **ASIA**
➤ Task: **Mapping**
➤ Variable 1: **24) POP MIL**
➤ View: **List: Rank**

POP MIL: Members of the military per 1000 population (WDI, 2005)

RANK	CASE NAME	VALUE
1	Korea, North	59.4
2	Singapore	55.5
3	Brunei	35.7
4	Laos	30.8
5	Cambodia	17.7
6	Korea, South	16.1
7	Armenia	13.2
8	Sri Lanka	13.0
9	Myanmar	12.9
10	Azerbaijan	10.6

As this list shows, North Korea maintains an army that is over three times larger than the army of South Korea. South Korea's army makes up a smaller percentage of its population, but this smaller size is largely due to the fact that the United States has a fairly large contingency of troops and weapons in the country.

Between 1948 and 1987, South Korea was ruled by three different dictators who violated human rights, suppressed workers, and assassinated opposition leaders. In 1981, the army of South Korea killed upward of 1,000 demonstrators in Kwangju, a southern province of the country.

In 1987, South Korea's military strongman Chun Doo Hwan stepped down in the face of widespread student protest and held presidential elections to select his successor. Since this time the South Korean political system has experienced gradual, but steady, improvement in the recognition of basic political rights. The map below allows you to compare political rights ratings in 1980 to ratings in 2004.

<table>
<tr><td align="right">Data File:</td><td>ASIA</td></tr>
<tr><td align="right">Task:</td><td>Mapping</td></tr>
<tr><td align="right">➤ Variable 1:</td><td>38) POL RIGT04</td></tr>
<tr><td align="right">➤ Variable 2:</td><td>47) POL RIGT80</td></tr>
<tr><td align="right">➤ View:</td><td>Map</td></tr>
<tr><td align="right">➤ Display:</td><td>Find Case: Korea, South</td></tr>
</table>

POL RIGT04 -- Rating of political rights on a scale of 1 to 7, 1 = most free, 7 = least free, for the year 2004. (FITW 2005)

KOREA, SOUTH (Most Free)

r = 0.683**

POL RIGT80 -- Rating of political rights on a scale of 1 to 7, 1 = most free, 7 = least free, for the year 1980. (FITW 2005)

KOREA, SOUTH (5)

The 2004 rating of 1 out of 7 is the freest rating possible on the freedom in the world index for political rights. This is a vast improvement from 1980 when the political rights rating was classified as 5, or one of the least-free ratings. South Koreans have experienced similar improvement in the area of civil liberties.

<table>
<tr><td align="right">Data File:</td><td>ASIA</td></tr>
<tr><td align="right">Task:</td><td>Mapping</td></tr>
<tr><td align="right">➤ Variable 1:</td><td>36) CIV LIBS04</td></tr>
<tr><td align="right">➤ Variable 2:</td><td>52) CIV LIBS80</td></tr>
<tr><td align="right">➤ View:</td><td>Map</td></tr>
<tr><td align="right">➤ Display:</td><td>Find Case: Korea, South</td></tr>
</table>

CIV LIBS04 -- Ratings of civil liberties on a scale of 1 to 7, 1 = most free, 7= least free, for the year 2004. (FITW 2005)

KOREA, SOUTH (2)

0.630**

CIV LIBS80 -- Ratings of civil liberties on a
scale of 1 to 7, 1 = most free, 7= least free,
for the year 1980. (FITW 2005)

KOREA, SOUTH (6)

South Korea's civil liberties rating is 2 out of a possible score of 7 (1 = most free). In the 1970s and early 80s, South Korea was well known for imprisoning political prisoners simply for publicly stating that they were sympathetic with North Korea or that they would like the North and South to be unified. Although this situation has improved dramatically since the 1980s, it is still not uncommon for South Koreans to be arrested for acting against the government's North Korea policy known as the National Security Law. Amnesty International reports that in 2005 there were still 11 people held for their political views under the National Security Law that bars collaboration or aid to North Korea.

An authoritarian heritage and fierce anti-communism have given South Korea a different idealogical spectrum than one might find in other NICs.

➤ *Data File:* **WVS02all**
➤ *Task:* **Cross-tabulation**
➤ *Row Variable:* **5) LT-RT-3**
➤ *Column Variable:* **1) COUNTRY**
➤ *View:* **Tables**
➤ *Display:* **Column%**

LT-RT-3   by   COUNTRY
Cramer's V: 0.159**

		COUNTRY								
		Germany	USA	Japan	Russia	S Korea	Mexico	Turkey	Nigeria	TOTAL
LT-RT-3	Left	552	196	195	490	385	174	944	656	3592
		32.9%	17.3%	19.0%	31.0%	32.1%	16.3%	22.0%	33.4%	25.8%
	Center	731	579	549	798	453	367	1888	537	5902
		43.6%	51.1%	53.5%	50.5%	37.8%	34.3%	44.0%	27.3%	42.3%
	Right	395	357	283	292	362	528	1460	773	4450
		23.5%	31.5%	27.6%	18.5%	30.2%	49.4%	34.0%	39.3%	31.9%
	Missing	358	68	335	920	0	466	315	56	2518
	TOTAL	1678	1132	1027	1530	1200	1069	4292	1966	13944
		100.0%	100.0%	100.0%	100.0%	100.0%	100.0%	100.0%	100.0%	

For the most part, ideology in South Korea appears to be the same as in most other countries and, if anything, leans a little to the political left. Despite this strong tradition of authoritarianism and anti-communism, South Korean politics have a fairly strong radical student movement. If we analyze ideology using the South Korea file, we begin to see a strong relationship between age and ideology.

➤ *Data File:* **WVS02–SOUTH KOREA**
➤ *Task:* **Cross-tabulation**
➤ *Row Variable:* **223) LT-RT-3**
➤ *Column Variable:* **218) AGE GROUP6**
➤ *View:* **Tables**
➤ *Display:* **Column %**

LT-RT-3   by   AGE GROUP6
Cramer's V: 0.192**

		AGE GROUP6						
		15-24	25-34	35-44	45-54	55-64	65+	TOTAL
LT-RT-3	Left	72	131	101	59	16	6	385
		43.9%	41.1%	34.9%	20.5%	14.3%	21.4%	32.1%
	Center	64	110	111	125	34	9	453
		39.0%	34.5%	38.4%	43.4%	30.4%	32.1%	37.8%
	Right	28	78	77	104	62	13	362
		17.1%	24.5%	26.6%	36.1%	55.4%	46.4%	30.2%
	TOTAL	164	319	289	288	112	28	1200
		100.0%	100.0%	100.0%	100.0%	100.0%	100.0%	

Notice that there is a very strong relationship here between ideology and age. 43.9% of the people between the ages of 15 and 24 place themselves on the political left, but this number declines significantly with each age group to the point that only 21.4% of those over 65 place themselves on the political left. The inverse relationship is also true for those on the political right. 17.1% of those who are between 15 and 24 place themselves on the right, while 46.4% of those who are over 65 place themselves on the political right.

The politics of South Korea are distinct, but the religious composition of society is also not what most people would expect.

> ➤ Data File: **ASIA**
>   ➤ Task: **Mapping**
> ➤ Variable 1: **43) %BUDDHIST**
>   ➤ View: **Map**
>   ➤ Display: **Find Case: Korea, South**

%BUDDHIST -- Percent of the population that is Buddhist. (WCE 2001)

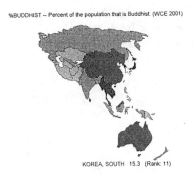

KOREA, SOUTH 15.3 (Rank: 11)

Buddhism still has a following in South Korea, but a religious census taken in 2000 indicates that the percentage of South Koreans who observe Buddhism is only 15.3%. Let's compare this to the percentage of Christians in South Korea.

>   Data File: **ASIA**
>   Task: **Mapping**
> ➤ Variable 1: **40) %CHRISTIAN**
> ➤ Variable 2: **41) %CATHOLIC**
>   ➤ View: **Map**
>   ➤ Display: **Find Case: Korea, South**

%CHRISTIAN -- Percent of the population that is Christian. (WCE 2001)

KOREA, SOUTH 40.8 (Rank: 11)

r = 0.649**

%CATHOLIC -- Percent of the population that is Catholic. (WCE 2001)

KOREA, SOUTH 7.9 (Rank: 8)

Most people are surprised to learn that South Korea has a very large percentage of the population that claims Christianity as their faith. 7.9% of South Koreans are Catholic and the remaining 32.9% are Protestant. Western missionaries in the 19th and early 20th centuries were very effective in this part of the world, and there is now a strong network of indigenous churches and church-related universities in South Korea.

Religious identification was important during the World Values Survey, but the percentages of people claiming an affiliation with a religion is different from what we found in the ASIA data file.

> *Data File:* **WVS02-SOUTH KOREA**
> *Task:* **Univariate**
> *Primary Variable:* **221) WHCH REL 2**
> *View:* **Pie**

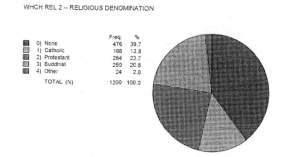

From this graph, the percentages look a little different. First of all, the percentage of Christians (Catholics and Protestants combined) looks higher (37.5%) than the variable we used in the ASIA data file. Second, the percentage of Buddhists appears to be higher (20.8%) than the variable we used in the ASIA data file.

This underscores the difficulty of measuring religion in any society. The variable from the ASIA data file comes from the *World Christian Encyclopedia*, which attempts to measure the number of people from different religions worldwide on the basis of church census records. The World Values Survey actually asks a sample of people in each country to name their affiliation. Both of these approaches are legitimate; they are just different approaches to measuring the same thing. But it is important to understand the difference when you are using data because each approach has certain inherent biases.

Let's see if there is an age-related pattern for religion in South Korea.

> *Data File:* **WVS02–SOUTH KOREA**
> *Task:* **Cross-tabulation**
> *Row Variable:* **221) WHCH REL 2**
> *Column Variable:* **218) AGE GROUP6**
> *View:* **Graph**
> *Display:* **Bar Stack**

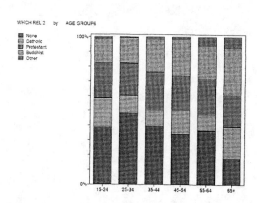

According to this analysis, there is an age pattern to religion in South Korea that the Bar Stack view does a nice job of illustrating. You will notice that the number of adherents to Buddhism increases with age and that the number of people who say they have no religious affiliation decreases with age. The percentages of Protestants and Catholics remain about the same across almost all age groups. Note

Comparative Politics

that this age analysis cannot tell us that "as people age they will be more likely to become Buddhist." While this is possible, there is another explanation for this pattern that should make us cautious. It is possible that the generation of people born 65 years ago were more likely to be Buddhist than generations that were born later.

So far we've analyzed unique political and social features of South Korea. Now let's take a look at South Korea's economic fortune. This first graph compares South Korea's growth in GDP since 1960 to the same growth rate of the East Asian region as a whole. You will remember from the previous chapter that East Asia has grown at the fastest rate of any region in the past 30 years.

➤ *Data File:* **HISTORY**
  ➤ *Task:* **Historical Trends**
➤ *Variables:* **41) GROW.EASIA**
  50) GR:S.KOREA

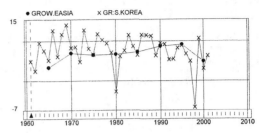

Economic Growth in South Korea and East Asia

The blue line indicates the growth rate of the region, and the green line indicates the annual growth rate for South Korea. Note that between 1965 and 1990, South Korea's growth rate exceeded the East Asian growth rate in all but a few years. During this period of time, South Korea experienced annual rates of growth exceeding 10% annually at least ten times. During the 1990s, South Korean growth was still robust, but even when it slowed to rates between 4% and 6% in the 1990s this still exceeded the growth rates of most advanced industrial democracies.

➤ *Data File:* **GLOBAL**
  ➤ *Task:* **Mapping**
➤ *Variable 1:* **135) GDP**
  ➤ *View:* **Map**
  ➤ *Display:* **Spot Fill**
    Find Case: Korea, South

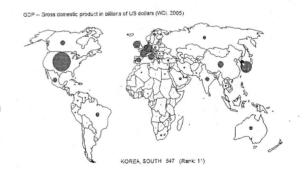

Growth rates like this quickly built the South Korean economy to the point that by 2005 it had become the eleventh largest economy in the world. South Korea's economy is now larger than in the economies of European countries like Spain and Portugal, and estimates of future growth indicate that it could soon surpass Canada's economy.

INDIA

India is also an NIC, but compared to South Korea it is slightly less democratic and much less developed. Artifacts from ancient Indian civilizations date as far back as 500,000 years making India one of the oldest civilizations in the world. Historical documentation of the earliest empires in India begins around 2500 B.C., but we will limit our historical overview to a more recent era. As they did with many other regions outside of Europe, the British colonized India between 1757 and 1857. The process of colonization began with the establishment of the British East India Company in 1757 in the coastal regions of India. This company, backed by the British government, established alliances with local Indian princes and managed to play one prince against another. This worked reasonably well for the British company until an alliance of disaffected Indian princes launched the Sepoy Rebellion of 1857. From that point forward the British government assumed formal control of India, and what would become present-day Pakistan until independence was granted to both of these nation-states in 1947.

> ➤ *Data File:* **ASIA**
> ➤ *Task:* **Mapping**
> ➤ *Variable 1:* **20) IND DATE**
> ➤ *View:* **Map**
> ➤ *Display:* **Find Case: India**

IND DATE – YEAR OF INDEPENDENCE (TWF, 1997)

INDIA 1947 (Rank: 26)

One of the dominant themes of 20th-century politics in India is the challenge of managing the most diverse nation-state in the world.

> ➤ *Data File:* **GLOBAL**
> ➤ *Task:* **Mapping**
> ➤ *Variable 1:* **461) MULTI-CULT**
> ➤ *View:* **List: Rank**

MULTI-CULT: Multiculturalism: Odds that any 2 persons will differ in their race, religion, ethnicity (tribe), or ethnic group

RANK	CASE NAME	VALUE
1	India	91
1	Congo, Dem. Republic	91
3	Bolivia	90
4	Uganda	89
4	Cameroon	89
6	Nigeria	88
7	South Africa	87
8	Côte d'Ivoire	86
9	Bhutan	85
9	Congo, Republic	85

This variable ranks the odds that any two people will differ in ethnic, religious, or cultural identity in a country. You should notice immediately that India is tied for first with the Congo as the most diverse nation-state in the world. Much of this diversity can be attributed to differences in religion.

Data File: **GLOBAL**
Task: **Mapping**
➤ Variable 1: **443) %HINDU**
➤ Variable 2: **440) %MUSLIM**
➤ View: **Map**

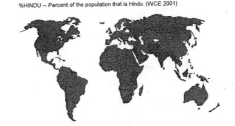

r = – 0.057

%MUSLIM -- Percent of the population that is Muslim. (WCE 2001)

These maps compare the percentage of Hindus in each nation of the world to the percentage of Muslims. Click on India and you will see that 72.9% of India's population is Hindu, compared to the 12.2% of the population that is Muslim. As you can see, Muslims are a good-sized minority group in India. Prior to independence, the percentage of the Muslim population living in India was actually much higher. Between 1885 and 1947, the Indian National Congress (INC) was formed by Indian nationalists to oppose British colonization of India. Until the 1920s this movement was led by Indian elites, but thanks to the work of Mohandas Karamchand Gandhi (Mahatma Gandhi), the INC re-invented itself as a broadly based social movement that included many classes, races, and religions. In spite of the success of this transformation, many Indian Muslims refused to accept Gandhi's Hindu leadership of the INC and demanded a separate Muslim state in negotiations for independence with the British. In August 1947, the British government granted independence to the secular state India and the Muslim state Pakistan. The so-called partition of India and Pakistan created a panic among Muslims living in India and Hindus living in Pakistan. Millions of Hindus living in Pakistan rushed to India, and millions of Muslims in India fled for Pakistan. More than 10 million people migrated between the two countries after the partition and nearly 500,000 people died in communal violence. If you find Pakistan on your map, you will see that there are now very few Hindus living in this country (1.2%). You will also notice that 96.1% of Pakistan is Muslim.

The bloody consequences of the partition set a very poor precedent for relations between India and Pakistan. The latter part of the 20th century witnessed persistent political tension between these two countries that even included episodes of open military conflict. In 1992 this tension reached a new peak when India declared that it had tested five nuclear weapons.

Chapter 10: Political Culture in South Korea and India

187

➤ *Data File:* **ASIA**
➤ *Task:* **Mapping**
➤ *Variable 1:* **22) NUKES**
➤ *View:* **Map**

NUKES -- OWNERSHIP OF NUCLEAR WEAPONS: 1=OWN NUCLEAR MATERIAL, 2=VOLUNTARILY ABANDONED WEAPONS, 3=OWN WEAPONS, 4=COMPELLED TO

Six countries in Asia now possess nuclear weapons or material. In 1998 Pakistan tested its first nuclear weapons and joined Russia, Kazakhstan, China, and India as a nuclear power in Asia.

Managing diversity also extends to ethnicity and caste in India. There are five major language groups in India (and many more minor languages), but social divisions in Indian society seem to be more strongly rooted in the system of social castes or classes. From top to bottom these are *Brahmans* (priestly castes), *Kshatriyas* (warrior castes), *Vaishyas* (trading and artisan castes), and *Shudras* (laboring and servant castes). Additionally, there is one other group which is sometimes referred to as the "fifth caste" but, technically, has no caste standing at all. Traditionally, members of this caste are referred to as "untouchables" or "out-castes"; today they are better known as *Dalits*, Scheduled Castes (SC's), other backward castes (OBC), or *Harijans*. So, when Indians seek to articulate their primary identity, it is quite difficult because Indian identity cuts across religion, ethnicity, and caste. In an effort to better understand Indian identity, the World Values Survey asked Indian citizens to select their primary identity in 1997.

IDENTITY -- Which of the following best describes you? [India]
1) Hindu; 2) Muslim; 3) OBC; 4) Indian above all; 5) Dalit; 6) Indian first, member of ethnic group second.

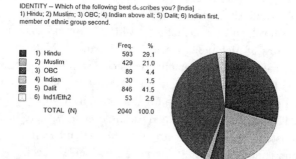

		Freq.	%
■	1) Hindu	593	29.1
▒	2) Muslim	429	21.0
■	3) OBC	89	4.4
▒	4) Indian	30	1.5
■	5) Dalit	846	41.5
□	6) Ind1/Eth2	53	2.6
	TOTAL (N)	2040	100.0

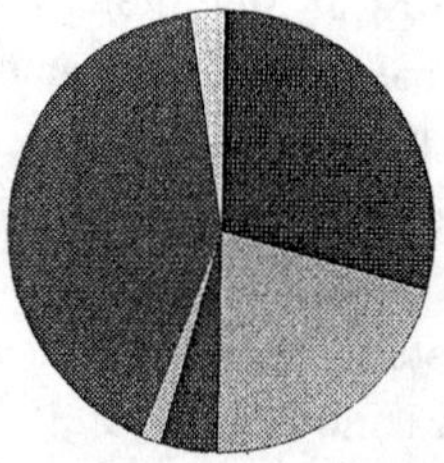

From this graph you will notice that both religion and caste are important. Indian citizens who were surveyed identify themselves with a particular caste, such as Dalit (41.5%), or with a religious group such as Muslim (21.0%) or Hindu (29.1%). Note that this does not mean that Dalits are not Hindus; rather, it means that Dalits see their Dalit caste as their primary identity. Very few people identify themselves as Indian (1.5%).

In addition to ethnic, religious, and caste diversity, India still struggles with overwhelming problems associated with a large percentage of the population living in poverty. Compared to many LDCs and marginal states, India appears to have a more equitable distribution of wealth in the population. The

following variable measures the percentage of the overall income garnered by the wealthiest 10% of the population.

➤ *Data File:* **GLOBAL**
➤ *Task:* **Mapping**
➤ *Variable 1:* **176) $ RICH 10%**
➤ *Display:* **Legend**
    Find Case: India
    Find Case: Korea, South

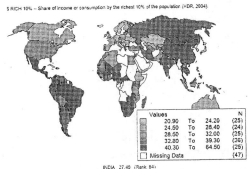

S RICH 10% -- Share of income or consumption by the richest 10% of the population (HDR, 2004).

Values			N
20.90	To	24.20	(25)
24.50	To	28.40	(24)
28.50	To	32.00	(25)
32.80	To	39.30	(26)
40.30	To	64.50	(25)
Missing Data			(47)

INDIA 27.40 (Rank: 84)

From this map you can see that the distribution of income in India is not as equitable as it is in South Korea or many European countries, but it is more equitable than it is in the United States. This result might lead one to believe that India is a relatively wealthy and equitable society, but this is a nation-state with more than 1 billion people; it is a nation that has not been able to develop its infrastructure on a pace with its rapid population growth or its more recent economic growth. The Pew Global Attitudes Project surveys citizen attitudes in a number of key areas including access to electricity, water, and sewage infrastructure. Let's take a look at the percentage of the population surveyed who says that they have access to electricity in South Korea and India.

➤ *Data File:* **PEW GLOBAL02**
➤ *Task:* **Cross-Tabulation**
➤ *Row Variable:* **5) HAVE ELCTR**
➤ *Column Variable:* **1) COUNTRY**
➤ *Subset Variable:* **1) COUNTRY**
    Include: 17) India
    22) S. Korea
➤ *Tables:* **Column%**

HAVE ELCTR   by   COUNTRY
Subset: COUNTRY Categories: India, S. Korea
Weight Variable: WEIGHT
Cramer's V: .0264**

		COUNTRY		
		India	S. Korea	TOTAL
HAVE ELCTR	Yes	1670	700	2370
		76.4%	100.0%	82.1%
	No	516	0	516
		23.6%	0.0%	17.9%
	TOTAL	2186	700	2887
		100.0%	100.0%	

To create a table that is limited to India and South Korea, make sure that you select 1) COUNTRY as a subset variable and select "NCLUDE" to include the categories of India and South Korea.

The table indicates that nearly all (76.4%) of Indians have access to electricity, but this is still far below the level of electricity access that South Korean citizens are accustomed to. The differences become more pronounced when citizens were asked about whether or not they had a flush toilet in their house.

Data·File: **PEW GLOBAL02**
Task: **Cross-Tabulation**
➤ Row Variable: **8) HAVETOILET**
Column Variable: **1) COUNTRY**
Subset Variable: **1) COUNTRY**
Include: **17) India**
22) S. Korea
Tables: **Column%**

HAVETOILET by COUNTRY
Subset: COUNTRY Categories: India, S. Korea
Weight Variable: WEIGHT
Cramer's V: 0.563**

		COUNTRY		
		India	S. Korea	TOTAL
HAVETOILET	Yes	636	661	1297
		29.1%	94.4%	44.9%
	No	1550	39	1590
		70.9%	5.6%	55.1%
	TOTAL	2186	700	2887
		100.0%	100.0%	

Access to a flush toilet can indicate personal wealth, but it also indicates access to sewer infrastructure, which is limited even in rapidly growing countries like India. This table indicates that only 29.1% of the population has a flush toilet in their household in India compared to 94.4% who have a toilet in South Korea. While this statistic might seem shocking to those living in the developed world, the picture is not without some hope when we compare access to healthy sources of drinking water in 1990 to 2002 in India.

➤ Data File: **GLOBAL**
➤ Task: **Mapping**
➤ Variable 1: **218) H2O TOT 02**
➤ Variable 2: **217) H2O TOT 90**
➤ Display: **Legend**
Find Case: India

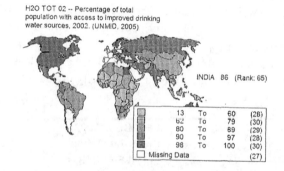

H2O TOT 02 -- Percentage of total population with access to improved drinking water sources, 2002. (UNMID, 2005)

INDIA 86 (Rank: 65)

13	To	60	(28)
62	To	79	(30)
80	To	89	(29)
90	To	97	(28)
98	To	100	(30)
Missing Data			(27)

r = 0.934**

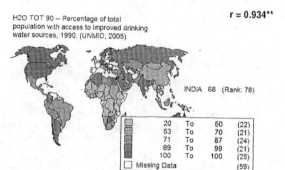

H2O TOT 90 -- Percentage of total population with access to improved drinking water sources, 1990. (UNMID, 2005)

INDIA 68 (Rank: 78)

20	To	50	(22)
53	To	70	(21)
71	To	87	(24)
89	To	99	(21)
100	To	100	(25)
Missing Data			(59)

According to data collected during these two time periods, the percentage of the population in India that has access to improved drinking water has increased from 68% to 86% in 12 years. This represents remarkable progress in a very short period of time.

The management of these vast differences in religion, ethnicity, language, and wealth in India may be assisted by India's tradition of democratic values and practices. India is one of the oldest democracies among developing nations. Shortly after independence, Gandhi was assassinated, leaving Jawaharlal

Nehru as the leader of the new nation. Nehru had been educated in Britain and was a committed Indian nationalist and social democrat (influenced by Britain's Labour Party). India adopted a democratic constitution and established a British parliamentary model of government with full adult suffrage. The INC was transformed from an anti-colonial movement to a full-fledged political party known as the Congress Party (CP). The CP managed its religious diversity by remaining committed to religious pluralism. Managing social conflict in India proved challenging for the new government, and Nehru was forced to rely on the police and armed services to maintain order.

Nehru died in office in 1964 and left the Congress Party without an apparent heir. Leaders within the party eventually tapped Nehru's daughter, Indira Gandhi, as the CP leader. Between 1966 until her assassination in 1984, Indian politics became more volatile and the anti-poverty campaigns of the CP failed to produce results. Looking for an approach to galvanize the Indian public and continue the CP's election successes, Indira Gandhi gradually turned from anti-poverty initiatives to religion and nationalism to mobilize the Indian population to support the Congress Party.

Since 1984 India's political system has rotated leadership between a number of party groups. The old Congress Party has held power for two five-year terms during this period, but the 1990s witnessed the rise of party groups that were more strongly rooted in religious or caste identities. The BJP (Indian People's Party) seeks to create a strong Hindu majority that protects Hindu rights that are threatened by religious diversity. The United Front consists of middle and lower caste groups that seek more political power and stronger social benefits.

Today, India's ratings for political rights and civil liberties reflect this long-standing democratic tradition and the reluctant embrace of civil liberties.

Data File: **GLOBAL**

Task: **Mapping**

➤ Variable 1: **312) POL RIGT04**

➤ View: **Map**

➤ Display: **Find Case: India**

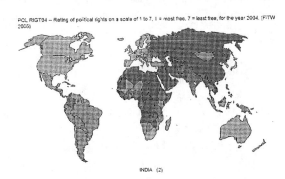

POL RIGT04 -- Rating of political rights on a scale of 1 to 7. 1 = most free. 7 = least free, for the year 2004. (FITW 2005)

INDIA (2)

India's political rights rating is a 2 out of 7. This means that India is highly democratic granting a full spectrum of political rights. Indians can change their government by means of a system of free and fair elections, though these elections in recent times have not occurred without a degree of social violence in some districts. There is increasing concern among human-rights watchers and pro-democracy advocates that the Hindu majority party, called BJP, may use its majority status to limit political rights, but this is not yet a formal problem. While political rights are generally respected in India, the realm of civil liberties is more problematic.

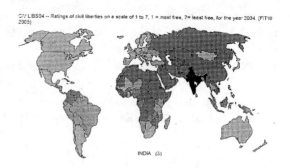

CIV LIBS04 -- Ratings of civil liberties on a scale of 1 to 7, 1 = most free, 7= least free, for the year 2004. (FITW 2005)

INDIA (3)

Data File: **GLOBAL**
Task: **Mapping**
➤ Variable 1: **305) CIV LIBS04**
  ➤ View: **Map**
  ➤ Display: **Find Case: India**

You will notice that India's rating in the civil liberties category is lower (3 out of 7). Freedom House (the organization that tracks political rights and civil liberties around the world) cites the following factors as being responsible for India's lower ratings in this category:

> *Police routinely torture suspects to extract confessions and abuse ordinary prisoners, particularly members of the lower castes. Custodial rape of female detainees continues to be a problem. While the National Human Rights Commission (NHRC) monitors custodial deaths (with 1,305 deaths being reported from April 2001 to March 2002) and other abuses, it has few enforcement powers.*

In December 2001, India's parliament building was attacked by a Pakistani-based terrorist group. This led to the passage of new anti-terrorism legislation in 2003 that gave police expanded powers to hold and prosecute suspected terrorists.

Although civil rights abuses have been a serious problem, India has begun to open its economy to world trade. This openness appears to have contributed to a phenomenal rate of growth during the 1990s.

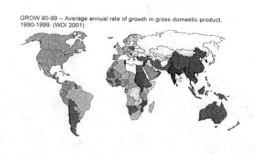

GROW 90-99 -- Average annual rate of growth in gross domestic product, 1990-1999. (WDI 2001)

INDIA 5.62 (Rank: 19)

Data File: **GLOBAL**
Task: **Mapping**
➤ Variable 1: **138) GROW 90–99**
  ➤ View: **Map**
  ➤ Display: **Find Case: India**

The map indicates that India's economy grew at an average annual rate of 5.62% during the decade of the 1990s. Interestingly enough, India's GDP growth has run parallel to the growth in GDP for South Asia since 1975, but the following analysis indicates that this changed in the 1990s.

> *Data File:* **HISTORY**
> > *Task:* **Historical Trends**
> *Variables:* **53) GDP:INDIA**
> > **55) GDP:SASIA**

GDP in India and South Asia

If you follow the trend line from 1975 to 1990, you will notice that the GDP of India and that of South Asia are very close. But by 1991 India starts to grow at a more rapid pace than the rest of the subcontinent and starts to pull away. While both India and South Korea are newly industrializing countries, India's economy does not bear many of the characteristics of South Korea's. GDP in India is still relatively low and the economy is still highly regulated.

> *Data File:* **GLOBAL**
> > *Task:* **Mapping**
> *Variable 1:* **266) ECON.FREE**
> > *View:* **Map**
> > *Display:* **Find Case: India**
> > **Find Case: Korea, South**

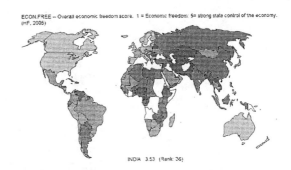

This rating of economic freedom places India with one of the higher ratings (3.53) for economic regulation. This puts India in the same company with former communist states like Russia and LDCs lke Niger and the Central African Republic. South Korea, by comparison, has a rating of 2.25, which is similar to the ratings of France and Japan. In addition to high levels of economic regulation, India has a problem with corruption.

> *Data File:* **GLOBAL**
> *Task:* **Mapping**
> *Variable 1:* **301) INDX:CORPT**
> > *View:* **Map**
> > *Display:* **Find Case: India**
> > **Find Case: Korea, South**

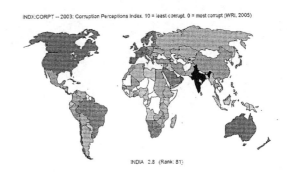

Of the 131 countries studied by the international organization Transparency International, India ranks 81st with a score of 2.8. South Korea is rated better and ranks 49th with a score of 4.3, but still needs to improve in this area as well.

Now that we understand the two NICs in our study, let's examine their political values to see if there is such a thing as distinctively "Asian values."

<u>Terms and Concepts</u>

Characteristics of South Korea and India
      Political rights
      Civil liberties
      Religion
      GDP
      GDP growth
      Caste

NAME:

COURSE:

DATE:

Workbook exercises and software are copyrighted. Copying is prohibited by law.

REVIEW QUESTIONS

Based on the first part of this chapter, answer True or False to the following items:

1. South Korea, due to its fear of an attack by North Korea, has the highest percentage of its population in the armed forces of any country in the Asia-Pacific region. T F

2. Most NICs are located in Europe. T F

3. Since 1980 South Korea has made little improvement in political rights or civil liberties. T F

4. In South Korea, the young tend to be more leftist than people of an older generation. T F

5. Catholicism is the largest religious group in South Korea. T F

6. The GDP of South Korea is greater than the GDP of Spain. T F

7. Hindus represent the largest religious group in India. T F

8. Most people in the Indian survey see their primary identity as Indian first. T F

9. Most people in India have flush toilets in their houses. T F

10. In the 1990s, India's economy grew at an average annual rate of 5.62%. T F

EXPLORIT QUESTIONS

I. Globalization became the buzzword of the 1990s with the integration of economies in Europe, the rapid explosion of global media like MTV, BBC, and CNN, the advent of the Internet, and the rapid economic growth of NICs. Globalization is a concept that has widely varying definitions, and it is both praised as an engine of economic development and vilified as a factor in the homogenization of a diverse world and the erosion of cultural and religious identity. Globalization is also offered up as an explanation for the rapid growth of NIC economies like India and South Korea. Let's test the hypothesis that globalization is responsible for the rapid economic growth of NICs like these two countries.

In 2001 the international consulting firm A. T. Kearney began publishing a "globalization index" that measures the level of global integration in 62 countries around the world. The globalization index measures the overall average level of economic, political, social, and technological engagement across nation-state borders. Take a look at the ranking of variable 265) GLOBAL in the GLOBAL data

Chapter 10: Political Culture in South Korea and India

file using the Mapping task, and construct a hypothesis and a null hypothesis that reflects the conventional wisdom that economic development in NICs is related to globalization.

State the hypothesis for H1 on the relationship between The Seven Worlds country type and globalization (refer back to worksheet section in Chapter 4 or 5 for a model of a hypothesis).

_____

_____

_____

State the null hypothesis for H1 (refer back to worksheet section in Chapter 4 or 5 for a model of a null hypothesis).

_____

_____

_____

Now let's test this hypothesis.

> ➤ Data File: **GLOBAL**
> ➤ Task: **ANOVA**
> ➤ Dependent Variable: **265) GLOBAL**
> ➤ Independent Variable: **130) WORLDS.7**
> ➤ View: **Means**

You may need to use both the Graph view and the Means view to answer the following questions.

11. The graph indicates that globalization is as high in NICs as it is in the most developed liberal democracies.   T   F

12. What is the mean level of globalization in liberal democracies?   _____

13. What is the mean level of globalization in NICs?   _____

14. NICs are more similar to LDCs than they are to liberal democracies.   T   F

15. Is the difference in globalization between the six country types significant?   Yes   No

On the basis of your findings, how would you change H1?

_____

_____

_____

II. Let's test the Asian values hypothesis—that Asian values are responsible for recent Asian economic successes. One component of Asian values is the preference for cooperation over conflict. To examine this we will hypothesize that in a socially harmonious society (one where the people prefer cooperation over conflict) citizens of different social classes are more likely to agree on economic issues. We will take the East Asian case of South Korea, an example of a society that is purported to have Asian values, and compare it to another NIC in South Asia—India. India, even though it is on the Asian continent, is a society that is largely influenced by the traditions of Hinduism and is not usually included in conversations about Asian values. During this analysis we will also include Japan, a liberal democracy, because the research often cites Japan as a more developed example of Asian values at work. If we find that South Korean values are not different from Indian values, then we would probably conclude that there is really no such thing as a distinct set of Confucian-inspired values that support economic development. On the other hand, if we find that South Korean values are quite different from Indian values, and similar to values in Japan, then we should probably hold open the possibility that Asian values may in fact exist.

For the analyses that follow, we will look at a number of economic issues and social classes. We hypothesize that in countries which exhibit Asian values, citizens of different social classes (working, middle, and upper) will not differ in their attitudes toward economic issues. Where there is no social harmony, we should see social class divisions on economic issues. If you want to know which nation-state is the most harmonious, look at the strength of relationship indicated by Cramer's V. The stronger the Cramer's V, the less harmonious the country.

For each analysis, fill in the percentaged results for the row that is specified in the table. Also fill in the value for Cramer's V and indicate whether the results are statistically significant (circle Y for Yes, N for No).

> ➤ *Data Files:* **WVS02–JAPAN, WVS02–S.KOREA, and WVS02–INDIA**
> ➤ *Task:* **Cross-tabulation**
> ➤ *Row Variable:* **BUS MGMT**
> ➤ *Column Variable:* **CLASS-3**
> ➤ *View:* **Tables**
> ➤ *Display:* **Column %**

Fill in the table below.

%OWNERS RUN	UPPER	MIDDLE	WORKING	V =	SIGNIFICANT?
JAPAN	_____%	_____%	_____%	_____	Y N
SOUTH KOREA	_____%	_____%	_____%	_____	Y N
INDIA	_____%	_____%	_____%	_____	Y N

16. A significant relationship between BUS MGMT and CLASS-3 in a given country means (circle one of the following)

     a. groups that agree on the same issue do not work in the same place.

     b. the different CLASS-3 groups are not in agreement on the issue of business management and the nation is therefore not "harmonious" with regard to that issue.

    c.   the different CLASS-3 groups are in agreement on the issue of business management and the nation is therefore "harmonious" with regard to that issue.

    d.   the countries disagree and are more likely to go to war.

17. The most harmonious country on this issue is
    a.   Japan.
    b.   South Korea.
    c.   India.

18. The least harmonious country on this issue is
    a.   Japan.
    b.   South Korea.
    c.   India.

19. On the business-ownership issue, which country is South Korea most similar to? Explain your answer.

_____

_____

_____

III. This time we'll look at the relationship between social class status and the issue of income equality. The question asks whether incomes should be made more equal or whether there should be greater incentives for individual effort.

          Data Files: **WVS02–JAPAN, WVS02–S.KOREA,** and **WVS02–INDIA**
               Task: **Cross-tabulation**
   ➤ *Row Variable:* **INCOME EQ3**
 ➤ *Column Variable:* **CLASS-3**
         ➤ *View:* **Tables**
      ➤ *Display:* **Column %**

Fill in the table below.

INC.EQUAL	UPPER	MIDDLE	WORKING	V =	SIGNIFICANT?
JAPAN	_____%	_____%	_____%	_____	Y N
SOUTH KOREA	_____%	_____%	_____%	_____	Y N
INDIA	_____%	_____%	_____%	_____	Y N

20. Which country is most harmonious on this issue?   _____

21. Which country is least harmonious on this issue?   _____

22. In the analysis of income equality, South Korea is most similar to
    a. Japan.
    b. India.
    c. Neither

IV. Now we'll look at the relationship between social class and the issue of competition. The question asks whether competition is good because it stimulates people to work hard and to develop new ideas, or whether competition is harmful because it brings out the worst in people.

> *Data Files:* **WVS02–JAPAN, WVS02–S.KOREA,** and **WVS02–INDIA**
> *Task:* **Cross-tabulation**
> ➤ *Row Variable:* **COMPETITN**
> ➤ *Column Variable:* **CLASS-3**
> ➤ *View:* **Tables**
> ➤ *Display:* **Column %**

Fill in the table below.

%BENEFICIAL	UPPER	MIDDLE	WORKING	V =	SIGNIFICANT?
JAPAN	_____%	_____%	_____%	_____	Y N
SOUTH KOREA	_____%	_____%	_____%	_____	Y N
INDIA	_____%	_____%	_____%	_____	Y N

23. In South Korea, the strongest differences on the value of competition are between workers in the (circle one of the following)
    a. upper class and middle class.
    b. upper class and working class.
    c. middle class and working class.
    d. There is no significant difference between the working class and other classes.

24. In India, the strongest differences on the value of competition are between workers in the (circle one of the following)
    a. upper class and middle class.
    b. upper class and working class.
    c. middle class and working class.
    d. There is no significant difference between the working class and other classes.

25. The most harmonious country on this issue is
    a. Japan.
    b. South Korea.
    c. India.

26. The least harmonious country on this issue is
    a. Japan.
    b. South Korea.
    c. India.

V.   Finally, let's take a look at attitudes toward globalization–that, is the process of increased economic, political, and social integration–in India and South Korea. But since we might know a little bit more about this issue in the United States, let's also include the U.S. in our analysis. The first question asks respondents whether or not the respondent thinks that globalization is a good thing or a bad thing. Once you have created the table with the 10) GLOBALZATN variable, create a second table with the 11) ANTI-GLOBL variable. The second question asks whether or not the respondent believes that anti-globalization protests are a good or bad thing. Print the globalization and anti-globalization tables, attach them to this exercise, and answer the questions listed below.

➤ *Data File:*	**PEW GLOBAL02**
➤*Task:*	**Cross-Tabulation**
➤ *Row Variable:*	**10) GLOBALZATN**
	11) ANTI-GLOBL
➤ *Column Variable:*	**1) COUNTRY**
➤ *Subset Variable:*	**1) COUNTRY**
Include:	**17) India**
	22) S. Korea
	40) US

27.   Which is the most accurate statement about globalization in the analysis of attitudes in India, South Korea, and the United States?

     a.   Most citizens favor globalization, but there are no significant differences between countries so we can't really compare them.

     b.   Most citizens in these three countries favor globalization. Citizens in India and South Korea favor globalization the most, followed by the United States. The differences between countries are significant.

     c.   Most citizens in these three countries oppose globalization, but there are no significant differences between countries so we can't really compare them.

28.   Which nation-state(s) seem pretty evenly divided on the issue of whether or not anti-globalization is a good thing? (Circle all that apply).

     a.   India

     b.   South Korea

     c.   United States

29.   Which country favors globalization the least?

     a.   India

     b.   South Korea

     c.   United States

     d.   We can't tell because the differences are not significant.

30.   Which country is most likely to think that anti-globalization protests are a bad thing?

     a. India

     b. South Korea

     c. United States

     d. We can't tell because the differences are not significant.

IN YOUR OWN WORDS

In your own words, please answer the following questions.

1. We have examined several economic issues in Japan, South Korea, and India to see whether or not social classes in the two East Asian countries are more harmonious on economic issues than those in India. Based on the previous analysis, are East Asian countries more harmonious on economic issues than India? Why might this be the case? Support your answer with evidence.

2. Does social harmony translate to relations between the sexes? Analyze the "gender gap" in India, Japan, and South Korea. Print all of the tables that have significant relationships and append them to this worksheet. Use the variable GENDER as the column variable and MAN'S JOB, MEN POLS, EDUC BOYS, and CONF:WOMEN as the row variables. As always, use column percentages. On the issues of men's and women's roles, are men and women in East Asia more harmonious in their views than men and women in India? On which issue is there the most harmony between genders? On which issue is there the least? Discuss your findings in the space below.

Part V

LESS DEVELOPED COUNTRIES AND MARGINAL STATES

Africa

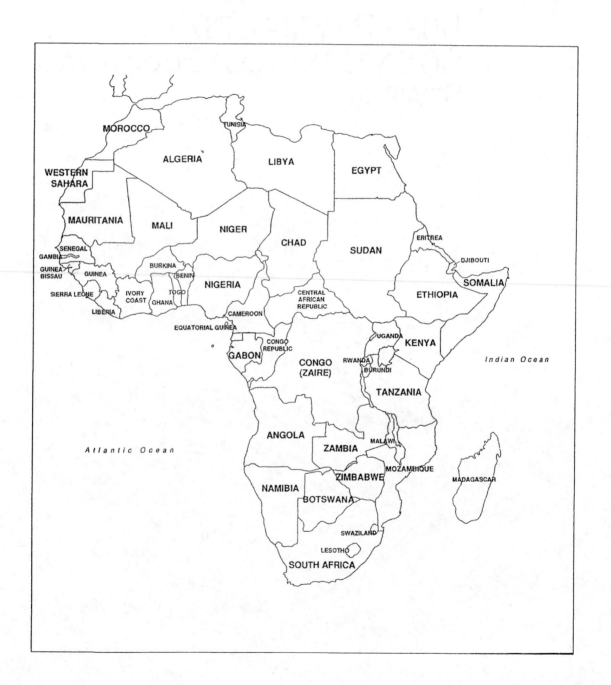

MOROCCO
TUNISIA
ALGERIA
LIBYA
EGYPT
WESTERN SAHARA
MAURITANIA
MALI
NIGER
CHAD
SUDAN
ERITREA
SENEGAL
DJIBOUTI
GAMBIA
GUINEA BISSAU
GUINEA
BURKINA
BENIN
NIGERIA
SOMALIA
SIERRA LEONE
IVORY COAST
TOGO
GHANA
ETHIOPIA
LIBERIA
CAMEROON
CENTRAL AFRICAN REPUBLIC
EQUATORIAL GUINEA
UGANDA
KENYA
CONGO REPUBLIC
GABON
CONGO (ZAIRE)
RWANDA
BURUNDI
Indian Ocean
TANZANIA
ANGOLA
MALAWI
ZAMBIA
MOZAMBIQUE
Atlantic Ocean
ZIMBABWE
MADAGASCAR
NAMIBIA
BOTSWANA
SWAZILAND
LESOTHO
SOUTH AFRICA

WAR, POLITICS, AND POVERTY IN LDCS AND MARGINAL STATES

We are building this nation, as in putting pieces of broken glass together.

JEAN-BERTRAND ARISTIDE, 1995,
FORMER PRESIDENT, HAITI

Tasks: Mapping, ANOVA, Scatterplot, Univariate, Cross-tabulation, Historical Trends
Data Files: AFRICA, GLOBAL, LATIN, HISTORY

When most people think about the nations of the Third World, they are usually thinking about a collection of nation-states that are economically, politically, and socially underdeveloped. But we have already seen that political scientists overlook important differences in the Third World category when they use this category for analysis. We now know that Newly Industrialized Countries (NICs) have higher levels of economic and social development and relatively stable political systems compared to other countries in the Third World categorization. As you remember from Chapter 3, there are three other categories of nation-states in the Third World besides NICs: less developed countries (LDCs), marginal states, and Islamic world. This chapter focuses on the features of LDCs and marginal states. Before we get too involved in analysis, let's open the GLOBAL data file and figure out where they are located.

> *Data File:* **GLOBAL**
> *Task:* **Mapping**
> *Variable 1:* **130) WORLDS.7**
> *Subset Variable:* **130) WORLDS.7**
> *Subset Categories:* **Include: 4) LDCs**
>   **6) Marginal**
> *View:* **Map**
> *Display:* **Legend**

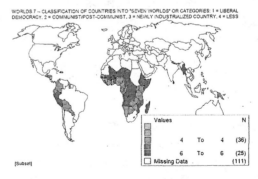

WORLDS 7 -- CLASSIFICATION OF COUNTRIES INTO "SEVEN WORLDS" OR CATEGORIES: 1 = LIBERAL DEMOCRACY, 2 = COMMUNIST/POST-COMMUNIST, 3 = NEWLY INDUSTRIALIZED COUNTRY, 4 = LESS

Values			N
4	To	4	(36)
6	To	6	(25)
Missing Data			(111)

[Subset]

Because we want to see only the LDCs and marginal states appear in the map, select 130) WORLDS.7 as the subset variable and check the box for categories 4) LDCs and 6) Marginal.

By now you are probably starting to notice that different types of states tend to be concentrated in certain regions. When we studied liberal democracies, we learned that most liberal democracies are located in Europe. Later we learned that communist/postcommunist states are concentrated in Europe and Asia. In the last couple of chapters we observed that NICs tend to be located in Latin America and Asia. Here we see that LDCs tend to be concentrated in Africa, but a few exist in Latin America and Asia as well.

To begin our analysis of the LDCs and marginal states, let's compare the overall freedom in the world rating using the ANOVA task. You remember that this rating is an average of the political rights and civil liberties ratings; it ranges from 1 to 7, where 1 is the most free and seven is the least free.

Data File: **GLOBAL**
➤ Task: **ANOVA**
➤ Dependent Variable: **480) FREEDOM2**
➤ Independent Variable: **130) WORLDS.7**
➤ View: **Graph: Summary**

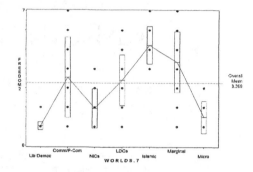

The analysis of these results is statistically significant. Let's focus our attention on the ratings for LDCs and marginal states. If you switch to the Means table, you will see that in terms of the ratings for civil rights and civil liberties, LDCs (3.417) are only slightly more free than communist/postcommunist countries (3.559). You will also notice that marginal states (4.360) are even less free than LDCs. Clearly, marginal states and LDCs are characterized by political and legal problems that make political freedom elusive. One of the reasons for this instability is the presence of warfare, but does this affect marginal states and LDCs in the same way?

Data File: **GLOBAL**
➤ Task: **Cross-tabulation**
➤ Row Variable: **459) WAR2**
➤ Column Variable: **130) WORLDS.7**
➤ View: **Bar Stack**

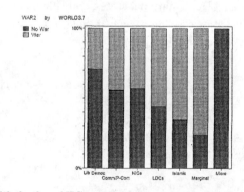

The graph illustrates that LDCs were a little more likely than NICs to be involved in warfare between 1990 and 2002, but marginal states were were more likely than any country type to be involved in warfare during this same period. So to summarize, there is less freedom in marginal states than in LDCs, but one of the reasons for this may be that marginal states experience a higher incidence of warfare. Let's examine the type of warfare that these countries may be involved in.

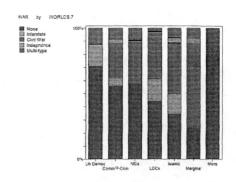

Data File: **GLOBAL**

Task: **Cross-tabulation**

➤ Row Variable: **458) WAR**

➤ Column Variable: **130) WORLDS.7**

➤ View: **Bar Stack**

This graph analyzes the type of warfare that each group of countries was involved in between 1990 and 2002. Interstate warfare consists of military conflict *between* nation-states, whereas civil war involves military conflict *within* a nation-state. A few nations were also involved in wars of independence. Finally, one category is reserved for those nation-states that were involved in more than one type of military conflict. From the graph you can see that marginal states have the highest incidence of civil war. If you switch to the table and click on the column percentage, you will see that 64.0% of all marginal states (16 out of 25 countries) were involved in civil war, while only 36.1% of LDCs were involved in this type of conflict. One of the factors for the "marginalization" of marginal states is the presence of civil wars in the majority of these countries. Although we have learned that the problems of a lack of political freedom in marginal states may be attributable to warfare, we have also learned that we really can't say the same thing about LDCs. The levels of civil war in LDCs don't seem to be all that different from the level of conflict found in NICs.

In addition to political instability, LDCs and marginal states are characterized by poverty. Let's compare the average GDP per capita for each type of country using the WORLDS.7 variable.

Data File: **GLOBAL**

➤ Task: **ANOVA**

➤ Dependent Variable: **133) GDPCAP PPP**

➤ Independent Variable: **130) WORLDS.7**

➤ View: **Means**

Means, Standard Deviations and Number of Cases of Dependent Var: GDPCAP PPP by Categories of Independent Var: WORLDS.7
Difference of means across groups is statistically significant (Prob. = 0.000)

	N	Mean	Std.Dev.
Lib Democ	24	27710.982	8023.393
Comm/P-Com	31	6224.717	4503.199
NICs	19	9210.532	5065.291
LDCs	35	3025.699	2131.618
Islamic	18	5632.952	5103.788
Marginal	19	1554.439	1288.400
Micro	6	8137.019	5896.064

The analysis of GDP and WORLDS.7 is significant. Notice that the average GDP per capita in less developed countries is $3,026 and $1,554 in marginal states. This compares to a GDP per capita that is almost six times higher in NICs ($9,211). All groups of countries are far below the super-rich liberal democracies ($27,711), but when we analyze GDP per capita, the LDCs and marginal states are clearly near the bottom. These are also economic systems that are growing very slowly or not growing at all.

One of the factors responsible for the relatively low economic development of LDCs and marginal states is that these economic systems still derive much of their economic productivity from agriculture.

Data File: **GLOBAL**
Task: **ANOVA**
➤ Dependent Variable: **207) % AGRIC $**
Independent Variable: **130) WORLDS.7**
➤ View: **Graph**

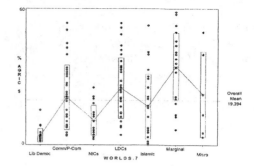

From this graph you can see that a relatively high percentage of the LDCs' and marginal states' economic productivity is derived from agriculture and that these results are significant. In fact, these nations exceed the average output in this area. If you switch to the Means view, you can see that 24.9% of LDCs, economic output comes from agriculture and that this percentage is 34.7% for marginal states. The devastating effects of warfare and the 9.8 percentage-point difference in agricultural output may be enough to explain the difference in GDP between the two types of nation-states.

From our previous analyses you will also suspect that LDCs and marginal states have lower levels of social development. The Human Development Index (HDI) is a good *composite measure* of social development. A composite measure combines a number of factors of interest into one number. The HDI combines life expectancy, education, and GDP per capita to measure the level of human development in a country. The higher the HDI number is, the greater the level of human development. Let's see how LDCs and marginal states compare in the area of human development.

Data File: **GLOBAL**
Task: **ANOVA**
➤ Dependent Variable: **127) HUM DEV02**
Independent Variable: **130) WORLDS.7**
View: **Graph**

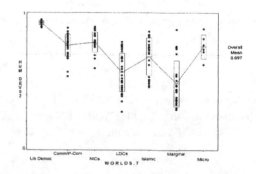

This graphic indicates that this analysis is significant and that LDCs and marginal states have the lowest levels of human development compared to all other groups of nation-states. If we switch to the Means view, we see that the average HDI for LDCs is .565 and that it is .483 for marginal states. By comparison we see that the HDI is .788 for NICs and .765 for communist/postcommunist countries. Islamic states are lower than the NICs (.682), and the liberal democracies have the highest HDI (.932).

Now that we have a general understanding of LDCs and marginal states, let's take a closer look at the regions where these states are concentrated. Earlier we saw a map that showed these countries are concentrated in Africa and Latin America, but what percentages of LDCs and marginal states are in these regions?

Data File:	**GLOBAL**
➤ Task:	**Cross-tabulation**
➤ Row Variable:	**464) REGION2**
➤ Column Variable:	**130) WORLDS.7**
➤ View:	**Tables**
➤ Display:	**Column %**

REGION2 by WORLDS.7
Cramer's V: 0.540**

REGION2	WORLDS.7							
	Lib Democ	Comm/P-Com	NICs	LDCs	Islamic	Marginal	Micro	TOTAL
Africa	0	0	2	22	9	17	1	51
	0.0%	0.0%	9.5%	61.1%	34.6%	68.0%	16.7%	29.7%
Mid. East	1	0	1	0	11	1	0	14
	4.2%	0.0%	4.8%	0.0%	42.3%	4.0%	0.0%	8.1%
Asia/Pacif	3	15	8	2	6	4	2	40
	12.5%	44.1%	38.1%	5.6%	23.1%	16.0%	33.3%	23.3%
West.Hemi	2	1	9	12	0	2	3	29
	8.3%	2.9%	42.9%	33.3%	0.0%	8.0%	50.0%	16.9%
Europe	18	18	1	0	0	1	0	38
	75.0%	52.9%	4.8%	0.0%	0.0%	4.0%	0.0%	22.1%
TOTAL	24	34	21	36	26	25	6	172
	100.0%	100.0%	100.0%	100.0%	100.0%	100.0%	100.0%	

The table helps us to understand the percentage of LDCs and marginal states in each region. A full 61.1% of LDCs and 68.0% of marginal states are in Africa. 33.3% of LDCs are in the Western Hemisphere (mostly South America and the Caribbean). The next largest group of LDCs or marginal states outside of Africa is four marginal states found in Asia. So, if we want to understand LDCs and marginal states, we will need to spend some time learning about Africa.

INTRODUCTION TO SUB-SAHARAN AFRICA

Africa is perhaps the richest, in terms of natural resources, and most diverse continent in the world, but its history and politics are as tragic as they are complex. The continent of Africa is quite distinct from other regions of the world. The nations of Africa were colonized by European powers during the 18th and 19th centuries. The map that follows indicates the owners of colonial possessions in Africa before World War I.

➤ Data File:	**AFRICA**
➤ Task:	**Mapping**
➤ Variable 1:	**24) COL.POWERS**
➤ View:	**Map**
➤ Display:	**Legend**

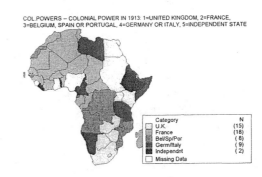

COL.POWERS – COLONIAL POWER IN 1913: 1=UNITED KINGDOM, 2=FRANCE, 3=BELGIUM, SPAIN OR PORTUGAL, 4=GERMANY OR ITALY, 5=INDEPENDENT STATE

Category	N
U.K.	(15)
France	(18)
Bel/Sp/Por	(8)
Germ/Italy	(9)
Independnt	(2)
Missing Data	

You will notice that only two countries escaped imperialist domination and remained independent: Ethiopia and Liberia. The latter nation was resettled by ex-slaves who returned from the Americas to found their own nation.

Europeans conquered 85% of Africa during the last 20 years of the 19th century. There were at least three reasons for colonial expansion in Africa: strategic interests, land greed, and the extraction of wealth and slaves.

Data File: **AFRICA**
Task: **Mapping**
➤ Variable 1: **25) COL.MOTIVE**
➤ View: **Map**
➤ Display: **Legend**

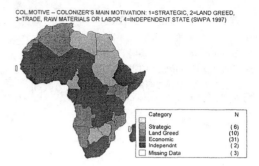

COL.MOTIVE – COLONIZER'S MAIN MOTIVATION: 1=STRATEGIC, 2=LAND GREED, 3=TRADE, RAW MATERIALS OR LABOR, 4=INDEPENDENT STATE (SWPA 1997)

Category	N
Strategic	(6)
Land Greed	(10)
Economic	(31)
Independnt	(2)
Missing Data	(3)

Colonized peoples of Africa were sold into slavery in Europe and America or used as slaves in their native lands to extract the wealth of their own land. Most Africans who were taken as slaves came from the western parts of Africa.

The boundaries carved out by colonizers consisted of huge land masses, rather than being organized around ethnic/tribal groups that existed at the time. As such, numerous ethnic/national groups were often combined into one country. The multiculturalism map we examined earlier in this workbook deserves another look.

➤ Data File: **GLOBAL**
➤ Task: **Mapping**
➤ Variable 1: **461) MULTI-CULT**
➤ View: **Map**
➤ Display: **Legend**

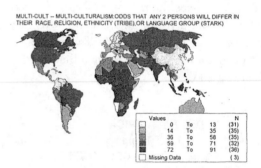

MULTI-CULT -- MULTI-CULTURALISM:ODDS THAT ANY 2 PERSONS WILL DIFFER IN THEIR RACE, RELIGION, ETHNICITY (TRIBE),OR LANGUAGE GROUP (STARK)

Values			N
0	To	13	(31)
14	To	35	(35)
36	To	58	(35)
59	To	71	(32)
72	To	91	(36)
Missing Data			(3)

As you can see, African nations are among the most diverse nations in terms of race, ethnicity, religion, and language. This raises serious questions about our ability to describe all but a few of the countries of Africa as nation-states. You will remember from the first chapter that the nation-state is a government that has sovereignty over a territory of relatively homogeneous people. The incredible diversity of Africa, which is compounded by arbitrary borders to its nation-states, challenges the European conception of a culturally homogeneous nation-state.

Colonialism in Africa did not begin to loosen its grip until the end of World War II.

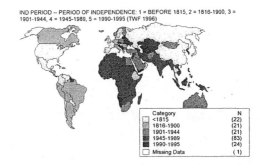

IND PERIOD -- PERIOD OF INDEPENDENCE: 1 = BEFORE 1815, 2 = 1816-1900, 3 = 1901-1944, 4 = 1945-1989, 5 = 1990-1995 (TWF 1996)

Data File:	GLOBAL
Task:	Mapping
➤ Variable 1:	456) IND PERIOD
➤ View:	Map
➤ Display:	Legend

Category	N
<1815	(22)
1816-1900	(21)
1901-1944	(21)
1945-1989	(83)
1990-1995	(24)
Missing Data	(1)

As a result, most of the nations of Africa did not receive their independence until the middle to later part of the 20th century.

The study of Africa is often divided into two regions. Northern Africa is often studied in conjunction with the Islamic states of the Middle East and South Asia. Southern Africa, or sub-Saharan Africa as it is more appropriately called, is the region below the Sahara Desert that makes up approximately two-thirds of the continent of Africa.

REGION -- REGION (HDR, 1998)

Data File:	GLOBAL
Task:	Mapping
➤ Variable 1:	463) REGION
➤ View:	Map
➤ Display:	Legend

Category	N
SUB-SAHARA	(43)
ARAB	(20)
ASIA/PACIF	(32)
WEST.HEMI.	(29)
EUROPE	(48)
Missing Data	

The REGION variable clearly shows these two parts of Africa. Sub-Saharan Africa is distinct from the northern part of Africa for a number of reasons. First, the religion and culture of sub-Saharan Africa differs from that of North Africa. This is clearly evident if you look at the maps showing the percentages of Muslims and Christians who live in each African country.

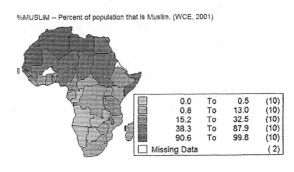

%MUSLIM -- Percent of population that is Muslim. (WCE, 2001)

➤ Data File:	AFRICA
➤ Task:	Mapping
➤ Variable 1:	9) %MUSLIM
➤ Variable 2:	10) %CHRISTIAN
➤ Views:	Map
➤ Display:	Legend

	0.0	To	0.5	(10)
	0.8	To	13.0	(10)
	15.2	To	32.5	(10)
	38.3	To	87.9	(10)
	90.6	To	99.8	(10)
Missing Data				(2)

r = –0.889**

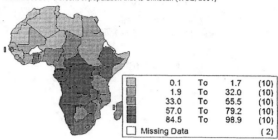

%CHRISTIAN -- Percent of population that is Christian (WCE, 2001)

0.1	To	1.7	(10)
1.9	To	32.0	(10)
33.0	To	55.5	(10)
57.0	To	79.2	(10)
84.5	To	98.9	(10)
Missing Data			(2)

Since the conquest of the Moors in the 7th century A.D., North Africa has been characterized by large populations of the Islamic faithful. Note that there is a strong negative correlation (–0.889**) between %MUSLIM and %CHRISTIAN. Where Islamic belief is strong, there is a relatively low percentage of Christians, and where Christian belief is strong, there is a relatively low percentage of Muslims.

Economically speaking, North Africa and sub-Saharan Africa are also quite distinct from one another. The variable GDP CAP 5 divides the countries of the world into five groups rank ordered according to each country's level of gross domestic product per capita.

➤ *Data File:* **GLOBAL**
➤ *Task:* **Mapping**
➤ *Variable 1:* **482) GDP CAP 5**
➤ *View:* **Map**
➤ *Display:* **Legend**

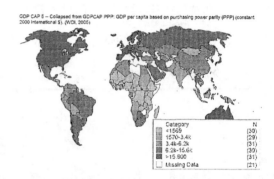

GDP CAP 5 -- Collapsed from GDPCAP PPP: GDP per capita based on purchasing power parity (PPP) (constant 2000 International $). (WDI, 2005)

Category	N
<1569	(30)
1570-3.4k	(29)
3.4k-6.2k	(31)
6.2k-15.6k	(30)
>15,900	(31)
Missing Data	(21)

You will notice that Central Africa not only is the poorest region of Africa, it also is the poorest part of the world. Let's switch back to the AFRICA file and examine the same GDP per capita measure.

➤ *Data File:* **AFRICA**
➤ *Task:* **Mapping**
➤ *Variable 1:* **14) GDP CAP 5**
➤ *View:* **Map**
➤ *Display:* **Legend**

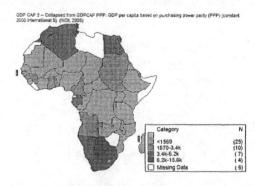

GDP CAP 5 -- Collapsed from GDPCAP PPP: GDP per capita based on purchasing power parity (PPP) (constant 2000 International $). (WDI, 2005)

Category	N
<1569	(25)
1570-3.4k	(10)
3.4k-6.2k	(7)
6.2k-15.6k	(4)
Missing Data	(6)

You will notice that North Africa is wealthier than sub-Saharan Africa. Also, you will notice that South Africa and the countries that border it are wealthier than the states of Central, East, and West Africa. The likeliest reason for this relatively low level of economic development in Central Africa has to do

Comparative Politics

with the extent to which the economy is devoted to agriculture as its primary production resource. Let's use the SCATTERPLOT task to look at the relationship between GDP per capita and the percentage of GDP derived from agriculture.

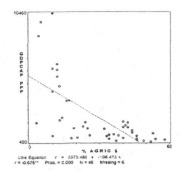

Data File: **AFRICA**
➤ Task: **Scatterplot**
➤ Dependent Variable: **17) GDPCAP PPP**
➤ Independent Variable: **15) % AGRIC $**
➤ View: **Reg. Line**

The scatterplot indicates that those countries in Africa that receive the highest percentage of their GDP from agriculture also tend to have the lowest levels of GDP per capita.

Poor economic conditions, ethnic and religious tension, and the legacy of colonialism have combined to produce a continent characterized by unstable politics. You will remember that many of the African nations in our study are marginal states. Let's see how the African states are distributed using the WORLDS.7 variable.

Data File: **AFRICA**
➤ Task: **Univariate**
➤ Primary Variable: **47) WORLDS.7**
➤ View: **Pie**

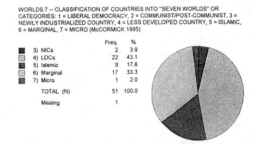

This analysis helps us to see that 33.3% of the nation-states in Africa are marginal states, 43.1% are LDCs, 17.6% are Islamic states, 3.9% are NICs, and 2% are microstates. You will remember that one of the characteristics of marginal states is the presence of warfare within that country. The variable 26) WAR categorizes each type of warfare according to its character.

Data File: **AFRICA**
Task: **Univariate**
➤ Primary Variable: **26) WAR**
➤ View: **Pie**

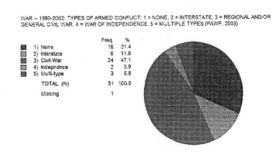

Note that the majority of nation-states in Africa were involved in some type of armed conflict between 1990 and 2002. Only 31.4% of the nations in Africa were not involved in any violent conflict during these years. Interstate conflict, that is, war between nation-states, is usually the dominant form of warfare in the modern era, but in Africa pure interstate warfare accounts for only 11.8% of the violent conflict experienced between 1990 and 2002. The most dominant type of conflict during the period was civil war, which consumed 47.1% of the nations of Africa. Wars of independence during 1990–2002 occurred in 3.9% of the countries, and 5.9% of the countries suffered more than one type of warfare during this period.

As a result of these conflicts, most of the parties to these conflicts have suffered tremendous tragedy in terms of the loss of life.

WARDEAD -- 1990-1995: CUMULATIVE DEATH TOLL OF ALL WARS (SWPA, 1997)

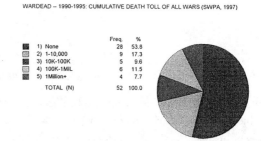

	Freq.	%
1) None	28	53.8
2) 1-10,000	9	17.3
3) 10K-100K	5	9.6
4) 100K-1MIL	6	11.5
5) 1Million+	4	7.7
TOTAL (N)	52	100.0

It is difficult to know how many people die from warfare. It is even more difficult to count the number of families that are affected by the loss of a family member, or to count the number of people who are severely injured in war. No one is responsible for counting these other victims, and numbers of dead are often manipulated by governments and armies for purposes of political propaganda. But awareness of the magnitude of human suffering caused by warfare is critical. It is estimated that throughout the world more than *5.6 million people died in warfare between the years of 1990 and 1995 alone*! That is a little less than 1 million people per year, and more than half of those (3.5 million) died in warfare on the African continent. The pie chart of war dead indicates that 4 out of 52 (or 7.7%) of the countries suffering the loss of life due to war lost more than 1 million people during this six-year period.

The end of the Cold War was a time of bitter conflict in Africa, but more recently trends indicate that the incidence of armed conflict is down worldwide since conflicts peaked in the 1990s.

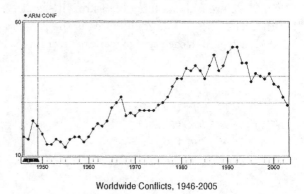

Worldwide Conflicts, 1946-2005

The reduction in armed conflicts has also resulted in a precipitous decline in battle fatalities throughout the world.

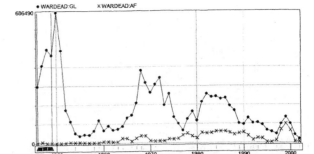

> *Data File:* **HISTORY**
>   > *Task:* **Historical Trends**
> *Variables:* **57) WARDEAD:GL**
>   **58) WARDEAD:AF**

Global deaths due to war have also declined since the 1990s, but it is clear that the majority of global deaths due to war since the 1990s have occurred in sub-Saharan Africa. This graphic also illustrates that the suffering experienced in the 1990s in Africa, were more severe than had been since the end of World War II, which is significant given the large number of countries that experienced wars of independence in the 1950s and 60s.

We now have a clearer idea of some of the political factors that contribute to the differences between LDCs and marginal states in Africa. In the last section of this chapter, we will look at the dynamics of political economy that can undermine development in some Latin American LDCs.

LDCS AND LAND IN LATIN AMERICA

We mentioned earlier that another factor that contributes to the poverty of LDCs is their dependence on agricultural production for the generation of wealth. While the involvement in agriculture is not as extensive as in Africa, a considerable percentage of the labor force in South and Central America still works in the agricultural sector of the economy. Let's turn to the LATIN file to get a closer look at this phenomenon.

> *Data File:* **LATIN**
>   > *Task:* **Mapping**
> *Variable 1:* **13) % AGRIC $**
> *Variable 2:* **10) GDPCAP PPP**
>   > *Views:* **Map**
>   > *Display:* **Legend**

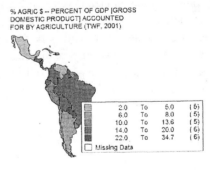

% AGRIC $ -- PERCENT OF GDP [GROSS DOMESTIC PRODUCT] ACCOUNTED FOR BY AGRICULTURE (TWF, 2001)

2.0 To	6.0	(5)
6.0 To	8.0	(5)
10.0 To	13.6	(5)
14.0 To	20.0	(6)
22.0 To	34.7	(6)

☐ Missing Data

r = −0.588**

GDPCAP PPP -- Gross Domestic Product
per capita based on purchasing power
parity (WDI 2001).

1464	To	2355	(5)	
2994	To	3674	(5)	
4344	To	5507	(6)	
5749	To	8297	(5)	
8652	To	15000	(6)	

☐ Missing Data

This continued organization of life around agricultural production is one of the factors that has been responsible for the continued poverty of the region. You will notice that the more a country's economy is agriculturally based, the more likely it is to be poor. The poorest countries have been those that have had difficulty making the transition to industry.

The life of a peasant farmer in South and Central America is extremely difficult. We can use the LATIN file to see the pattern of land ownership.

LANDOWNERS: 80 percent of total farmland is owned by:
1 = up to 55% of the farms, 2 = up to 30% of the farms,
3 = less than 20% of the farms (SWPD, 1997)

Data File: **LATIN**
Task: **Mapping**
➤ Variable 1: **20) LANDOWNERS**
➤ View: **List: Rank**

RANK	CASE NAME	VALUE
1	El Salvador	<20%
1	Guatemala	<20%
1	Dominican Republic	<20%
1	Ecuador	<20%
5	Chile	<30%
5	Colombia	<30%
5	Peru	<30%
8	Uruguay	<55%
8	Panama	<55%
8	Mexico	<55%

In El Salvador, Guatemala, Dominican Republic, and Ecuador, more than 80% of the farmland is owned by less than 20% of the farmers. Eighty percent of the land is owned by less than 30% of the farmers in Chile, Colombia, and Peru. This pattern of ownership means that many farmers are left to subsist on hillside plots or plots too small to produce enough for their families while wealthy farmers control vast tracts of fertile land. In the past, this disparity of land ownership has led to more serious consequences in the distribution of overall wealth. The variable 14) $ RICH 10% describes how much of a nation's income is received by the richest 10% of the population.

	Data File:	**LATIN**
	Task:	**Mapping**
➤	Variable 1:	**14) $ RICH 10%**
	➤ View:	**List: Rank**

$ RICH 10%: Share of income or consumption by the richest 10 % of the population (HDR, 2004)

RANK	CASE NAME	VALUE
1	Guatemala	48.30
2	Chile	47.00
3	Brazil	46.70
4	Colombia	46.50
5	Nicaragua	45.00
6	Paraguay	43.60
7	Panama	43.30
8	Mexico	43.10
9	Honduras	42.20
10	Ecuador	41.60

The first thing you will notice is that in a few countries 10% of the population receives almost half of the national income. This means that in a country like Guatemala, 90% of the people divide up 51.7% of the national income.

So far we have seen some of the factors that make LDCs and marginal states distinctive. We have learned that most of them are former colonies and that most of them have agricultural economies and considerable disparities of wealth between the rich and the poor. We have also learned that marginal states are much more likely to have been afflicted by warfare. We noted that LDCs and marginal states have much lower levels of human development than any other group of nation-states, but we haven't really examined the social implications of this lower level of development. In the worksheet section, it will be your turn to do this analysis.

Terms and Concepts

LDC
Marginal state
Composite measure
Human Development Index
Sub-Saharan Africa
Colonial power in Africa
Armed conflict trends
War deaths in Africa
Agriculture in LDCs

CHAPTER
11

REVIEW QUESTIONS

Based on the first part of this chapter, answer True or False to the following items:

1. Most marginal states are located in Africa.   T   F

2. LDCs are concentrated in Asia and Latin America.   T   F

3. Marginal states have less freedom (in terms of political rights and civil liberties) than LDCs.   T   F

4. Africa is the most culturally homogeneous continent in the world.   T   F

5. There are significant religious differences between Saharan and sub-Saharan Africa.   T   F

6. Applying the term *nation-state* to the countries of Africa is problematic because most of them aren't composed of relatively homogeneous people.   T   F

7. In Latin America, the higher the percentage of an economy that depends on agriculture, the lower the level of GDP per capita in that country.   T   F

EXPLORIT QUESTIONS

I. In this worksheet we will examine some of the social conditions within Africa because that is where most of the LDCs and marginal states are located. Many researchers who study economic development have discovered that one of the keys to development is to give women a stake in the power structure and the economy. The variable FEM.PROF. measures the number of women for every 100 men who are involved in professional and technical occupations. This includes professions like law, medicine, engineering, and computer science. Thus the number 100 means that there are 100 women in professional occupations for every 100 men in professional occupations. For this variable we have data for 39 of 52 African countries, from a survey that was conducted in 1995.

> ➤ *Data File:* **AFRICA**
> > ➤ *Task:* **Mapping**
> ➤ *Variable 1:* **11) FEM.PROF.**
> > ➤ *View:* **List: Rank**

Chapter 11: War, Politics, and Poverty in LDCs and Marginal States

Write down the five top countries and the ratio of women per 100 men in professional and technical occupations.

COUNTRY	WOMEN IN PROFESSIONS
_____	_____
_____	_____
_____	_____
_____	_____
_____	_____

II. Why do you think there is so much variation in the number of women in professions in Africa? Let's explore two hypotheses: (1) African countries with high rates of female education will be more likely to have higher numbers of women in professions; (2) In countries where women are more involved in the economy in general (not just professions), they are more likely to seek representation in the legislature.

> Data File: **AFRICA**
> ➤ Task: **Scatterplot**
> ➤ Dependent Variable: **11) FEM.PROF.**
> ➤ Independent Variable: **13) M/F EDUC.**
> ➤ View: **Reg. Line**

8. What is the correlation coefficient for this scatterplot?   r = _____

9. Are these results statistically significant?   Yes   No

10. Do these results support the hypothesis that as education rates for women increase, so will their participation in professions?   Yes   No

> Data File: **AFRICA**
> Task: **Scatterplot**
> ➤ Dependent Variable: **12) %FEM.LEGIS**
> ➤ Independent Variable: **37) FEMECON1**
> ➤ View: **Reg. Line**

11. What is the correlation coefficient for this scatterplot?   r = _____

12. Are these results statistically significant?   Yes   No

13. Does the rate of females in the economy seem to be related to the percentage of women in the legislature?   Yes   No

III. Now let's look at the relationship between involvement in professions and the role of women in positions of political leadership in Africa. The variable FEM MINIST gives the percentage of the government's cabinet seats held by women.

> Data File: **AFRICA**
> Task: **Scatterplot**
> ➤ Dependent Variable: **35) FEM MINIST**
> ➤ Independent Variable: **11) FEM.PROF.**
> ➤ View: **Reg. Line**

14. What is the correlation coefficient for this scatterplot?   r = _____

15. Are these results statistically significant?   Yes   No

16. Does the rate of female political leadership seem to be related to the women's involvement in professions?   Yes   No

IV. The most pressing health problem in the world is the proliferation of the AIDS virus. The variable HIV/AIDS measures the percentage of the population with HIV/AIDS. Before we can consider what might be an effective strategy, we must understand the problems. Is illiteracy or GDP associated with HIV/AIDS in Africa? What about government spending on health?

> ➤ Data File: **GLOBAL**
> ➤ Task: **Mapping**
> ➤ Variable 1: **92) HIV LOW**
> ➤ View: **Rank**

17. Based on a low estimate, how many African nations are in the top ten nations with HIV/AIDS?   _____

> ➤ Data File: **AFRICA**
> ➤ Task: **Scatterplot**
> ➤ Dependent Variable: **38) HIV:PREV**
> ➤ Independent Variable: **34) IL:FEM<25**
> ➤ View: **Reg. Line**

18. The scatterplot suggests that
   a. as illiteracy among women under 25 increases, the percentage of those with HIV/AIDS decreases.
   b. as illiteracy among women under 25 increases, the percentage of those with HIV/AIDS increases.
   c. as literacy among women under 25 increases, the percentage of those with HIV/AIDS increases.
   d. as literacy among women under 25 increases, the percentage of those with HIV/AIDS decreases.
   e. Both a and c are true.

Now let's see if HIV/AIDS is associated with levels of wealth in African nation-states.

Data File:	**AFRICA**
Task:	**Scatterplot**
Dependent Variable:	**37) HIV:PREV**
➤ Independent Variable:	**17) GDPCAP PPP**
➤ View:	**Reg. Line**

19. What is the correlation coefficient for this scatterplot?   r = _____

20. Are these results statistically significant?   Yes   No

21. Does GDP per capita seem to be related to the HIV/AIDS rate?   Yes   No

Now let's examine the role that health expenditure and international aid plays in the number of HIV/AIDS cases, but before we start on the analysis let's be sure that we understand the variables that we are working with. Match the variable from the AFRICA file in the list below with its best description by placing the variable number in the blank provided.

0) NO SUCH VARIABLE

36) HEALTH_CAP

38) HIV:PREV

39) HIV:WOMEN

40) HIV:KIDS

43) AID/CAP

48) CONDM FEM

72) CONDM MALE

DESCRIPTION   **VARIABLE NUMBER**

22. The number of childhood (ages 0–14) HIV/AIDS cases: _____

23. The prevalence of adults (ages 15–49) living with HIV/AIDS (%):   _____

24. Percentage of males who know that condom use can reduce the
    transmission of HIV: _____

25. Female adults with HIV as a percentage of the population ages 15–49
    with HIV:

                                                                                                      _____

26. Government health expenditure in dollars: _____

27. Percentage of females who know that condom use can prevent the
    transmission of HIV:

                                                                                                      _____

28. Health expenditure per capita (current US $):   _____

29. Aid per capita (current US $):

                                                                                                      _____

Now examine the relationship between HIV/AIDS cases and health expenditure for each variable relationship.

Data File:	**AFRICA**
Task:	**Scatterplot**
➤ *Dependent Variables:*	**38) HIV:PREV**
	39) HIV:WOMEN
	40) HIV:KIDS
➤ *Independent Variable:*	**36) HEALTH_CAP**
➤ *View:*	**Reg. Line**

30. 36) HEALTH_CAP and 38) HIV:PREV   r = _____   Significant? Yes   No

31. 36) HEALTH_CAP and 39) HIV:WOMEN   r = _____   Significant? Yes   No

32. 36) HEALTH_CAP and 40) HIV:KIDS   r = _____   Significant? Yes   No

Now examine the relationship between HIV/AIDS cases and international aid for each variable relationship.

Data File:	**AFRICA**
Task:	**Scatterplot**
Dependent Variables:	**38) HIV:PREV**
	39) HIV:WOMEN
	40) HIV:KIDS
➤ *Independent Variable:*	**43) AID/CAP**
➤ *View:*	**Reg. Line**

33. 43) AID/CAP and 38) HIV:PREV   r = _____   Significant? Yes   No

34. 43) AID/CAP and 39) HIV:WOMEN   r = _____   Significant? Yes   No

35. 43) AID/CAP and 40) HIV:KIDS   r = _____   Significant? Yes   No

Data File:	**AFRICA**
Task:	**Scatterplot**
Dependent Variables:	**38) HIV:PREV**
	39) HIV:WOMEN
	40) HIV:KIDS
➤ *Independent Variable:*	**48) CONDM FEM**
➤ *View:*	**Reg. Line**

36. 48) CONDM FEM and 38) HIV:PREV   r = _____   Significant? Yes   No

37. 48) CONDM FEM and 39) HIV:WOMEN   r = _____   Significant? Yes   No

38. 48) CONDM FEM and 40) HIV:KIDS   r = _____   Significant? Yes   No

Data File:	**AFRICA**
Task:	**Scatterplot**
Dependent Variables:	**38) HIV:PREV**
	39) HIV:WOMEN
	40) HIV:KIDS
➤ *Independent Variable:*	**72) CONDM MALE**
➤ *View:*	**Reg. Line**

39. 72) CONDM MALE and 38) HIV:PREV   r = _____   Significant?   Yes   No

40. 72) CONDM MALE and 39) HIV:WOMEN   r = _____   Significant?   Yes   No

41. 72) CONDM MALE and 40) HIV:KIDS   r = _____   Significant?   Yes   No

IN YOUR OWN WORDS

In your own words, please answer the following questions.

1. Summarize the results of your analysis of HIV/AIDS. Which factors (literacy, GDP per capita, health spending, condom knowledge, and international aid per capita) are associated with a lower number of cases of HIV/AIDS? From this analysis, would you conclude that enough is being done to confront the HIV/AIDS crisis in Africa? Be sure to support your answer with evidence. Print out three scatter-plots that support your analysis.

2. What are the key features of the movement of refugees in Africa? Is it state weakness, war, health, or economic problems? Using the two variables 44) REFUGEES and 46) ASYLUM as dependent variables, write a paragraph that analyzes the movement of refugees in Africa. You may use any variable in the AFRICA data file that you think might be associated with the movement of refugees in Africa. Print out the two best explanations and attach them to this worksheet. The variable REFUGEES indicates the number of refugees from a given country. The variable ASYLUM indicates the number of refugees that are now residing in the country.

CHAPTER **12**

SOCIAL CAPITAL IN NIGERIA AND GHANA

People are people through other people.

XHOSA PROVERB OFTEN QUOTED
BY ARCHBISHOP DESMOND TUTU

Tasks: Mapping, Univariate, Historical Trends, Cross-tabulation
Data Files: PEW GLOBAL02, GLOBAL, AFRICA, PGAP02–NIGERIA, PGAP02–GHANA

In the previous chapter we described the experience of LDCs and marginal states at the nation-state level. In comparative politics it is important to understand the realities of nation-states in this category, it is also important to know what people really think about their lives, communities, and experiences. Forty years ago political scientists began very limited surveys across nation-state borders to understand how communities differed in their attitudes toward things like family, government, economics, and politics. In the first twenty years of this work, researchers focused their study on the public in familiar liberal democracies such as the United States and those nation-states in Europe. In the 1990s, systematic studies of world values began to include nations from the developing world, and by 2002 we began to glean a better understanding of the public in LDCs, NICs, and nations in the Islamic world. Now we can get an idea of how citizens in different countries think about important issues.

➤ *Data File:* **PEW GLOBAL02**
➤ *Task:* **Cross-tabulation**
➤ *Row Variable:* **12) US-TERROR**
➤ *Column Variable:* **2) WORLDS.7**
➤ *View:* **Tables**
➤ *Display:* **Column%**

US-TERROR   by   WORLDS.7
Weight Variable: WEIGHT
Cramer's V: 0.382**

		WORLDS.7						
		Lib.Democ	Comm/P-Com	NIC	LDC	Islamic	Marginal	TOTAL
US-TERROR	Favor	3871	3794	5294	4973	1494	784	20210
		78.4%	82.1%	62.3%	72.6%	26.9%	60.8%	63.7%
	Oppose	1067	829	3199	1876	4051	506	11528
		21.6%	17.9%	37.7%	27.4%	73.1%	39.2%	36.3%
	Missing	285	3365	1035	451	1262	186	6584
	TOTAL	4937	4624	8492	6849	5545	1290	31738
		100.0%	100.0%	100.0%	100.0%	100.0%	100.0%	

The Pew survey indicates tells us a lot about how the U.S.-led war on terror is supported around the world. In most country types there is fairly strong support for the war on terror. Liberal democracies (78.4%) and communist/postcommunist countries (82.1%) exhibit the highest degree of support for the war on terrorism. The level of support is slightly lower for LDCs (72.6%) and more than 15% lower in NICs. Perhaps the most striking finding of all is the very low opinion of this war in the Islamic world.

We'll talk about this issue in the next chapter, but it is clear that the Islamic public has not been persuaded that this is a war that Islamic nation-states should support.

Surveys like the World Values Study and the Pew Global Attitudes study help us to understand a great deal more than we knew before about what real people in these countries really think about important issues. Surveys like the Global Attitudes and World Values can help to confirm or refute assumptions that we might make about public perceptions in less developed countries. Let's take a look at a few examples.

When we examine the core values that support democratic practices, we find that the public is remarkably similar across nation-state boundaries.

Data File:	**PEW GLOBAL02**
Task:	**Cross-tabulation**
➤ *Row Variable:*	**13) IM:CRITGOV**
➤ *Column Variable:*	**2) WORLDS.7**
➤ *View:*	**Tables**
➤ *Display:*	**Column%**

IM:CRITGOV   by   WORLDS.7
Weight Variable: WEIGHT
Cramer's V: 0.096**

		Lib.Democ	Comm/P-Com	NIC	LDC	Islamic	Marginal	TOTAL
IM:CRITGOV	Very/Some	2360	3509	8451	6539	4672	1241	26771
		95.1%	85.2%	92.3%	91.0%	87.6%	89.2%	90.2%
	Not much	123	608	702	849	660	150	2893
		4.9%	14.8%	7.7%	9.0%	12.4%	10.8%	9.8%
	Missing	2739	3873	373	112	1476	85	8658
	TOTAL	2483	4116	9154	7188	5332	1391	29664
		100.0%	100.0%	100.0%	100.0%	100.0%	100.0%	

The preceding question asks citizens in all 44 countries whether or not it is important to be able to criticize the government. There are some significant differences across all country groups, but what is also notable is that more than 90% of the population in the LDCs surveyed believe that the freedom to criticize government is an important value. As you learned in the last chapter, the challenge of living in an LDC is that not everyone is free to act on the basis of their political beliefs.

Data File:	**PEW GLOBAL02**
Task:	**Cross-tabulation**
➤ *Row Variable:*	**14) CRIT GOV**
➤ *Column Variable:*	**2) WORLDS.7**
➤ *View:*	**Tables**
➤ *Display:*	**Column%**

CRIT GOV   by   WORLDS.7
Weight Variable: WEIGHT
Cramer's V: 0.202**

		Lib.Democ	Comm/P-Com	NIC	LDC	Islamic	Marginal	TOTAL
CRIT GOV	Very/Some	2212	2929	6667	4846	2902	1060	20616
		89.9%	72.6%	73.1%	67.6%	54.3%	78.0%	69.9%
	Not Well	250	1108	2458	2326	2438	299	8878
		10.1%	27.4%	26.9%	32.4%	45.7%	22.0%	30.1%
	Missing	2761	3952	402	128	1468	117	8828
	TOTAL	2462	4037	9125	7172	5340	1360	29494
		100.0%	100.0%	100.0%	100.0%	100.0%	100.0%	

If you compare the two previous tables, you can see the difference between citizen aspirations and the realities that they confront. Notice that in liberal democracies there is about a 5.2% gap between those who believe that citizens should be able to criticize government (95.1%), and those who feel that you can criticize the government in practice (89.9%). This gap is much wider in LDCs, where 91.0% believe that it is important to be able to criticize the government, but only 67.6% of the citizens surveyed feel free enough to do so.

Knowledge of citizen opinion is important when we are trying to understand the nature of political institutions, the economy of a country, and the social context of people's existence. You'll remember that our definition of less developed countries provided in Chapter 3 indicates that these nation-states have some potential to build political, economic, and social stability, but face many long-term obstacles. Most of these obstacles are in some way related to a lack of political stability, economic stagnation, and social conflict.

SOCIAL CAPITAL

One of the leading reasons for the violence and instability experienced by LDCs and marginal states is the suspicion and fear bred by a legacy of colonial rule, violence, and mistrust between indigenous peoples and their colonizers. European colonizers often used one ethnic group against another to divide and conquer a territory. Not every ethnic group was at peace before the Europeans' conquest of Africa and Latin America, but the pattern of pitting one group against the other exacerbated latent political conflicts between the various ethnic groups in each country. This is perhaps one reason that Nigerians and Ghanaians have a very difficult time trusting others in their respective countries.

➤ *Data File:* **GLOBAL**
➤ *Task:* **Mapping**
➤ *Variable 1:* **393) TRUST?**
➤ *View:* **List: Rank**

TRUST?: Percent who say, "Most people can be trusted." (WVS, 2002)

RANK	CASE NAME	VALUE
1	Denmark	66.5
2	Sweden	66.3
3	Iran	65.3
4	Norway	65.3
5	Netherlands	60.1
5	Finland	57.4
7	China	54.5
8	Indonesia	51.6
9	New Zealand	49.1
10	Japan	43.1

If you scroll down the table, you will notice that both Ghanaians and Nigerians have some of the lowest levels of trust among their citizens. They rank 48th and 35th out of the 79 countries surveyed on this question for the World Values Survey. Social trust of fellow citizens is one indicator of what political scientist Robert Putnam refers to as "social capital."[1] Social capital is the reserve of goodwill and trust citizens have toward one another that allows them to engage in democratic behaviors. In a study of Italy, Putnam theorizes that democracy works best when citizens with different backgrounds and perspectives can trust one another. On the face of it, this makes sense. If you generally trust people, you will be more inclined to tolerate election results that do not work in your favor. While you may not agree with the decisions of your government, if you trust that people will not harm you, you are much more likely to allow them to govern if they are properly chosen by the community as a whole. Social capital in and of itself, though, does not necessarily precede democratic behavior. Democracy is usually very risky business if you are part of a group that feels threatened, so a track record of benevolent government and loyal opposition can help to build the social capital necessary for democracy.

In this chapter and the worksheet section that follows, we will examine social capital and political development in two LDCs: Nigeria and Ghana. Ghana has had slightly more success in recent times with political, economic and social development than Nigeria. Is it possible that social capital may play a factor in this key difference? Before we get into analysis, let's work to understand a little more about these two LDCs.

---

[1] Robert Putnam, *Making Democracy Work: Civic Traditions in Modern Italy* (Princeton, NJ: Princeton University Press, 1993).

COMPARING GHANA AND NIGERIA

Ghana is a former British slave colony and center of commerce for West Africa that has gradually taken small, but significant steps toward greater political and economic stability over the past 20 years. Ghana achieved its independence from the UK in 1957 and was ruled by a series of oppressive, incompetent, and deceptive military leaders until 1981.

Nigeria was also a British colony until it received its independence in 1960. Between 1960 and 2006 Nigeria has been ruled by successive military dictators for 30 of those 46 years. The nation-state has experienced more than a dozen coups during this time and a major civil war. From 1967 to 1970 Nigeria was ravaged by warfare when the provinces of southeast Nigeria tried to secede from the rest of the country. The southeasterners, mostly members of the Igbo ethnic minority, hoped to take the provinces rich in newly discovered oil with them to establish a more prosperous nation-state. The so-called Biafran war resulted in mass starvation, and accusations of genocide were leveled at the central government by the Igbo people. By 1970 the rebellion was put down, but the ethnic tension between the Igbo, Hausa-Fulani, and Yoruba peoples characterizes the politics of Nigeria to this day. Let's see how Freedom House rated the political rights and civil liberties of Ghana and Nigeria in 1975.

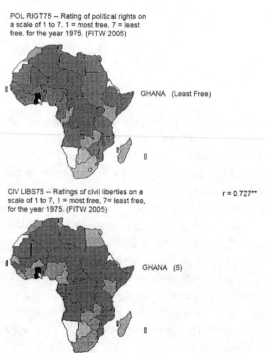

➤ Data File: **AFRICA**
➤ Task: **Mapping**
➤ Variable 1: **79) POL RIGT75**
➤ Variable 2: **84) CIV LIBS75**
➤ View: **Map**
➤ Display: **Find Case: Ghana**
Nigeria

POL RIGT75 -- Rating of political rights on a scale of 1 to 7. 1 = most free. 7 = least free. for the year 1975. (FITW 2005)

GHANA (Least Free)

CIV LIBS75 -- Ratings of civil liberties on a scale of 1 to 7, 1 = most free, 7= least free, for the year 1975. (FITW 2005)

r = 0.727**

GHANA (5)

As a result of the challenges of transition from colonialism to self-government, in the 1970s the politics of Ghana and Nigeria were characterized by strong authoritarian rule and limited civil liberties. Ghana received a rating of 7 for political rights and a rating of 5 for civil liberties in 1975. Nigerians fared similarly in 1975 with a political rights rating of 6 and a civil liberties rating of 5. After 1975, the situation in both of these countries began a gradual process of change that began to bear some fruit by the 1990s.

In 1981, a Ghanaian air force lieutenant by the name of Jerry Rawlings overthrew the corrupt civil government and began work on the restructuring of the economy, and the process of political and constitutional reform that legalized political parties for the election of 1992. In spite of these advances, Rawlings'

Comparative Politics

leadership of Ghana through the 1980s and his orchestration of a sham election in 1992 compromised his reform efforts. In 1996 Ghanaians elected the opposition leader John Kufuor to the presidency, which marked the first democratic transition from one leader to another in Ghana. Since 1996 Ghana has experienced successive democratic elections, and its political rights and civil liberties ratings now rank among the most free in Africa.

The expansion of political rights and civil liberties since the 1970s has been more tentative in Nigeria. In 1993 it appeared that Nigeria might be emerging from a long period of military rule under General Ibrahim Babangida. Based on the accounts of independent election observers, a Muslim Yoruba named Moshood Abiola won the election in 1993, but the military negated the results of the election and continued its pattern of political dominance with the arrest of Abiola until he died in detention in 1998. In 1999 former army general Olusegun Obasanjo was elected president in a popular election and subsequently re-elected in a somewhat tainted election in 2003. Let's see how Ghana and Nigeria are rated now in light of recent political developments in each of these countries.

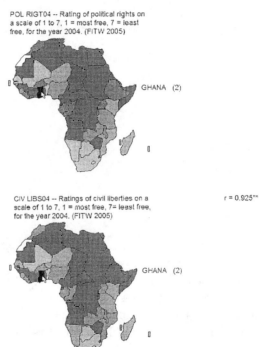

Data File: **AFRICA**

Task: **Mapping**

➤ Variable 1: **28) POL RIGT04**

➤ Variable 2: **30) CIV LIBS04**

➤ View: **Map**

➤ Display: **Find Case: Ghana**
Nigeria

POL RIGT04 -- Rating of political rights on a scale of 1 to 7, 1 = most free, 7 = least free, for the year 2004. (FITW 2005)

GHANA (2)

CIV LIBS04 -- Ratings of civil liberties on a scale of 1 to 7, 1 = most free, 7= least free, for the year 2004. (FITW 2005)

r = 0.925**

GHANA (2)

Recent election success has helped to improve Ghana's political rights ratings from a 7 in the 1970s to 2 by 2005. Ghana's civil liberties ratings have also made similar progress from a rating of 5 in the 1970s to a rating of 2 today. Ghana has made significant progress in the protection of political rights, the reduction of corruption, the protection of minority groups, and the prosecution of religious and interethnic violence.

Nigerians have made some advances in the extension of political rights, with a rating of 4 in 2005, and the protection of civil liberties, also with a rating of 4, but there are still a significant number of problems. Election irregularities such as ballot-box stuffing, multiple voting, falsification of results, and voter intimidation were observed by local and international election observers. Amnesty International and other human-rights groups reported several politically motivated assassinations and violent clashes between political groups prior to the election. Interethnic and religious violence is sometimes tolerated by the authorities, and violence and kidnappings have escalated in the oil-rich Niger Delta. Local groups in the Delta have organized a guerrilla militia to protest government corruption and "take back" the local population's fair share of oil revenue from the government and global oil companies. Recent elections have raised the hopes of Nigerians, but the patterns of social conflict, political authoritarianism, and economic deprivation and corruption still pose significant obstacles to development in Nigeria.

Data File: **AFRICA**
Task: **Mapping**
➤ Variable 1: **86) CORRUPT 04**
➤ Variable 2: **87) CORRUPT 96**
➤ View: **Map**
➤ Display: **Legend**
Find Case: **Ghana**
Nigeria

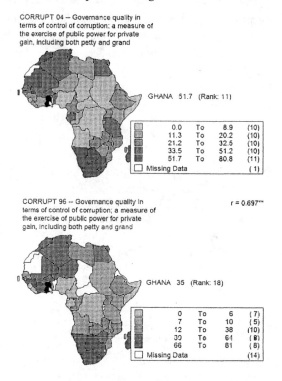

The international organization Transparency International tracks public corruption using the experience of local and international businesspersons, public surveys, and academic researchers. A score of 100 would represent a 'clean' government and a score of 1 would represent the most corrupt government. The pattern of corruption over the past two decades reflects the political and civil circumstances of each country. Ghana shows considerable improvement from 1996 to 2005 as its corruption rating has improved from the 18th to the 11th highest rated country in Africa. This is still not a great rating in global terms, but it represents significant progress in a short time. Nigeria, on the other hand, continues to struggle with corruption. In 1996 Nigeria was ranked 33rd out of 38 countries for corruption and in 2005 it was rated 42nd out of 51. Corruption can have significant deleterious effects on economic development.

Data File: **AFRICA**
Task: **Mapping**
➤ Variable 1: **85) GROW 90-99**
➤ Variable 2: **17) GDPCAP PPP**
➤ View: **Map**
➤ Display: **Legend**
Find Case: **Ghana**
Nigeria

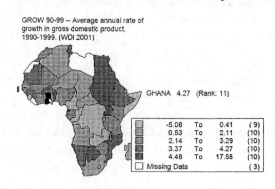

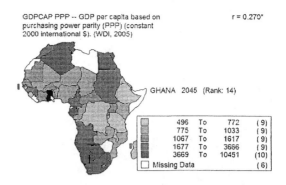

GDPCAP PPP -- GDP per capita based on purchasing power parity (PPP) (constant 2000 international $). (WDI, 2005)

r = 0.270*

GHANA 2045 (Rank: 14)

496	To	772	(9)
775	To	1033	(9)
1067	To	1617	(9)
1677	To	3666	(9)
3669	To	10451	(10)
Missing Data			(6)

Ghana has capitalized on its position as a producer of cocoa and gold and its economic growth rate in the 1990s exceeded 4%. Its GDP per capita is $2,045 per year and is ranked 14th on the African continent. This is very positive for Ghana; but it still places Ghana at a ranking 107th out of 172 nation-states worldwide. Nigeria, with its vast oil reserves, has even more access to natural resources than Ghana, but public corruption has squandered these opportunities. As a result of corruption and unstable politics, Nigeria grew at an average annual rate of only 3.05% in the 1990s, and it still has one of the lowest GDP per capita levels ($911 per year) on the continent of Africa. The management of scarce resources can be very difficult where there are severe social divisions in any country.

For the final part of this analysis, let's take a look at the social structure of Ghana and Nigeria.

Data File: **AFRICA**
Task: **Mapping**
➤ Variable 1: **8) MULTI-CULT**
➤ View: **Map**
➤ Display: **Legend**
Find Case: Ghana
Nigeria

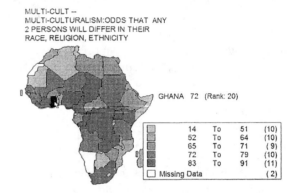

MULTI-CULT --
MULTI-CULTURALISM:ODDS THAT ANY 2 PERSONS WILL DIFFER IN THEIR RACE, RELIGION, ETHNICITY

GHANA 72 (Rank: 20)

14	To	51	(10)
52	To	64	(10)
65	To	71	(9)
72	To	79	(10)
83	To	91	(11)
Missing Data			(2)

While it is still a highly diverse nation-state, compared to Nigeria, Ghana is relatively homogeneous. The predominant ethnic group, Akan, constitutes 44% of the national population, and the WCE census reveals that 62.6% of the population is Christian. In Ghana there are only a few conflicts between ethnic groups, and the religious climate is more homogeneous and tolerant than many West African nations. Ghana is still a diverse nation, but it is not the most diverse on the continent of Africa. Nigeria remains one of the most diverse nation-states on the planet, and it is evenly divided between Christians and Muslims.

Data File: *AFRICA*
Task: **Mapping**
Variable 1: **9) %MUSLIM**
➤ Variable 2: **10) %CHRISTIAN**
➤ View: **Map**
➤ Display: **Legend**
Find Case: Nigeria

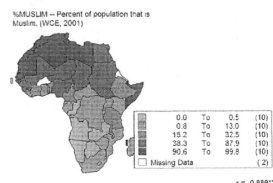

%MUSLIM -- Percent of population that is Muslim. (WCE, 2001)

0.0	To	0.5	(10)
0.8	To	13.0	(10)
15.2	To	32.5	(10)
33.3	To	37.9	(10)
90.6	To	99.8	(10)
Missing Data			(2)

r = -0.889**

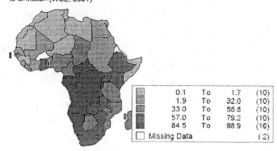

%CHRISTIAN -- Percent of population that is Christian (WCE, 2001)

0.1	To	1.7	(10)
1.9	To	32.0	(10)
33.0	To	56.5	(10)
57.0	To	79.2	(10)
84.5	To	98.9	(10)
☐ Missing Data			(2)

This even division between these two religious groups and the historic tensions between Igbo, Yoruba, and Hausa-Fulani may be at the root of many of Nigeria's contemporary problems. These divisions will likely continue to exacerbate the political conflict that has characterized this country for some time to come.

Ghana is a fairly typical LDC in may respects. Although it has increasingly stable political and economic institutions, Ghana does not have a very long track record of political stability relative to the many other nations that we have studied in previous chapters. The economy is still largely dependent on agriculture and natural resources, rather than industry, and this society has only recently begun to work out social conflicts by means of the ballot box. Ghana represents a hopeful example of an LDC moving in the direction of greater stability, but it still has a number of obstacles. Our analysis here has just scratched the surface, and we still can only begin to understand why democracy seems to be taking root in Ghana and why the Nigerian system remains in turmoil. In fact, we don't know anything about what Ghanaians or Nigerians actually think about their own situation. Now it is your turn to find out.

Terms and Concepts
social capital
social trust
survey research in LDCs

Understand the following concepts as they apply to Ghana and Nigeria:
  civil liberties and political rights, 1975
  civil liberties and political rights, 2005
  economic growth
  corruption
  GDP per capita
  ethnic diversity
  religious diversity

REVIEW QUESTIONS

Based on the first part of this chapter, answer True or False to the following items:

1. Nigerians have a lower level of trust in fellow citizens than do Ghanaians.   T   F

2. Systematic surveys that compare attitudes across borders have been used
    by political scientists only within the last 40 years.   T   F

3. In LDCs, the difference between those who believe that one should be able to
    criticize the government and those who actually feel able to criticize the government
    is smaller than it is in any other category of country.   T   F

4. Ghana and Nigeria were both British colonies, are both in West Africa, and are both
    making rapid progress toward democracy.   T   F

5. The civil liberties and political rights situation in Ghana has improved significantly
    since 1975.   T   F

6. The civil liberties and political rights situation in Nigeria has improved slightly
    since 1975.   T   F

7. Oil wealth in Nigeria has helped to make Nigeria the wealthiest country, in terms of
    GDP per capita, in Africa.   T   F

8. Corruption appears to be worse in Ghana than it is in Nigeria.   T   F

9. Nigeria is evenly divided between Muslims and Christians.   T   F

10. According to our analysis in the chapter, a majority of Ghana's population is Christian.   T   F

EXPLORIT QUESTIONS

I.   One of the things discussed in this chapter is the idea we can use surveys to help us to check our own
     assumptions about the problems that others identify as important to their own country. For example,
     we might perceive that ethnic conflict is a major problem, but if citizens of Nigeria don't think of this as
     a major problem, then one may want to think about the situation in a slightly different way, or re-examine
     our assumptions about the nature of conflict in a given country. In the analysis that follows we will com-

pare the nation-states of Nigeria and Ghana in order to better understand how citizens define significant problems in their own country.

Use the PEW GLOBAL02 data file to perform the series of cross-tabulations indicated. For each result, fill in the percentaged results for the row that is specified in the table below. Finally, be sure to indicate the Cramer's V statistic and whether or not the result is significant (circle Y for Yes, N for No).

> *Data File:* **PEW GLOBAL02**
>> *Task:* **Cross-tabulation**
> *Row Variables:* **15) ETHN CONF; 16) MORALDEC; 17)WATERQUAL;**
>> **18) TERRORISM; 19) HIV/AIDS; 20) SCHOOLQUAL; 21) LEAVECNTRY**
> *Column Variable:* **1) COUNTRY**
> *Subset Variable:* **1) COUNTRY**
> *Subset Category:* **Include: 14) GHANA; 26) NIGERIA; and 34) S. AFRICA**
>> *View:* **Tables**
>> *Display:* **Column%**

> Instead of opening a new data file for each analysis, when you use this data file, you can simply re-open the cross-tabulation menu by clicking on the arrow button ↶ and enter a new row variable for each analysis. You do not need to re-enter the column variable or the subset variable each time, as long as you set this up correctly the first time.

Fill in the table below.

	GHANA	NIGERIA	S. AFRICA	CRAMER'S V	SIGNIFI-CANT?
15) ETHN CONF % Very Big	_____%	_____%	_____%	_____	Y N
16) MORALDEC % Very Big	_____%	_____%	_____%	_____	Y N
17) WATERQUAL % Very Big	_____%	_____%	_____%	_____	Y N
18) TERRORISM % Very Big	_____%	_____%	_____%	_____	Y N
19) HIV/AIDS % Very Big	_____%	_____%	_____%	_____	Y N
20) SCHOOLQUAL % Very Big	_____%	_____%	_____%	_____	Y N
21) LEAVECNTRY % Very Big	_____%	_____%	_____%	_____	Y N

11. Which country has the highest percentage of citizens who believe that ethnic conflict is a very big problem?   _____

12. Of the three countries in this analysis, in which countries do a majority of the population identify ethnic conflict as a very big problem? (Circle all that apply)

    a. Ghana   b. Nigeria   c. South Africa

13. According to this survey, what is the biggest problem facing Ghana (in other words, what is the problem that the highest percentage of the population identifies as a very big problem)?   _____

14. According to this survey, what is the biggest problem facing Nigeria?   _____

15. According to this survey, what is the biggest problem facing South Africa?   _____

16. According to this survey, what is least likely to be identified as the biggest problem facing Ghana (in other words, what is the problem that the lowest percentage of the population identifies as a very big problem)?   _____

17. According to this survey, what is least likely to be identified as the biggest problem facing Nigeria?   _____

18. According to this survey, what is least likely to be identified as the biggest problem facing South Africa?   _____

II. Based on the previous analysis, it appears that one of the problems that is of significant concern to Nigerians and Ghanaians is the problem of interethnic conflict. The 2002 Nigeria subset of the Pew Global Attitudes Project asks some specific questions about this in an effort to understand the nature of this conflict. But before we get into the analysis, you will need a little background on ethnicity in Nigeria.

Although Europeans were involved in the West African slave trade from the 16th century until the 19th century, the British Empire controlled what is now present-day Nigeria from 1886 until its independence in 1960. Nigeria consisted not only of small tribes but of nations and empires as well until the European conquest. More than 250 ethnic groups reside in Nigeria, but at least three large groups have dominated the political landscape in Nigeria since independence: the Hausa-Fulani, the Igbo, and the Yoruba.

Prior to the time of the British conquest, the Hausa-Fulani had established an extensive empire in Northern Nigeria. This was a nation devoted to the practice of Islam, whose Hausa branch had a long history of domination and empire between A.D. 1000 and 1200. The Fulanis dominated in the period of British conquest, but the two groups became so intertwined that the two are generally referred to as the Hausa-Fulani. The Hausa-Fulani succeeded in remaining relatively insulated from British domination. The British allowed them a degree of autonomy in self-government and, unlike the southern part of the country, did not allow Christian proselytizing in the North.

The Igbo (pronounced "eebo") and the Yoruba reside in the southern part of the nation. Unlike the Hausa-Fulani, the Igbo were politically decentralized and independent. They had settled widely throughout the country and were integrally involved in the early military governments in Nigeria. They are described by other ethnic groups in Nigeria as "pushy" and "aggressive." The Igbo have also been very adept at appropriating Western education, commerce, and political practices. Unlike the Hausa-Fulani, the Igbo were very receptive to Christian missionary efforts and are also said to be strongly egalitarian.

The Yoruba live in the southwestern part of the country in and around the capital, Lagos. The Yoruba have a long tradition of promoting commerce in the context of their network of city-states and have had highly stratified societies and relatively authoritarian political structures. Like the Igbo, the Yoruba have been very receptive to Western missionaries and schools imported to the region during the 19th and 20th centuries.

For political reasons, it is very difficult to get an exact count by ethnicity (see Table 12.1). Each group is interested in overrepresenting its numbers so that it may lay claim to a greater share of political power, so the only two estimates we have are unreliable. The 1952–53 and 1963 censuses were both notorious for their inaccuracy because census enumerators sought to inflate the populations of different regions in order to increase the number of seats allocated to these regions. To this day, there still is no accurate census on the population of Nigeria. The 1963 census and the 2001 CIA estimates have very similar results, but these results differ from most scholarly samples of the Nigerian population.

Table 12.1 Ethnic Identities in Nigeria, 1963
and 2001

Group	1963 Census	2001 CIA Estimate
Hausa-Fulani	29.5%	29%
Yoruba	20.3%	21%
Igbo	16.6%	18%
Other	33.6%	32%

Let's see how the Pew Global Attitudes Project surveyed ethnicity in Nigeria.

> *Data File:*   **PGAP02-NIGERIA**
> *Task:*   **Univariate**
> *Primary Variable:*   **1) ETHNICITY**
> *View:*   **Pie**

Print out this graph and attach it to this worksheet.

19. If the CIA census numbers are correct, which groups appear to be overrepresented in the survey?

    a. Hausa

    b. Igbo

    c. Yoruba

    d. Other

20. If the CIA census numbers are correct, which groups appear to be underrepresented in the survey?

    a. Hausa

    b. Igbo

    c. Yoruba

    d. Other

21. In the space provided below, how closely does this sample of the Nigerian population from the PGAP02-Nigeria file come to census estimates from the Nigerian government in 1963 and CIA estimates from 2001?

_____

_____

_____

_____

Now let's do some analysis. How does one's ethnic affiliation influence how one views one's own culture and other cultural groups within Nigeria?

If ethnicity matters in one's view of the influence of other ethnic groups, then we would observe a relationship between one's own ethnicity and the perception of the influence of other groups.

        Data File: **PGAP02-NIGERIA**
       ➤ *Task:*   **Cross-tabulation**
   ➤ *Row Variables:*   **3) ETHNOCENTR; 4) IGBO GRP; 5) HAUSA GRP; 6) YORUBA GRP**
 ➤ *Column Variable:*   **1) ETHNICITY**
       ➤ *View:*   **Tables**
    ➤ *Display:*   **Column%**

Fill in the table below.

	HAUSA	IGBO	YORUBA	OTHER	CRAMER'S V	SIGNIFI-CANT?
3) ETHNOCENTR % Com.Agree	____%	____%	____%	____%	_____	Y N
4) IGBO GRP % VG/Good	____%	____%	____%	____%	_____	Y N
5) HAUSA GRP % VG/Good	____%	____%	____%	____%	_____	Y N
6) YORUBA GRP % VG/Good	____%	____%	____%	____%	_____	Y N

Let's say that the belief that the influence of another ethnic group is good is an indicator of trust. Consider the following questions:

22. Which ethnic group has the highest percentage of its population that completely agree with the statement "Our people are not perfect, but our culture is superior to others"? _____

23. Which ethnic group has the lowest percentage of its population that completely agree with the statement "Our people are not perfect, but our culture is superior to others"? _____

24. In general, a majority of Nigerians believe that the influence of all groups other than their own is good or very good.   T   F

25. Which ethnic group is least likely to say that the influence of the Igbo is very good or good?

     a. Hausa   b. Igbo   c. Yoruba   d. Other

26. Which ethnic group is least likely to say that the influence of the Hausa is very good or good?

     a. Hausa   b. Igbo   c. Yoruba   d. Other

27. Which ethnic group is least likely to say that the influence of the Yoruba is very good or good?

     a. Hausa   b. Igbo   c. Yoruba   d. Other

III. Another issue of interest to us is to understand how well values related to democracy, corruption, and good governance are understood across the lines of culture and ethnicity. In short, is there a relationship between one's ethnicity and values related to governance in Nigeria and Ghana? Let's find out.

NIGERIA SURVEY

> ➤ *Data File:*   **PGAP02-NIGERIA**
> ➤ *Task:*   **Cross-tabulation**
> ➤ *Row Variables:*   **10) GOVT DUTY; 11) GOVTWASTES; 12) BENEFITALL; 14) CORRUPTLDR;**
>   **15) OURCOUNTRY; 16) CORRPTGOVT**
> ➤ *Column Variable:*   **1) ETHNICITY**
> ➤ *View:*   **Tables**
> ➤ *Display:*   **Column%**

For each result, fill in the percentaged results for the row that is specified in the table below. Also indicate whether the results are statistically significant (circle Y for Yes, N for No).

Fill in the table below.

	HAUSA	IGBO	YORUBA	OTHER	V =	SIGNIFI-CANT?
10) GOVT DUTY % Agree	_____%	_____%	_____%	_____%	_____	Y N
11) GOVTWASTES % Agree	_____%	_____%	_____%	_____%	_____	Y N
12) BENEFITALL % Agree	_____%	_____%	_____%	_____%	_____	Y N
14) CORRUPTLDR % Very Big	_____%	_____%	_____%	_____%	_____	Y N
15) OURCOUNTRY % Agree	_____%	_____%	_____%	_____%	_____	Y N
16) CORRPTGOVT % Often	_____%	_____%	_____%	_____%	_____	Y N

28. Do ethnic groups in Nigeria differ significantly in all six areas?   Yes   No

29. Which ethnic group is least likely to think that government should benefit all?   _____

30. Which ethnic group is most likely to think that government should benefit all?   _____

31. Is one ethnic group more likely to believe that corrupt leaders are more of a problem than any other group?   _____

32. Which ethnic group is most likely to have paid bribes recently?   _____

33. Which ethnic group is least likely to have paid bribes recently?   _____

Now use the PGAP02-GHANA file to do the same analysis in Ghana. You will remember from the preliminary part of the chapter that, compared to Nigeria, Ghana has relatively harmonious relations between the variety of ethnic groups, but a majority of citizens still cite ethnic group conflict as a very big problem in Ghana. In order to understand a bit more about the largest ethnic groups in Ghana, create a pie chart of the key ethnic groups in Ghana using the variable 1)ETHNICITY, print out the chart and append it to this worksheet.

The ethnic groups identified by a CIA census and field study in 1998 identified the following ethnic groups:

Akan 44%
Moshi-Dagomba 16%
Ewe 13%
Ga 8%
Other 19%

34. If the census numbers are correct, which groups appear to be overrepresented in the Ghana survey?

    a. Akan

    b. Moshi-Dagomba

    c. Ewe

    d. Ga

    e. Other

35. If the census numbers are correct, which groups appear to be underrepresented in the Ghana survey?

    a. Akan

    b. Moshi-Dagomba

    c. Ewe

    d. Ga

    e. Other

36. In the space provided below, how closely does this sample of the Ghanaian population come to census estimates from the CIA in 1998?

_____

_____

_____

_____

Now that we understand a little bit about the ethnic groups in Ghana, let's take a look at how ethnicity is related to democracy, corruption, and good governance in Ghana. In short, is there a relationship between one's ethnicity and values related to governance in Ghana? Let's find out.

GHANA SURVEY

➤ *Data File:*   **PGAP02-GHANA**
➤ *Task:*   **Cross-tabulation**
➤ *Row Variables:*   **7) GOVT DUTY; 8) GOVTWASTES; 9) BENEFITALL;**
                            11) CORRUPTLDR; 12) OURCOUNTRY; 13) CORRPTGOVT
➤ *Column Variable:*   **1) ETHNICITY**
➤ *View:*   **Tables**
➤ *Display:*   **Column%**

For each result, fill in the percentaged results for the row that is specified in the table below. Also indicate whether the results are statistically significant (circle Y for Yes, N for No).

Fill in the table below.

	AKAN	DAGOMBA	EWE	GA	OTHER	CRAMER'S V	SIGNIFI-CANT?
7) GOVT DUTY % Agree	_____%	_____%	_____%	_____%	_____%	_____	Y N
8) GOVTWASTES % Agree	_____%	_____%	_____%	_____%	_____%	_____	Y N
9) BENEFITALL % Agree	_____%	_____%	_____%	_____%	_____%	_____	Y N
11) CORRUPTLDR % Very Big	_____%	_____%	_____%	_____%	_____%	_____	Y N
12) OURCOUNTRY % Agree	_____%	_____%	_____%	_____%	_____%	_____	Y N
13) CORRPTGOVT % Often	_____%	_____%	_____%	_____%	_____%	_____	Y N

37. Do ethnic groups in Ghana differ significantly in all six areas?   Yes   No

38. Which ethnic group is most likely to think that government should benefit all?   _____

39. Which ethnic group is least likely to believe that government should benefit all?   _____

40. Is our group more likely to think that corrupt leaders are more of a problem than other groups?   _____

41. Which ethnic group seems to pay bribes more often?   _____

IN YOUR OWN WORDS

In your own words, please answer the following questions.

1. Based on your analysis of ethnicity and issues in Nigeria, please respond to the statement "The conflict between ethnic groups is a racist fantasy. There is no such thing as ethnic conflict. Conflict between different groups in Nigeria is the same the world over: a conflict between the 'haves' and the 'have nots.'" Be sure to base your answer on the analysis of data that you conducted in this chapter.

2. Based on your analysis of Ghana and Nigeria, does the evidence serve to explain the margin of success that Ghana has experienced over Nigeria in its efforts to develop economically, politically, and socially? Why or why not?

Part VI

THE ISLAMIC WORLD

The Islamic World

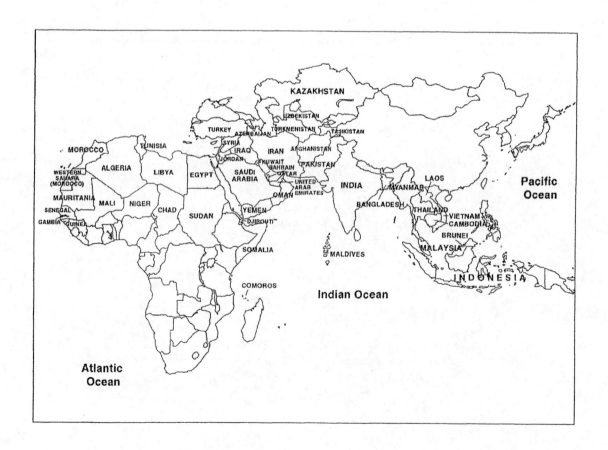

CHAPTER 13

FEATURES OF THE ISLAMIC WORLD

> *Islamic fundamentalists in Arab countries preach their ideology because they consider Islam the elevator to take power.*
>
> HASSAN II, 1995,
> KING OF MOROCCO

Tasks: Mapping, Cross-tabulation, Univariate, Scatterplot, ANOVA
Data Files: GLOBAL, PEW GLOBAL02, WVS02all, WVS02–PAKISTAN, WVS02–TURKEY, PEW GLOBAL02

In 1979, Islamic fundamentalists overthrew the shah of Iran and established a theocratic government, or Islamic Republic, rooted in the theological principles outlined in the holy book of Islam, the Qur'an (or Koran). Western observers were taken by surprise by the militancy of the students who were the vanguard of the Islamic revolution in Iran. As a result of this event, countries where Islam dominates the religious landscape are increasingly understood as a separate type of political system. The Islamic world consists of states that govern themselves by Islamic law or have a large majority of the population who are Islamic believers.

Let's use the WORLDS.7 variable in the GLOBAL data file to examine the Islamic countries throughout the world. To include only Islamic countries in the following map, use ExplorIt's [Subset] option, as described below.

➤ *Data File:* **GLOBAL**
➤ *Task:* **Mapping**
➤ *Variable 1:* **130) WORLDS.7**
➤ *Subset Variable:* **130) WORLDS.7**
➤ *Subset Category:* **Include: 5) Islamic**
➤ *View:* **Map**

WORLDS.7 – CLASSIFICATION OF COUNTRIES INTO "SEVEN WORLDS" OR CATEGORIES: 1 = LIBERAL DEMOCRACY, 2 = COMMUNIST/POST-COMMUNIST, 3 =

[Subset]

The option for selecting a subset variable is located on the same screen you use to select other variables. For this example, additionally select 130) WORLDS.7 for the subset variable. A window will appear that shows you the categories of the subset variable. Select 5) Islamic as your subset category and choose the [Include] option. Then click [OK] and continue as usual. With this particular subset selected, the results will be limited to countries in the Islamic world. The subset selection continues until you do one of the following: exit the task, delete the subset variable, or use the [Clear All] button to clear all variables.

This map includes only those countries that have a large percentage of Islamic adherents *and* a political system that is influenced by the Koran. You will notice that most of these countries are concentrated in North Africa, the Middle East, and parts of South Asia. Let's take a look at the percentage of the population who are Islamic believers for all countries.

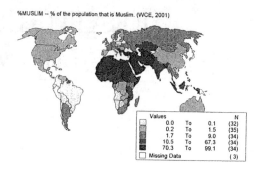

%MUSLIM -- % of the population that is Muslim. (WCE, 2001)

Data File:	**GLOBAL**
Task:	**Mapping**
➤ Variable 1:	**440) %MUSLIM**
➤ View:	**Map**
➤ Display:	**Legend**

Values				N
0.0	To	0.1		(32)
0.2	To	1.5		(35)
1.7	To	9.0		(34)
10.5	To	67.3		(34)
70.3	To	99.1		(34)
Missing Data				(3)

Note: Before selecting the %MUSLIM variable, use the [Clear All] button to remove the subset selected in your previous analysis.

Here we see that the concentrations of Islamic believers are found in North Africa and almost all of South Asia. If you use the [List: Rank] option to view the specific percentages for nations, you see that the population in more than 14 countries is greater than 95% Muslim; 40 countries are at least 50% Muslim. There is also a high concentration of Islamic believers in the republics of the former USSR. If Islamic revival in other parts of the world is any indication of the future of the southern republics of the former Soviet Union, then we can expect that these states will also develop an "Islamic" character.

The study of Islamic states as a distinct political phenomenon is antithetical to Western notions of religion and politics. Political scientist John McCormick notes that the Judeo-Christian understanding of religion and politics is that they are separate realms:

> "Render . . . unto Caesar the things which are Caesar's and unto God the things that are God's" (Matthew 22:21) . . . is a principle that most liberal democracies follow. For many Muslims, by contrast, Islam is the state, there is no separation of state (dawla) and religion (din) (in theory at least), and all Muslims are part of a larger entity . . . that transcends race and national borders.

McCormick and other scholars of this region suggest that Westerners see political Islam as being more analogous to an ideology than a religion because Islam has a complete body of law for ordering society. The Pew Global Attitudes Project helps us to see this dynamic across the Seven Worlds classification of countries. The survey of Muslims living in different kinds of countries asked whether or not they thought that it was important for religious leaders to get more involved in politics.

➤ Data File:	**PEW GLOBAL02**
➤ Task:	**Cross-tabulation**
➤ Row Variables:	**22) RELIG&POL**
➤ Column Variable:	**2) WORLDS.7**
➤ View:	**Tables**
➤ Display:	**Column%**

RELIG&POL by WORLDS.7
Weight Variable: WEIGHT
Cramer's V: 0.165**

		WORLDS.7						
		Lib.Democ	Comm/P-Com	NIC	LDC	Islamic	Marginal	TOTAL
RELIG&POL	S.Agree	0	101	164	488	1870	314	2935
		0.0%	17.6%	17.2%	31.7%	41.2%	47.2%	35.5%
	Agree	0	148	327	332	1388	125	2320
		0.0%	25.8%	34.3%	21.7%	30.6%	18.8%	28.1%
	Disagree	0	153	314	262	562	128	1419
		0.0%	26.5%	32.9%	17.1%	12.4%	19.3%	17.2%
	S.Disagree	0	174	149	453	714	97	1587
		0.0%	30.2%	15.6%	29.6%	15.7%	14.7%	19.2%
	Missing	5223	7413	8573	5766	2273	813	30060
	TOTAL	0	576	954	1534	4535	664	8262
		100.0%	100.0%	100.0%	100.0%	100.0%	100.0%	

Comparative Politics

The survey indicates that 63.6% of Muslims living around the world believe that religious leaders should become more involved in politics. The number is considerably lower in communist/postcommunist countries, but it rises to 71.8% in Islamic countries. As a result, you will notice that the states of the Islamic world tend to be distinct from other categories of states around the world. For example, examine the types of government that are found in Islamic nations.[1]

> ➤ Data File: **GLOBAL**
> ➤ Task: **Cross-tabulation**
> ➤ Row Variable: **450) GOVERNMENT**
> ➤ Column Variable: **130) WORLDS.7**
> ➤ View: **Tables**
> ➤ Display: **Column %**

GOVERNMENT by WORLDS.7
Cramer's V: 0.494**

| | | WORLDS.7 | | | | | | | |
		Lib Democ	Comm/P-Com	NICs	LDCs	Islamic	Marginal	Micro	TOTAL
GOVERNMENT	Old Demos	24	0	15	16	3	2	5	65
		100.0%	0.0%	71.4%	44.4%	11.5%	8.0%	83.3%	37.8%
	Transition	0	22	4	10	2	10	1	49
		0.0%	64.7%	19.0%	27.8%	7.7%	40.0%	16.7%	28.5%
	One Party	0	8	1	4	5	1	0	19
		0.0%	23.5%	4.8%	11.1%	19.2%	4.0%	0.0%	11.0%
	Autocratic	0	0	1	6	14	3	0	24
		0.0%	0.0%	4.8%	16.7%	53.8%	12.0%	0.0%	14.0%
	Civil War	0	4	0	0	2	9	0	15
		0.0%	11.8%	0.0%	0.0%	7.7%	36.0%	0.0%	8.7%
	TOTAL	24	34	21	36	26	25	6	172
		100.0%	100.0%	100.0%	100.0%	100.0%	100.0%	100.0%	

If you look down the column labeled Islamic, you see that 53.8% of all nation-states having Islamic political systems are autocratic. By far, this is the highest percentage of any world classification. The next highest category, less developed countries, is only about 16.7% autocratic. The second most common category for Islamic states is one-party states (19.2%), and there are very few that are democracies or in transition to democracies.

The "autocratic" categorization of Islamic states hides the fact that there is a lot of variety in the political and legal systems of the Islamic world. If we limit our analysis to those nation-states with majority Islamic populations, we can see that there is still a lot of political variety within these nations.

> Data File: **GLOBAL**
> ➤ Task: **Univariate**
> ➤ Primary Variable: **453) ISLAMPOL**
> ➤ View: **Pie**

ISLAMPOL -- POLITICAL SYSTEM OF THE ISLAMIC WORLD (TWF, 2001)

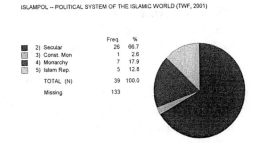

	Freq.	%
2) Secular	26	66.7
3) Const. Mon	1	2.6
4) Monarchy	7	17.9
5) Islam Rep.	5	12.8
TOTAL (N)	39	100.0
Missing	133	

The Islamic political model is distinct from other models of politics in that it does not seem to aspire to democratic forms of organization. But even in this unique category, the models of government are numerous. Secular Islamic states (66.7% of states with majority Muslim populations) seek to marginalize the Islamic faith and moderate its hold on politics while often retaining many of the legal requirements of the faith.

---

[1] There are a few instances in this chapter where the cross-tabulation result using the GLOBAL file produces the statement "Warning: Potential significance problem." This is to alert you that the statistical significance value may not be reliable due to the small number of cases used in the analysis. The likelihood of this warning message appearing will also increase as the number of cells in the table increases—the greater the number of cells, the more likely the warning message will appear. For our purposes in this chapter, we will often ignore this warning.

Another obvious form is monarchy, which comprises 17.9% of states if you combine absolute monarchies and constitutional monarchies. It should be noted that the Islamic countries are the only countries in the world to retain absolute monarchy as a form of political organization. Finally, in the latter part of the 20th century, several countries organized themselves as Islamic Republics. Most of these are concentrated in South Asia. Let's look at this same variable using the MAPPING task. Perhaps there is a regional pattern to the political organization of the Islamic states.

<table>
<tr><td align="right">Data File:</td><td>GLOBAL</td></tr>
<tr><td align="right">➤ Task:</td><td>Mapping</td></tr>
<tr><td align="right">➤ Variable 1:</td><td>453) ISLAMPOL</td></tr>
<tr><td align="right">➤ View:</td><td>Map</td></tr>
<tr><td align="right">➤ Display:</td><td>Legend</td></tr>
</table>

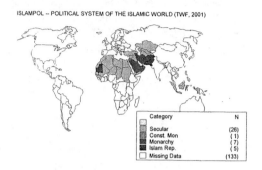

There doesn't seem to be much of a pattern, although three of the five Islamic Republics (Pakistan, Iran, and Afghanistan) are clustered in South Asia. At least two Islamic nation-states, Afghanistan and Iraq, are in the midst of transitions brought about by war with the United States. The continued Islamic character of these states is not disputed, but the particular form that Islam takes within the boundaries of these states is uncertain. In the case of Afghanistan, the United States, together with warlords throughout the country, overthrew the Taliban in December 2001 and established an interim authority to govern the country. The Taliban, and other Islamic fundamentalist groups throughout the Islamic world, advocate an unequivocally Islamic approach to politics. These groups want all legal norms and structures of the country to conform to Islamic law, which is derived from the Koran. The Koran outlines a structure for holy living in the context of culture, economy, politics, and the family. It remains to be seen whether or not the presence of U.S. forces in the Islamic world will serve to moderate this belief in these societies or further inflame devotion to this form of political Islam.

The most difficult decisions in Iraq and Afghanistan have involved how the state must decide on a constitution. There are essentially three types of legal systems that Iraq and Afghanistan could have chosen as they cast about for models of constitutional organization: those that are European in nature, those that are strictly Islamic, and those that include aspects of both. Let's examine the legal systems of Islamic countries.

<table>
<tr><td align="right">Data File:</td><td>GLOBAL</td></tr>
<tr><td align="right">Task:</td><td>Mapping</td></tr>
<tr><td align="right">➤ Variable 1:</td><td>454) ISLAMLEGAL</td></tr>
<tr><td align="right">➤ View:</td><td>Map</td></tr>
<tr><td align="right">➤ Display:</td><td>Legend</td></tr>
</table>

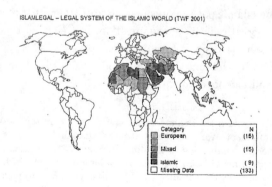

As the legend for the legal systems map shows, 15 countries with majority Islamic populations have adopted a European legal system, 15 have a mixed legal system, and 9 have an Islamic legal system. Unsurprisingly, 4 of the 5 states that have Islamic political systems also have Islamic legal systems. Many of the absolute monarchies, such as Saudi Arabia and the United Arab Emirates, also abide by Islamic law. On the other hand, the secular political systems like Egypt and Turkey abide by European legal traditions. But what is responsible for these differences? Let's check to see if the type of legal system is at all related to the percentage of Muslims in a society.

<table>
<tr><td align="right">Data File:</td><td>GLOBAL</td></tr>
<tr><td align="right">➤ Task:</td><td>ANOVA</td></tr>
<tr><td align="right">➤ Dependent Variable:</td><td>440) %MUSLIM</td></tr>
<tr><td align="right">➤ Independent Variable:</td><td>454) ISLAMLEGAL</td></tr>
<tr><td align="right">➤ View:</td><td>Graph</td></tr>
</table>

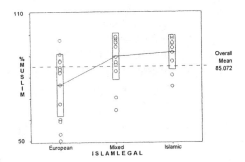

Mixed and Islamic legal systems are associated with the presence of a larger Muslim population. If you click on the [Statistics:Means] button, you will see the mean population of Muslims in a country for each legal system. In European legal systems, you see that the average population of Muslims is 76.3%. Mixed legal systems have 90.3% Muslims, and Islamic legal systems have 91.0%. The differences in mean Muslim population between these three types of legal systems are significant.

If the relationship between the percentage of Islamic faithful in a society and the type of constitution it adopts is causal (and we have no evidence here that it is), then it seems unlikely that the legal systems of Iraq and Afghanistan will be European in character. 98.1% of Afghanistan's population and 96% of Iraq's population are Muslim, so it seems unlikely that a legal system that advocates the separation of faith and politics will be deemed legitimate.

Let's examine the political rights and civil liberties of this group of countries more closely. One of the features of the Islamic world is its tendency toward authoritarianism. You remember from our examination of the type of government that there are very few democracies in the Islamic world. That would suggest that the political rights ratings would be relatively weak.

<table>
<tr><td align="right">Data File:</td><td>GLOBAL</td></tr>
<tr><td align="right">Task:</td><td>ANOVA</td></tr>
<tr><td align="right">➤ Dependent Variable:</td><td>312) POL RIGT04</td></tr>
<tr><td align="right">➤ Independent Variable:</td><td>130) WORLDS.7</td></tr>
<tr><td align="right">➤ View:</td><td>Means</td></tr>
</table>

Means, Standard Deviations and Number of Cases of Dependent Var: POL RIGT04 by Categories of Independent Var: WORLDS.7
Difference of means across groups is statistically significant (Prob. = 0.000)

	N	Mean	Std.Dev.
Lib Democ	24	1.000	0.000
Comm/P-Com	34	4.029	2.380
NICs	21	2.048	1.117
LDCs	36	3.694	1.564
Islamic	25	5.720	0.936
Marginal	25	4.800	1.848
Micro	6	1.500	0.837

The weak level of support for political rights in these countries is indicated by the relatively poor political rights ratings for the Islamic world. Notice that the average political rights rating for the Islamic world is 5.720. This is more than a full point worse than marginal states and almost two points worse than the average for communist/post-communist regimes. Since September 11th, 2001, liberal democratic nations in the West have become more fearful of the Islamic extremist movements that have become active in the 1990s. As a result, the liberal democracies of the West have been more willing to turn a blind eye to the repression of basic political rights and civil liberties perpetrated by more secular governments as they attempt to root out terrorism. Countries like Egypt, Saudi Arabia, Turkey, and Pakistan all have very active programs that oppose Islamic fundamentalism and many of these programs undermine basic human rights. Needless to say, the record of civil liberties in the Islamic world is almost as dismal as the rating for political rights.

Data File: **GLOBAL**
Task: **ANOVA**
➤ *Dependent Variable:* **305) CIV LIBS04**
➤ *Independent Variable:* **130) WORLDS.7**
➤ *View:* **Means**

Means, Standard Deviations and Number of Cases of Dependent Var: CIV LIBS04 by Categories of Independent Var: WORLDS.7
Difference of means across groups is statistically significant (Prob. = 0.000)

	N	Mean	Std Dev
Lib Democ	24	1.167	0.482
Comm/P-Com	34	3.676	2.026
NICs	21	2.381	1.117
LDCs	36	3.556	1.107
Islamic	25	5.280	0.936
Marginal	25	4.480	1.558
Micro	6	1.667	0.816

The average civil liberties rating for the Islamic world (5.280) is even worse than that for marginal states (4.480). Clearly the political rights and civil liberties ratings in the Islamic world are far from the robust protections guaranteed in liberal democracies (1.167) or even the modest efforts of NICs (2.381). But the continued strife in this region leaves us with limited hope that these ratings will be improved in the short run.

What about war? Are Islamic countries more likely or less likely to be involved in wars than other regions of the world?

Data File: **GLOBAL**
➤ *Task:* **Cross-tabulation**
➤ *Row Variable:* **458) WAR**
➤ *Column Variable:* **130) WORLDS.7**
➤ *View:* **Tables**
➤ *Display:* **Column %**

WAR by WORLDS.7
Cramer's V: 0.241*

WAR		Lib Democ	Comm/P-Com	NICs	LDCs	Islamic	Marginal	Micro	TOTAL
None		17	19	12	16	9	6	6	85
		70.8%	55.9%	57.1%	44.4%	34.6%	24.0%	100.0%	49.4%
Interstate		4	2	0	6	4	0	0	16
		16.7%	5.9%	0.0%	16.7%	15.4%	0.0%	0.0%	9.3%
Civil War		2	9	7	13	10	16	0	57
		8.3%	26.5%	33.3%	36.1%	38.5%	64.0%	0.0%	33.1%
Independnce		0	1	0	0	1	1	0	3
		0.0%	2.9%	0.0%	0.0%	3.8%	4.0%	0.0%	1.7%
Multi-type		1	3	2	1	2	2	0	11
		4.2%	8.8%	9.5%	2.8%	7.7%	8.0%	0.0%	6.4%
TOTAL		24	34	21	36	26	25	6	172
		100.0%	100.0%	100.0%	100.0%	100.0%	100.0%	100.0%	

In spite of the pan-Islamic ideal of a brotherhood of all Islamic countries, Islamic countries have experienced a great deal of interstate conflict. Between 1990 and 2002, 15.4% of Islamic states were involved in interstate conflict. Wars between Iran and Iraq and between Iraq and Kuwait explain much of this conflict, but the region is still not very secure, and a common faith in Islam has not helped it to overcome its conflicts. Civil wars have also plagued these countries. Afghanistan, Algeria, Sudan, Turkey, Iraq, and Egypt have all suffered tremendous loss of life as a result of internal strife.

If Islamic countries have higher levels of war, this must have an impact on their gross domestic product. You would expect that Islamic countries spend a greater percentage of their government budgets on armed forces. Let's see if this is the case.

Data File: **GLOBAL**
➤ Task: **Scatterplot**
➤ Dependent Variable: **325) MIL/BUDGET**
➤ Independent Variable: **440) %MUSLIM**
➤ View: **Reg. Line**

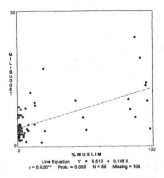

The correlation between government spending on the armed forces and the percentage of Muslims is very strong (r = 0.620**). Notice the cases located above the regression line and on the right side of the screen. These dots represent Islamic states that spend a lot of their budget for military purposes. If you click on these dots, you immediately notice that most are oil-producing nations. Thus, they have a great deal of money to spend on defense and are distinctly above the norm. Conversely, if you click on the cases located below the regression line and on the right side of the screen, you find Islamic countries that are not oil producers. Close scrutiny of this scatterplot suggests that oil production may, in fact, play a more important role in military spending than does the religious character of Islamic nation-states.

Speaking of oil wealth, let's analyze the characteristics of the Islamic economies using the ANOVA task.

Data File: **GLOBAL**
➤ Task: **ANOVA**
➤ Dependent Variable: **133) GDPCAP PPP**
➤ Independent Variable: **130) WORLDS.7**
➤ View: **Means**

Means, Standard Deviations and Number of Cases of Dependent Var: GDPCAP PPP by Categories of Independent Var: WORLDS.7
Difference of means across groups is statistically significant (Prob. = 0.000)

	N	Mean	Std.Dev.
Lib Democ	24	27710.982	8023.393
Comm/P-Com	31	6224.717	4503.199
NICs	19	9210.532	5065.291
LDCs	35	3025.699	2131.618
Islamic	18	5632.952	5103.788
Marginal	19	1554.439	1288.400
Micro	6	8137.019	5896.064

According to this table, the Islamic world has a relatively high GDP per capita ($5,633) compared to communist/postcommunist states ($6,225), LDCs ($3,026), and marginal states ($1,554). So, this average level of GDP per capita puts the nation-states of the Islamic world just behind NICs ($9,211) and microstates ($8,137). This probably seems appropriate given that some states in the Islamic world produce oil, but if we don't look carefully at averages we can easily be misled. In this case we would probably conclude that "Islamic states are pretty well off." Let's rank these states in terms of GDP per capita.

GDPCAP PPP: GDP per capita based on purchasing power parity (PPP) (constant 2000 international $). (WDI, 2005) Subset: WORLDS.7 Categories: Islamic

Data File: **GLOBAL**
➤ Task: **Mapping**
➤ Variable 1: **133) GDPCAP PPP**
➤ Subset Variable: **130) WORLDS.7**
➤ Subset Category: **Include: 5) Islamic**
➤ View: **List: Rank**

RANK	CASE NAME	VALUE
1	Bahrain	16512
2	Kuwait	15698
3	Oman	12833
4	Saudi Arabia	11994
5	Tunisia	6508
6	Iran	6277
7	Algeria	5550
8	Jordan	4063
9	Egypt	3669
10	Morocco	3393

From the ranking you will see that only 4 of the 26 states are actually above the mean GDP per capita of $8,675. All of these nations derive a substantial majority of their income from oil revenue. In fact, several countries are so far above the mean that they have made the average much higher than it would otherwise be. If you scroll down the list, you will see that there are ten countries that have a lower average GDP per capita than the average for LDCs, and nine that are lower than the mean GDP per capita for marginal states. The use of means can mask the variation within a variable, so we need to proceed with caution if we are attempting to draw conclusions based on means. Without a close examination of the mean GDP per capita, we might have concluded that the Islamic countries were on the verge of joining the NICs. Instead, we learned that oil production significantly skews the average level of wealth of the Islamic nations.

From the analysis of other groups of nation-states, we know that developing nations with a higher percentage of their economies devoted to industry tend to have a higher level of GDP. Let's see if this is true in the case of the Islamic world.

Data File: **GLOBAL**
➤ Task: **Scatterplot**
➤ Dependent Variable: **133) GDPCAP PPP**
➤ Independent Variable: **208) % INDUS $**
➤ Subset Variable: **130) WORLDS.7**
➤ Subset Category: **Include: 5) Islamic**
➤ View: **Reg. Line**

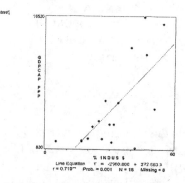

In the analysis of the Islamic world, GDP per capita is associated with the percentage of the economy devoted to industry (r = 0.710**). Oil production is considered an industrial activity, and thus we see that the countries in the upper right corner of the scatterplot—that is, the United Arab Emirates, Qatar, Brunei, Bahrain, and Kuwait—have the highest percentage of their economy devoted to industry, produce the most oil, and have the highest GDP per capita.

In this chapter we have learned that religion, warfare, and oil have all served to shape the unique politics of the Islamic world. In the worksheet section that follows, you will examine this complex relationship in greater detail.

Terms and Concepts

Koran
Political ideology of Islam
Islamic world characterisitics:

Political systems

Legal systems

Military spending

Political rights

Civil liberties

War

GDP per capita

CHAPTER

13

Workbook exercises and software are copyrighted. Copying is prohibited by law.

REVIEW QUESTIONS

Based on the first part of this chapter, answer True or False to the following items:

1. Most Islamic nations are in North Africa, South Asia, and the Middle East.　　　　　　　　T　　F

2. One reason that Islamic conceptions of politics are different from those of the West is that Islamic teaching does not separate religion and politics.　　　　T　　F

3. Due to the basic principles outlined in the Koran, the majority of Islamic states are democratic or in transition to democracy.　　　　T　　F

4. Absolute monarchy is the most common political system in countries with a majority of Muslims.　　　　T　　F

5. Of the countries in the Seven Worlds classification, Islamic states are among the least likely to have been at peace between 1990 and 2002.　　　　T　　F

6. The GDP per capita indicates that all of the states of the Islamic world have caught up with NICs.　　　　T　　F

EXPLORIT QUESTIONS

I. In the first part of this chapter, we explored some of the distinctive social, political, and economic characteristics of the Islamic world. Now let's look at the issue of social development.

> ➤ *Data File:* **GLOBAL**
> ➤ *Task:* **ANOVA**
> ➤ *Dependent Variable:* **33) POP GROWTH**
> ➤ *Independent Variable:* **130) WORLDS.7**
> ➤ *View:* **Graph**

7. Are the differences between Islamic countries and other countries significant with respect to population growth?　　　Yes　　No

8. List the three groups of countries with the highest population growth rates.

    COUNTRY TYPE   GROWTH RATE

    a. _____   _____

    b. _____   _____

    c. _____   _____

Now analyze the following variables to see what might be associated with the higher levels of population growth. Focus your comparison on the three groups of countries with the highest population growth rates, and print out the Means table for each of the analyses and attach it to your worksheet.

>   Data File: **GLOBAL**
>   Task: **ANOVA**
> Dependent Variables: **28) BIRTHRATE**
>   **44) FERTILITY**
>   **32) MORTAL<5**
>   **104) CONTRACEPT**
>   **34) DEATHRATE**
>   **108) IM:DPT**
>   **40) LIFE EXPCT**
> Independent Variable: **130) WORLDS.7**

9. If we compare the three groups of countries with the highest population growth rates (see your answer to Question 8), which of these three has the lowest birth rate? _____

10. Which of these three groups of countries has the lowest fertility rate? _____

11. Which of these three groups of countries has the lowest mortality rate for children under 5? _____

12. Which of these three groups of countries has the highest rate of contraceptive use? _____

13. Which of these three groups of countries has the lowest death rate? _____

14. Which of these three groups of countries has the highest immunization rate for diphtheria? _____

15. Finally, which of these three groups has the highest life expectancy rating? _____

16. Based on the analysis of these seven variables, which of the following seems to be the most plausible explanation for the Islamic countries' population growth rates?

    a.   High population growth rates are probably caused by high birth rates, high fertility rates, and low contraceptive use.

    b.   High population growth rates may also be caused by improving health conditions (such as more doctors, hospitals, immunization programs, and preventive health education) that result in higher rates of contraception, fewer infant deaths, and a lower death rate at all ages.

17. Based on the analysis of these seven variables, which of the following seems to be the more plausible explanation for the high population growth rates in the non-Islamic countries in your analysis?

    a.   High population growth rates are probably caused by high birth rates, high fertility rates, and low contraceptive use.

    b.   High population growth rates may also be caused by improving health conditions (such as more doctors, hospitals, immunization programs, and preventive health education) that result in higher rates of contraception, fewer infant deaths, and a lower death rate at all ages.

II. Now let's continue our comparison of the Islamic world with LDCs and marginal states in the areas of education and patterns of consumption. Complete the analyses and fill in the table below.

                   Data File: **GLOBAL**
                      Task: **ANOVA**
  ➤ *Dependent Variable:* **339) EDUC INDEX**
                                 359) LITYOUTH:F
                                 360) LITYOUTH:M
  ➤ *Independent Variable:* **130) WORLDS.7**

	EDUC INDEX	LITYOUTH:F	LITYOUTH:M
LDCs	_____	_____	_____
ISLAMIC	_____	_____	_____
MARGINAL	_____	_____	_____
SIGNIFICANT?	Y N	Y N	Y N

18. According to the analysis of the education index,

    a.   Islamic countries have a higher level of education than LDCs or marginal states.

    b.   Islamic countries have a lower level of education than LDCs or marginal states.

    c.   Islamic countries' education rate is about the same as the rate for LDCs, but higher than for marginal states.

    d.   Islamic countries' education rate is in between the rates for LDCs and marginal states.

19. According to the analysis of literacy rates among males,

    a. Islamic countries have a higher rate of male literacy than LDCs or marginal states.

    b. Islamic countries have a lower rate of male literacy than LDCs or marginal states.

    c. Islamic countries' literacy rate for males is about the same as the rate for LDCs, but higher than for marginal states.

    d. Islamic countries' literacy rate for males is in between LDCs and marginal states.

20. According to the analysis of literacy rates among females,

    a. Islamic countries have a higher rate of female literacy than LDCs or marginal states.

    b. Islamic countries have a lower rate of female literacy than LDCs or marginal states.

    c. Islamic countries' literacy rate for females is about the same as the rate for LDCs, but higher than for marginal states.

    d. Islamic countries' literacy rate for females is in between the rates for LDCs and marginal states.

Health and education are both indicators of social development, but patterns of consumption and use of technology can also tell us a lot about social and economic development.

> *Data File:* **GLOBAL**
> *Task:* **ANOVA**
> ➤ *Dependent Variables:* **178) CARS/1000**
> **188) COMPUTER**
> **205) TV/1000**
> **184) CELL PHN02**
> **185) WEB/1000**
> ➤ *Independent Variable:* **130) WORLDS.7**

	CARS	COMPUTER	TV	CELL	INTERNET
LDCS	_____	_____	_____	_____	_____
ISLAMIC	_____	_____	_____	_____	_____
MARGINAL	_____	_____	_____	_____	_____
SIGNIFICANT?	Y N	Y N	Y N	Y N	Y N

21. On the basis of the analysis of consumer products (cars and TVs), which of the following groups of states (among the groups in our analysis) seems to have the highest average levels of ownership of these products?

    a.   LDCs

    b.   Islamic world

    c.   marginal states

    d.   None of the above; the differences between groups of states is not significant.

22. On the basis of the analysis of technology (computers, cell phones, and Internet hosts), which of the following groups of states (among the groups in our analysis) seems to have the highest average levels of ownership of these products?

    a.   LDCs

    b.   Islamic world

    c.   marginal states

    d.   None of the above; the differences between groups of states is not significant.

III. So far we have examined features of the Islamic world at what is referred to as the "aggregate level" of analysis. This means that we have not examined the results of questions asked of actual citizens of an Islamic country. For years, survey data from these kinds of countries were difficult to obtain, but in the latest release of the World Values Survey we have the results of surveys conducted in Pakistan and Turkey. This has allowed political scientists to get answers to a number of questions that we have had about religion and politics in the Islamic world. First, let's see how important religion is across a variety of nation-states.

> ➤ *Data File:* **WVS02all**
> ➤ *Task:* **Cross-tabulation**
> ➤ *Row Variable:* **10) RELI IMPT?**
> ➤ *Column Variable:* **1) COUNTRY**
> ➤ *View:* **Tables**
> ➤ *Display:* **Column %**

23. Which two nation-states have the highest percentage of citizens who say that religion is very important?

COUNTRIES	PERCENTAGE
_____	_____
_____	_____

24. Which two nation-states have the highest percentage of citizens who say that religion is not at all important?

COUNTRIES   PERCENTAGE

_____   _____

_____   _____

25. Now use the data files from Pakistan (WVS02–PAKISTAN) and Turkey (WVS02–TURKEY) to determine which society is more secularized. Use the variable RELI IMPT? Which society is more secular? Please give your reason for coming to this conclusion.

IV. One of the issues that many of the Islamic faithful are concerned about is the encroachment of Western secular culture on Islamic values and the corruption of the young. Let's examine whether or not these concerns are well founded. Do the young consider religion to be as important as the old do? Is watching TV associated with lower levels of religious salience?

> ➤ *Data Files:*   **WVS02–PAKISTAN**
>   **WVS02–TURKEY**
> ➤ *Task:*   **Cross-tabulation**
> ➤ *Row Variable:*   **RELI IMPT?**
> ➤ *Column Variables:*   **AGE GROUP**
>   **WATCH TV (Pakistan only)**
> ➤ *View:*   **Tables**
> ➤ *Display:*   **Column %**

Fill in the table below.

AGE GROUP

	15–24	25–34	35–44	45–54	55+	V =	SIGNIFI-CANT?
PAKISTAN 4) RELI IMPT? % Very	_____%	_____%	_____%	_____%	_____%	_____	Y N
TURKEY 3) RELI IMPT? % Very	_____%	_____%	_____%	_____%	_____%	_____	Y N

WATCH TV

	NO TV	1–2 HRS	2–3 HRS	3+ HRS	CRAMER'S V	SIGNIFI-CANT?
PAKISTAN 4) RELI IMPT? % Very	_____%	_____%	_____%	_____%	_____	Y N

The relationship between TV watching and religiosity may speak to a wider pattern of backlash against the incursion of Western culture into the living rooms of Muslim families. Let's take a look at some further research that was done by the Pew Global Attitudes Project on this topic. The Pew Opinion research center asked Muslims around the world whether or not they believe that "religious leaders should play a larger role in politics."

➤ *Data File:* **PEW GLOBAL02**
➤ *Task:* **Cross-tabulation**
➤ *Row Variables:* **22) RELIG&POL**
➤ *Column Variable:* **2) WORLDS.7**
➤ *View:* **Tables**
➤ *Display:* **Column%**

For each result, fill in the percentaged results for the row that is specified in the table below. Also indicate whether the results are statistically significant (circle Y for Yes, N for No).

	COMM/ P-COM	NIC LDC	ISLAMIC	MARGINAL	CRAMER'S V	SIGNIFI-CANT?
22) RELIG&POL %Agree	_____%	_____%	_____%	_____%	_____	Y N

The degree to which one think that religious leaders should get more involved in politics may be a good indicator of non-Western Islamic worldview. Of this is the case, then we may hypothesize that those who believe that religious leaders should be more involved in politics are also opposed to Western influences like American television, music, and movies. Let's test this hypothesis with Muslims around the world.

Data File: **PEW GLOBAL02**
Task: **Cross-tabulation**
➤ *Row Variables:* **23) AMERICN TV**
➤ *Column Variable:* **22) RELIG&POL**
➤ *View:* **Tables**
➤ *Display:* **Column%**

	AGREE	DISAGREE	CRAMER'S V =	SIGNIFI-CANT?
23) AMERICAN TV % Agree	_____%	_____%	_____	Y N

Interpret the results of these analyses in the "*In Your Own Words*" section.

IN YOUR OWN WORDS

In your own words, please answer the following questions.

1. In the first part of this worksheet section, you analyzed indicators of social and economic development. Compare Islamic states, marginal states, and LDCs. Which group of countries seems to be "more developed" in economic and social terms? Be sure to support your answer with evidence.

2. What is the role that exposure to Western media might play in the process secularization in the Islamic world? Is there a relationship between a Muslim's worldview and that person's view of American media? As always, discuss your answer in light of the evidence.

CHAPTER **14**

ISLAM AND POLITICS IN PAKISTAN AND TURKEY

> *For whether we like it or not, whether it must be so or not, the world seems to be increasingly looking at the values and mores of the West and the values and traditions of Islam as mutually exclusive and confrontational.*
>
> BENAZIR BHUTTO,
> FIRST WOMAN PRIME
> MINISTER OF PAKISTAN

Tasks: Mapping, ANOVA, Cross-tabulation, Scatterplot
Data Files: PEW GLOBAL02, GLOBAL, WVS02all, WVS02–PAKISTAN, WVS02–TURKEY

The attacks on the World Trade Center and the Pentagon on September 11, 2001, vaulted little-known terrorist and Islamic fundamentalist Osama bin-Laden to the forefront of world media attention. His video tapes condemned Western occupation of Muslim holy lands, U.S. and Israeli hostility toward the Palestinians, and Western media values that are perceived as hostile to Islam. In 2004, the Pew Center published a survey that solicited the opinions of citizens inside and outside the Islamic world. The results were shocking to Westerners.

> ➤ *Data File:* **PEW GLOBAL04**
> ➤ *Task:* **Cross-tabulation**
> ➤ *Row Variables:* **9) BIN LADEN?**
> ➤ *Column Variable:* **1) COUNTRY**
> ➤ *View:* **Bar Stack**

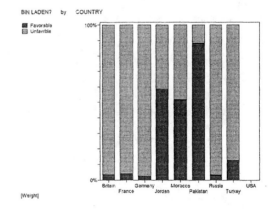

In Britain, France, Russia, and Germany the results are not surprising. Less than 4% of the population surveyed in these countries had a favorable view of Bin Laden. But in countries like Jordan and Morocco a majority of the population had a favorable view of Bin Laden. In Pakistan, a key U.S. ally in the war against Bin Laden's followers in neighboring Afghanistan, Islamic world Westerners were surprised to learn that 88.3% of the population has a favorable view of Bin Laden.

In the mid-1990s when this book was first published, the section on the Islamic world was viewed as a peculiarity. Scholars in Comparative Politics acknowledged that the politics, social arrangements of the Islamic world were unique, but most were not sure that it warranted its own category. However, one of the biggest changes since the end of the Cold War is the growing realization in the United States and Europe that the Islamic world is distinct from the West in almost every way; that powerful liberal democracies are dependent upon the Islamic world meet its energy needs; and that North Americans and Europeans know very little about the Islamic world.

Comparative polling evidence indicates that there is an enormous gap in mutual understanding between the Islamic world and the United States. The Pew 2004 survey also asked these populations whether or not the war on terror was a sincere effort to reduce international terrorism.

Data File: **PEW GLOBAL04**
Task: **Cross-tabulation**
➤ Row Variables: **10) US SINCERE**
➤ Column Variable: **2) WORLDS.7**
➤ View: **Tables**
➤ Display: **Column%**

US SINCERE by WORLDS.7
Weight Variable: WEIGHT
Cramer's V. 0.293**

		WORLDS.7			
		Lib.democ	Comm/P-Com	Islamic	TOTAL
US SINCERE	Sincere	1891	354	564	2808
		57.6%	38.5%	16.1%	36.4%
	Both	72	87	405	564
		2.2%	9.5%	11.5%	7.3%
	Insincere	1320	477	2538	4336
		40.2%	52.0%	72.4%	56.2%
	Missing	168	84	752	1004
	TOTAL	3283	918	3507	7708
		100.0%	100.0%	100.0%	

The majority of citizens in the liberal democracies believe that the war on terror is a sincere effort to reduce global terrorism, but this is not the case in the Islamic countries surveyed where only 16.1% believe the motives of the U.S. are sincere.

But it would be a mistake to conclude that all Islamic countries are similar in their view of Bin Laden or the United States. If you refer back to our first graph on Bin Laden, you will notice that in Turkey only 12.8% have a favorable opinion of Bin Laden, while in Pakistan the result is nearly the opposite with almost 90% of the population surveyed having a favorable view.

So let's focus our efforts on the comparison of two countries with large Islamic populations: Pakistan and Turkey.

➤ Data File: **GLOBAL**
➤ Task: **Mapping**
➤ Variable 1: **440) %MUSLIM**
➤ View: **Map**
➤ Display: **Find Case: Pakistan**
Find Case: Turkey

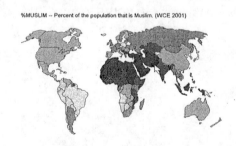

%MUSLIM -- Percent of the population that is Muslim. (WCE 2001)

PAKISTAN 96.1 (Rank: 11)

Select Pakistan in the map and you will see that the percentage of the Muslim population in Pakistan is 96.1% and that Pakistan is one of the Islamic states in our Seven Worlds categorization. Now select Turkey, and you will see that Turkey has an almost identical population of Muslims (97.2%). In the next few pages we will give a brief overview of these two countries as examples of nation-states in the Islamic world.

PAKISTAN

If you remember our discussion of the history of India in Chapter 10, then you know that Pakistan was part of the British colonial empire during the 18th, 19th, and early 20th centuries.

Data File: **GLOBAL**
Task: **Mapping**
➤ Variable 1: **455) IND DATE**
➤ View: **Map**
➤ Display: **Find Case: Pakistan**

IND DATE -- YEAR OF INDEPENDENCE (TWF 1996)

PAKISTAN 1947 (Rank: 101)

Pakistan gained its independence with the partition of the Indian colony by the British as the UK granted independence to the subcontinent. From 1947 to 1971, Pakistan was divided by India between East and West. After a nine-month civil war, East Pakistan achieved independence from Pakistan in 1971 and became the state of Bangladesh. During more than half of Pakistan's years of independence, military dictators ruled the country and overthrew the fledgling democratic process for its "failure to resist corruption." In 1990 and 1996, the first female prime minister of Pakistan, Benazir Bhutto, was sacked by the military for alleged corruption. The most recent military coup occurred in 1999 when democratically elected President Nawaz Sharif was deposed by the military chief of staff, General Pervez Musharraf. As a result of the military dominance and the weak political system, Pakistan's freedom ratings are quite poor.

Data File: **GLOBAL**
Task: **Mapping**
➤ Variable 1: **312) POL RIGT04**
➤ Variable 2: **314) POL RIGT95**
➤ View: **Map**
➤ Display: **Find Case: Pakistan**

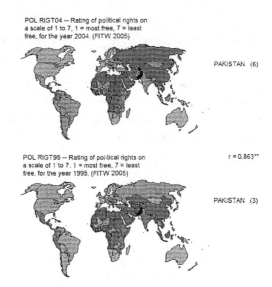

POL RIGT04 -- Rating of political rights on a scale of 1 to 7, 1 = most free, 7 = least free, for the year 2004. (FITW 2005)

PAKISTAN (6)

POL RIGT95 -- Rating of political rights on a scale of 1 to 7, 1 = most free, 7 = least free, for the year 1995. (FITW 2005)

r = 0.863**

PAKISTAN (3)

From the map you can see that Pakistan currently has a political rights rating of 6. The decline in political rights from 3 in 1995 to 6 in 2004 is the result of the military overthrow of the democratically elected government that occurred in Pakistan in 1999. This is also due, in part, to Musharraf's continued military dominance of the Pakistani government and a referendum on his leadership in 2002 that was perceived as a political sham by election observers. The condition of civil liberties in Pakistan is only marginally better.

Data File: **GLOBAL**
Task: **Mapping**
➤ Variable 1: **305) CIV LIBS04**
➤ Variable 2: **307) CIV LIBS95**
➤ View: **Map**
➤ Display: **Find Case: Pakistan**

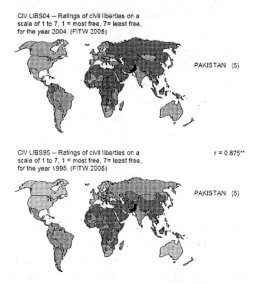

CIV LIBS04 -- Ratings of civil liberties on a scale of 1 to 7, 1 = most free, 7= least free, for the year 2004. (FITW 2005)

PAKISTAN (5)

CIV LIBS95 -- Ratings of civil liberties on a scale of 1 to 7, 1 = most free, 7= least free, for the year 1995. (FITW 2005)

r = 0.875**

PAKISTAN (5)

Freedom House rates Pakistan 5 out of 7 for its performance in the area of civil liberties. The judicial system in Pakistan consists of civil and criminal courts and a special Sharia court designed to enforce Islamic law. According to Freedom House,

> *The Sharia court enforces the 1979 Hudood Ordinances, which criminalize non-marital rape, extramarital sex, and several alcohol, gambling, and property offenses. . . . Anecdotal evidence suggested that police continued to routinely engage in crime; used excessive force in ordinary situations; arbitrarily arrested and detained citizens; extorted money from prisoners and their families; accepted money to register cases on false charges; raped female detainees and prisoners; committed extrajudicial killings; and tortured detainees, often to extract confessions.*

Between 1999 and 2001, Musharraf and the Pakistani government were under considerable pressure from the international community and the United States to return to democracy, but since September 11th, Pakistan has become an ally of the United States in the war against terror and criticism of political rights and civil liberties practices in the country has been muted.

While Pakistan's political rights and civil liberties conditions seem to be deterioriating, the opposite seems true in Turkey.

TURKEY

Turkey's political institutions have taken many forms over the past 2000 years, but the zenith of Turkey's geopolitical power was the Ottoman Empire, which lasted in various forms from 1288 until the modern state was formed in 1923 by the father of modern Turkey, Mustafa Kemal Ataturk.

Data File: **GLOBAL**

Task: **Mapping**

➤ Variable 1: **455) IND DATE**

➤ View: **Map**

➤ Display: **Find Case: Turkey**

IND DATE -- YEAR OF INDEPENDENCE (TWF 1996)

TURKEY 1923 (Rank: 112)

Since 1923, Turkey's pattern of governance looks remarkably similar to Pakistan's. Turkey has also experienced democratic governance with interludes of military intervention in 1960 and 1980. Most of the conflict between the military and elected officials has centered on the role of Islam in society, with the military insisting on a secular state compared to various Islamic groups that have sought to extend Sharia to Turkish society. Despite this conflict, and a civil war with a Kurdish minority in the 1990s, the condition of political and civil rights in Turkey has begun to improve.

Data File: **GLOBAL**

Task: **Mapping**

➤ Variable 1: **312) POL RIGT04**

➤ Variable 2: **314) POL RIGT95**

➤ View: **Map**

➤ Display: **Find Case: Turkey**

POL RIGT04 -- Rating of political rights on a scale of 1 to 7. 1 = most free, 7 = least free. for the year 2004. (FITW 2005)

TURKEY (3)

POL RIGT95 -- Rating of political rights on a scale of 1 to 7. 1 = most free, 7 = least free. for the year 1995. (FITW 2005)

r = 0.863**

TURKEY (5)

With a rating of 3, Turkey is now one of the freest political systems in the Islamic world, which represents real progress since it received a rating of 5 in 1995. Regular elections have occurred in Turkey since 1983, and the possibility of membership in the European Union has encouraged military leaders to refrain from direct control of the political process. By EU estimates the military still wields too much control on decisions related to security and foreign policy. The government has also been very slow in the recognition of Kurdish rights in the wake of the civil war with the Kurds. Despite these problems, Freedom House notes a general pattern of improvement in political rights since the mid-1990s. In the area of civil liberties, Turkey is about the same.

Data File: **GLOBAL**
Task: **Mapping**
➤ Variable 1: **305) CIV LIBS04**
➤ Variable 2: **307) CIV LIBS95**
➤ View: **Map**
➤ Display: **Find Case: Turkey**

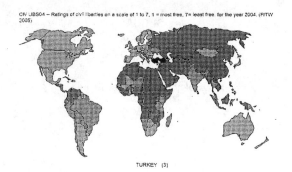

CIV LIBS04 -- Ratings of civil liberties on a scale of 1 to 7. 1 = most free, 7= least free. for the year 2004. (FITW 2005)

TURKEY (3)

Turkish civil liberties have improved over the past few years since it received a rating of 5 in 1995. In terms of civil liberties protections, Turkey is now among the most protected nation-states in the Islamic world. As recently as 2001 Turkey was sanctioned for serious violations of human rights, but, under increasing pressure because of its desire to join the European Union, Turkey has adopted a series of constitutional and legal reforms that have improved the civil liberties situation. In 2001, members of the Human Rights Association were beaten and detained, five of their branches were shut down, and 12 members were charged under the government's Anti-Terror Law. Interestingly enough, Islamists have also experienced persecution in Turkey as the government seeks to restrain Islamic fundamentalism. According to Human Rights Watch, the ban on women's wearing of the *hijab* (headscarf) was "applied with increasing severity against students and civil servants." Teachers and doctors were dismissed for wearing the headscarf on duty, and new regulations prohibited students from taking the June university examinations while wearing a *hijab*.

In Freedom House's 2005 report, Turkey was commended for its improvement of civil rights protections, although some significant concerns remain:

> *The constitution protects freedom of association, but broad language leaves room for restrictions despite some tightening through recent reforms. Some local officials use bureaucracy to prevent registration of demonstrations, and police regularly disperse peaceful public gatherings, often using excessive force. Nevertheless, civil society plays an increasing role in Turkish politics. Regulation of the activities and membership of nongovernmental organizations (NGOs) has relaxed with recent reforms, although restrictions remain, particularly for pro-Kurdish groups.*

In most of the earlier chapters we have walked you through an analysis of each country's social and economic features. In this chapter we save this analysis for you in the worksheet section. Now we will move on to an analysis of the condition of women in the Islamic world. This issue has received a great deal of attention in the international media and will be the focus of the remainder of this chapter.

Many international organizations argue that Islam treats women in a degrading fashion, limits their personal freedom, and even justifies acts of violence and torture toward women. The Islamic faithful counter that Western standards are used unfairly in the evaluation of women in Islamic countries. They claim that women are treated as special creations of God, who are not subjected to the pornography, obscenity, and immorality commonly found in the West. Some Islamic scholars even claim that poor treatment of women in many Islamic countries is not the fault of Islam, which treats all people with dignity, but is brought on by poverty and ignorance. We cannot resolve this debate here, but we can analyze the plight of women in Islamic states and compare it to the plight of women in other poor states (such as the marginal states) to see if they are worse off. We will hypothesize that unequal treatment of women is not due to the religious character of countries but, rather, to their level of development.

To examine this relationship, we'll use the "gender equity index," which combines a number of factors (such as education, employment opportunities, equal treatment) in the assessment of women's equality in a nation.

Data File: **GLOBAL**
Task: **Mapping**
➤ Variable 1: **342) GENDER EQ**
➤ View: **Map**
➤ Display: **Legend**

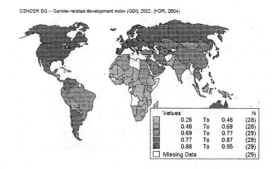

For this index, 0 is the lowest possible score and 1.0 is the highest score. The higher the score, the more gender equality exists. What we want to do is look at the relationship between the gender equity index and the WORLDS.7 variable.

Data File: **GLOBAL**
➤ Task: **ANOVA**
➤ Dependent Variable: **342) GENDER EQ**
➤ Independent Variable: **130) WORLDS.7**
➤ View: **Graph**

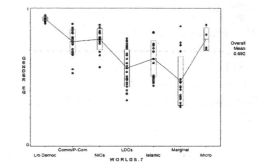

Carefully examine the graph line and think about how you might summarize the relationship between these two variables. What does this graph tell us? We can now easily compare different groups of countries. In this graph you can see that the first category, liberal democracies, has the highest level of gender equity. The average score for communist and postcommunist countries is below the liberal democracies and slightly below newly industrialized countries. And now, for the purpose of this analysis, notice that Islamic countries have a higher average level of gender equity than marginal states and LDCs. You can also look at these mean values themselves in the form of a table.

Data File: **GLOBAL**
Task: **ANOVA**
Dependent Variable: **342) GENDER EQ**
Independent Variable: **130) WORLDS.7**
➤ View: **Means**

Means, Standard Deviations and Number of Cases of Dependent Var: GENDER EQ
by Categories of Independent Var: WORLDS.7
Difference of means across groups is statistically significant (Prob. = 0.000)

	N	Mean	Std.Dev.
Lib Democ	24	0.928	0.015
Comm/P-Com	26	0.763	0.091
NICs	19	0.780	0.078
LDCs	33	0.566	0.138
Islamic	17	0.635	0.134
Marginal	20	0.471	0.182
Micro	4	0.781	0.083

If you are continuing from the previous example, select the [Means] button.

This table shows the actual mean value of gender equity within each category of the independent variable (Seven Worlds). As we can see, liberal democracies have the highest score, 0.928. The marginal states have the lowest mean gender equity score, 0.471. The Islamic nations are far below the liberal democracies, with a mean gender equity score of 0.635, but they are higher than LDCs (0.566) and marginal states. Finally, the differences between these states are significant.

The study of Islamic states as a distinctive group of countries is in a relatively early stage in political science. In the worksheet section, you will look at some of the first political science survey research conducted in those states.

Terms and Concepts

Public opinion of Bin Laden
Islamic World attitudes toward the U.S.
Civil liberties and political rights in Turkey and Pakistan
Gender equity index
Gender equity in Turkey and Pakistan

WORKSHEET

NAME:

COURSE:

DATE:

CHAPTER

14

REVIEW QUESTIONS

Based on the first part of this chapter, answer True or False to the following items:

1. Osama Bin Laden is viewed favorably by a majority of the population in European nation-states.   T   F

2. A majority of people living in the Islamic nations surveyed by the Pew Global Attitudes Project do not believe that the U.S. war on terrorism is sincere.   T   F

3. More than 90% of the populations of Turkey and Pakistan are Muslim.   T   F

4. The two Islamic countries in our study (Turkey and Pakistan) became independent nation-states in the 19th century.   T   F

5. Pakistan's record of political rights has improved since the 1990s.   T   F

6. Turkey's record of political rights has improved since the 1990s.   T   F

7. The differences in gender equity across the various types of countries are statistically significant.   T   F

EXPLORIT QUESTIONS

I. In the earlier part of this chapter we analyzed the variables for civil rights and civil liberties in the GLOBAL file, but we didn't examine the economic and social conditions of Turkey and Pakistan. Are these two countries above or below the Islamic world average for economic and social development? In the table below you will need to compare the results of the variable for each of the two countries to the Islamic world's average for that variable. Use the GLOBAL file and the ANOVA task to get the Islamic world average for each variable, and the MAPPING task to get the specific rating for Turkey and Pakistan.

Chapter 14: Islam and Politics in Pakistan and Turkey

273

ECONOMIC DEVELOPMENT

VARIABLE	ISLAMIC WORLD	TURKEY	PAKISTAN
135) GDP	_____	_____	_____
133) GDPCAP PPP	_____	_____	_____
208) % INDUS $	_____	_____	_____
157) TECH_EXP	_____	_____	_____

For the purpose of answering the following questions, assume that a nation-state must be higher than the Islamic world average on three out of four of the previous variables to be considered "more developed," or lower than average on three out of four to be "less developed." If a nation-state is only higher or lower on two out of four, then we will say that this nation-state is "as developed" as the Islamic world average.

8. According to the analysis of economic development variables, it seems that

    a. Turkey is more developed than the average Islamic country.

    b. Turkey is less developed than the average Islamic country.

    c. Turkey is as developed as the average Islamic country.

9. According to the analysis of economic development variables, it seems that

    a. Pakistan is more developed than the average Islamic country.

    b. Pakistan is less developed than the average Islamic country.

    c. Pakistan is as developed as the average Islamic country.

GENERAL SOCIAL DEVELOPMENT

VARIABLE	ISLAMIC WORLD	TURKEY	PAKISTAN
28) BIRTHRATE	_____	_____	_____
32) MORTAL<5	_____	_____	_____
40) LIFE EXPCT	_____	_____	_____
34) DEATHRATE	_____	_____	_____

In this analysis we will use the same criteria as for Questions 8 and 9. Except in the analysis of social development, health, and education, we will need to be more careful. Unlike our analysis of the economy, higher numbers do not always indicate greater development. Developed nations tend to have lower birth rates, lower infant mortality, higher life expectancy, and lower death rates. *Keep this in mind as you answer the following questions.*

10. According to the analysis of social development variables, it seems that

   a. Turkey is more developed than the average Islamic country.

   b. Turkey is less developed than the average Islamic country.

   c. Turkey is as developed as the average Islamic country.

11. According to the analysis of social development variables, it seems that

   a. Pakistan is more developed than the average Islamic country.

   b. Pakistan is less developed than the average Islamic country.

   c. Pakistan is as developed as the average Islamic country.

CONSUMPTION AND TECHNOLOGY

VARIABLE	ISLAMIC WORLD	TURKEY	PAKISTAN
178) CARS/1000			
205) TV/1000			
188) COMPUTER			
185) WEB/1000			

12. According to the analysis of consumption and technology, it seems that

   a. Turkey is more developed than the average Islamic country.

   b. Turkey is less developed than the average Islamic country.

   c. Turkey is as developed as the average Islamic country.

13. According to the analysis of consumption and technology, it seems that

   a. Pakistan is more developed than the average Islamic country.

   b. Pakistan is less developed than the average Islamic country.

   c. Pakistan is as developed as the average Islamic country.

II. In the preliminary part of this chapter, we saw that Islamic, marginal, and less developed countries have the lowest scores on the gender equity scale. These findings suggest that economic development and political instability may contribute more to the low levels of equality for women than the religious character of the country. But a gender equity index is just one variable that can be used to test this theory. Let's examine a few other items that assess gender equality in nation-states. As you answer these questions, be sure to refer back to the chapter discussion or gender equity.

> Data File: **GLOBAL**
> ➤ Task: **ANOVA**
> ➤ Dependent Variable: **347) %FEM.LEGIS**
> ➤ Independent Variable: **130) WORLDS.7**
> ➤ View: **Graph**

14. Based on the ANOVA graphic alone, do countries appear to differ in the percentage of women who are represented in the national legislature?   Yes   No

15. List the type of country that has the highest level of women's representation in the legislature.   _____

> Data File: **GLOBAL**
> Task: **ANOVA**
> Dependent Variable: **347) %FEM.LEGIS**
> Independent Variable: **130) WORLDS.7**
> ➤ View: **Means**

16. List the type of country that has the lowest level of women's representation in the legislature. Also indicate the mean (i.e., average) percentage of women in the legislature for that type.   Country Type _____

                                                          Mean Percentage _____

17. Are the differences between types of nations and the levels of women's representation in the legislature statistically significant?   Yes   No

18. Because Islamic countries have lower rates of female representation in the legislature than marginal countries and less developed countries, this suggests that the religious character of countries may play an important role in gender equity.   T   F

19. Based on these results, one might conclude that (circle one of the following)

   a. economic development appears to be more important than religious character in determining the level of female representation in the legislature.

   b. the religious character of nation-states appears to be more important than economic development in determining the level of female representation in the legislature.

   c. both the religious character of nation-states and their level of economic development seem to have an impact on the level of female representation in the legislature.

III. Islam does generally limit the opportunities for the advancement of women, but do women also endorse these limitations? Let's analyze the role that gender plays in attitudes toward gender roles.

> ➤ *Data Files:* **WVS02–PAKISTAN**
> **WVS02–TURKEY**
> ➤ *Task:* **Cross-tabulation**
> ➤ *Row Variables:* **EDUC BOYS**
> **MAN'S JOB**
> **TALK POLIT**
> **MEN POLS**
> ➤ *Column Variable:* **GENDER**
> ➤ *View:* **Tables**
> ➤ *Display:* **Column %**

Fill in the table below.

PAKISTAN

	MALE	FEMALE	V =	SIGNIFICANT?
5) EDUC BOYS				
% Strongly agree	_____%	_____%	_____	Y N
% Strongly disagree	_____%	_____%		
7) MAN'S JOB				
% Agree	_____%	_____%	_____	Y N
% Disagree	_____%	_____%		
8) TALK POLIT				
% Frequently	_____%	_____%	_____	Y N
% Never	_____%	_____%		
9) MEN POLS				
% Strongly agree	_____%	_____%	_____	Y N
% Strongly disagree	_____%	_____%		

TURKEY

	MALE	FEMALE	V =	SIGNIFICANT?
4) EDUC BOYS				
% Strongly agree	_____%	_____%	_____	Y N
% Strongly disagree	_____%	_____%		
6) MAN'S JOB				
% Agree	_____%	_____%	_____	Y N
% Disagree	_____%	_____%		
7) TALK POLIT				
% Frequently	_____%	_____%	_____	Y N
% Never	_____%	_____%		
8) MEN POLS				
% Strongly agree	_____%	_____%	_____	Y N
% Strongly disagree	_____%	_____%		

IN YOUR OWN WORDS

In your own words, please answer the following questions.

1. In terms of economic and social factors, are Pakistan and Turkey generally more developed or less developed than the average Islamic country? Use evidence to support your answer.

2. Review the results from the survey analyses of Pakistan and Turkey. In a brief paragraph, evaluate the following hypothesis: There is no relationship between the gender of an individual and that individual's support for more limited opportunities for women in education, the economy, and politics. Use evidence from your analysis to support your conclusions.

APPENDIX: VARIABLE NAMES AND SOURCES

The codebook of variable names listed here is abridged and does not include every data file. or an unabridged codebook please download it from the website: http://www.thomsonedu.com/politicalscience/Le_Roy. Select the "Student Companion Page" for the complete listing of all variables included in this data set.

Note for MicroCase users: These data files may be used with the MicroCase Analysis System. If you are moving variables from these files into other MicroCase files, or vice-versa, you may need to reorder the cases. Also note that files that have been modified in MicroCase will not function properly in Student ExplorIt.

◆ DATA FILE: AFRICA ◆

1) COUNTRY	30) CIV LIBS04	59) %FEM/LEG99
2) AREA	31) CIV LIBS2	60) LIT:FEM 90
3) POPULATION	32) EDUC INDEX	61) PRIM FEM
4) POP GROWTH	33) IL:FEM>15	62) GIRL LABOR
5) LIFE EXPCT	34) IL:FEM<25	63) LITYOUTH:F
6) HUM DEVLP3	35) FEM MINIST	64) PRIM FIN:F
7) EDUCATION	36) HEALTH_CAP	65) UNIV:FEM
8) MULTI-CULT	37) FEMECON1	66) SEC:FEM
9) %MUSLIM	38) HIV:PREV	67) PRIM:FEM
10) %CHRISTIAN	39) HIV:WOMEN	68) HIV:TEEN
11) FEM.PROF.	40) HIV:KIDS	69) HIV LOW
12) %FEM.LEGIS	41) MALARIA1	70) HIV HIGH
13) M/F EDUC.	42) TUBERC1	71) HIV PREG
14) GDP CAP 5	43) AID/CAP	72) CONDM MALE
15) % AGRIC $	44) REFUGEES	73) AID/EXPND
16) GDP	45) WAR2	74) AID/GNI
17) GDPCAP PPP	46) ASYLUM	75) POL RIGT95
18) GDP GROW	47) WORLDS.7	76) POL RIGT90
19) ECON DEVEL	48) CONDM FEM	77) POL RIGT85
20) FREEDOM	49) HIV KNOW:F	78) POL RIGT80
21) GOVERNMENT	50) HIV KNOW:M	79) POL RIGT75
22) IND DATE	51) SEX MUTIL	80) CIV LIBS95
23) IND PERIOD	52) SEXMUT URB	81) CIV LIBS90
24) COL.POWERS	53) SEXMUT RUR	82) CIV LIBS85
25) COL.MOTIVE	54) WOMEN WORK	83) CIV LIBS80
26) WAR	55) F/M EMPLOY	84) CIV LIBS75
27) WARDEAD	56) FEM POWER	85) GROW 90-99
28) POL RIGT04	57) %FEM.HEADS	86) CORRUPT 04
29) POL RIGHT2	58) %FEM/LEG95	87) CORRUPT 96

◆ DATA FILE: ASIA ◆

1) COUNTRY	4) POP GROWTH	7) EDUCATION
2) AREA	5) LIFE EXPCT	8) MULTI-CULT
3) POPULATION	6) HUM DEVLP3	9) GDP PPP

A1

◆ DATA FILE: ASIA cont'd ◆

10) GDPCAP PPP
11) ECON GROW
12) ECON DEVEL
13) GROW 90-99
14) INDUS GROW
15) ECON REG
16) SAVINGS
17) $ RICH 10%
18) FREE3
19) GOVERNMENT
20) IND DATE
21) IND PERIOD
22) NUKES
23) MISSILES
24) POP MIL

25) ARMD FORCE
26) KID THRIFT
27) NATL PRIDE
28) BIRTHRATE
29) ECON REG2
30) MIL/GNI
31) WORLDS.7
32) CHEM ARMS
33) BIOL ARMS
34) COMMUNIST
35) CIV LIBS
36) CIV LIBS04
37) POL RIGT
38) POL RIGT04
39) %MUSLIM

40) %CHRISTIAN
41) %CATHOLIC
42) %HINDU
43) %BUDDHIST
44) POL RIGT95
45) POL RIGT90
46) POL RIGT85
47) POL RIGT80
48) POL RIGT75
49) CIV LIBS95
50) CIV LIBS90
51) CIV LIBS85
52) CIV LIBS80
53) CIV LIBS75

◆ DATA FILE: CSES–GERMANY02 ◆

1) PTY VOTE
2) LT-RT-3
3) GENDER
4) EDUCATION
5) RELIGION
6) CH.ATTEND

7) RELIGIOUS?
8) UNION?
9) VOTE?
10) GOV PERF
11) POWER.DIFF
12) VOTE.DIFF

13) DEMOCRACY
14) CORRUPTION
15) POL INFO
16) WEIGHT

◆ DATA FILE: CSES–UK05 ◆

1) PTY VOTE
2) LT-RT-3
3) GENDER
4) EDUCATION
5) RELIGION
6) CH.ATTEND

7) RELIGIOUS?
8) UNION?
9) VOTE?
10) GOV PERF
11) POWER.DIFF
12) VOTE.DIFF

13) DEMOCRACY
14) CORRUPTION
15) POL INFO
16) WEIGHT

◆ DATA FILE: EUROPE ◆

1) COUNTRY
2) AREA
3) POPULATION
4) POP GROWTH
5) LIFE EXPCT
6) HUM DEVLP3
7) EDUCATION
8) MULTI-CULT
9) C.CONFLICT
10) GDP
11) GDPCAP PPP
12) GROW 90-99

13) FREE 3
14) GOVERNMENT
15) GOVERNMEN2
16) IND DATE
17) IND PERIOD
18) LEFT/RIGHT
19) INJUSTICE
20) COLD WAR
21) NATO
22) EUROPE
23) PRESS.FREE
24) CAP PUN 06

25) CAP PUN 95
26) ELECT96
27) ELECT04
28) ELECT FMLY
29) %TURNOUT
30) %TURNOUT2
31) %EXT.LEFT
32) STS.EXLEFT
33) %SOCIALIST
34) STS.SOCIAL
35) %SOC.DEM
36) STS.SOCDEM

◆ DATA FILE: EUROPE cont'd ◆

37) %GREEN
38) STS.GREEN
39) %LIBERAL
40) STS.LIBERL
41) %CENTER
42) STS.CENTER
43) %CH.DEM
44) STS.CHDEM
45) %CONSERVAT
46) STS.CONSRV
47) %EXT.RIGHT
48) STS.EXRIGH
49) %REGIONAL
50) STS.REGION

51) %OTHER
52) STS.OTHER
53) FREEDOM
54) COMMUNIST
55) ECON.FREE
56) REGULATION
57) COMM TYPE
58) CIV LIBS
59) POL RIGHT
60) GDPCAP PP3
61) GDP CAP GR
62) GDP GROW
63) DEBT %GDP
64) TRADE %GDP

65) POL INTRST
66) TALK POL
67) CIV LIBS04
68) CIV LIBS95
69) CIV LIBS90
70) CIV LIBS85
71) CIV LIBS80
72) CIV LIBS75
73) POL RIGT04
74) POL RIGT95
75) POL RIGT90
76) POL RIGT85
77) POL RIGT80
78) POL RIGT75

◆ DATA FILE: GLOBAL ◆

1) COUNTRY
2) AREA
3) COASTLINE
4) % ARABLE
5) %IRRIGATED
6) %PERM CROP
7) %MEAD-PAST
8) %FOR-WOOD
9) FOREST 90
10) FOREST 00
11) CEREAL
12) POPULATION
13) POP/FEM
14) POP/MALE
15) WOMEN/MEN
16) %POP FEM
17) % UNDER 15
18) %POP 15-64
19) % OVER 64
20) POPDENSITY
21) URBAN %75
22) UBRAN %02
23) URBAN %15
24) URBAN GROW
25) RURAL POP
26) RURAL GROW
27) AGE.DEPEND
28) BIRTHRATE
29) MORTL<5 60
30) MORTL<5 90
31) MORT<5 RED
32) MORTAL<5

33) POP GROWTH
34) DEATHRATE
35) DEATH 70
36) BIRTH 70
37) LIFE EX 70
38) LIFEX FEM
39) LIFEX MALE
40) LIFE EXPCT
41) LIFE FEM
42) FERTILE 60
43) FERTILE 90
44) FERTILITY
45) FERT RED1
46) FERT RED2
47) MORTAL FEM
48) MORTAL MEN
49) NETMIGRT
50) REMIT WORK
51) REMIT RCPT
52) ASSAULT
53) MURDER
54) RAPE
55) ROBBERY
56) BURGLARY
57) THEFT
58) DRUG
59) POLICE
60) PRISONERS
61) CAP PUN 95
62) CAP PUN 06
63) CIRRHOSIS
64) SUICIDE

65) AIDS
66) DRUGS
67) ALCOHOL IP
68) SPIRITS
69) BEER DRINK
70) WINE DRINK
71) CIGARETTES
72) ALCOHOL
73) UNDERNOUR
74) FOOD90-92
75) FOOD:00-02
76) DIET:79-81
77) DIET:00-02
78) FOOD_PROD
79) FOOD_PROD2
80) HIV:ALL
81) HIV:TEEN
82) HIV:PREV
83) AIDS:DEATH
84) AIDS:ORPHN
85) AIDS:LIFE
86) NOAID:LIFE
87) HIV:BLOOD
88) HIV:INFO
89) HIV:DRUGS
90) HIV:DISCR
91) HIV:CONDOM
92) HIV LOW
93) HIV HIGH
94) HIV PREG
95) CONDM MALE
96) CONDM FEM

97) HIV KNOW:M
98) HIV KNOW:F
99) HIV:WOMEN
100) %HIV/AIDS
101) ANTI RVIR%
102) TUBERCULOS
103) TUBE DEATH
104) CONTRACEPT
105) SEX MUTIL
106) SEXMUT URB
107) SEXMUT RUR
108) IM:DPT
109) IM:MEASLES
110) IM:MEASL<1
111) IM:DTP<1
112) IM:HEPB<1
113) %UNDRWGHT
114) ORPHAN ALL
115) DOCTORS
116) BIRTH HELP
117) ABORTION
118) ABORT LEGL
119) MOM HEALTH
120) AB. UNWANT
121) HUM DEV75
122) HUM DEV80
123) HUM DEV85
124) HUM DEV90
125) HUM DEV95
126) HUM DEV00
127) HUM DEV02
128) ECON DEVEL
129) THREEWORLD
130) WORLDS.7
131) QUAL. LIFE
132) CALORIES
133) GDPCAP PPP
134) GDPCAP PP3
135) GDP
136) GDP CAP GR
137) GDP GROW
138) GROW 90-99
139) DEBT %GDP
140) ACCNT_BAL
141) FDI NET
142) FDI_GROSS
143) GROSS SAVE
144) AID/EXPND
145) EXP/GDP

146) TRADE %GDP
147) TRADE GOOD
148) IMP/GDP90
149) IMP/GDP02
150) EXP/GDP90
151) EXP/GDP02
152) AGRIC EXP
153) AGRIC IMP
154) FOOD_IMP
155) FOOD EXP
156) FUEL EXP
157) TECH_EXP
158) TOUR %IMP
159) MFG EXP
160) MFG IMP
161) TOUR EXPE
162) PR_EXP90
163) PR_EXP02
164) MFG_EXP90
165) MFG_EXP02
166) COMMEXP
167) COMMIMP
168) POP<1$DAY
169) AID/GNI
170) AID/CAP
171) FOOD$INDEX
172) FOOD INDEX
173) KID WORK
174) WOMEN WORK
175) UNEMPL:UNV
176) $ RICH 10%
177) INEQUALITY
178) CARS/1000
179) PC/100
180) PHONES/100
181) TELP/P1 90
182) TELP/P1 02
183) CELL PHN90
184) CELL PHN02
185) WEB/1000
186) INTRNT:HST
187) PRODELECT
188) COMPUTER
189) RAIL LINES
190) RAIL PSNGR
191) RAIL PSG
192) RAIL TON
193) RAILT/CP
194) AUTO

195) AUTO/CP
196) COM VEH
197) COM V/CP
198) HWY VEH
199) HWY V/CP
200) ROADS/AREA
201) RADIO
202) RADIO/CP
203) RADIOS/CP
204) TELEVISN
205) TV/1000
206) NEWS/CP
207) % AGRIC $
208) % INDUS $
209) % SERVC $
210) %WORK AG
211) %WORK IN
212) F/M EMPLOY
213) H2O URB 90
214) H20 URB 02
215) H2O RUR 90
216) H2O RUR 02
217) H2O TOT 90
218) H2O TOT 02
219) SAN RUR 90
220) SAN RUR 02
221) SAN TOT 90
222) SAN TOT 02
223) SAN URB 90
224) SAN URB 02
225) ENERGY.DEP
226) CARB DIOX
227) ELEC/COAL
228) ELEC/HYDRO
229) ELEC/GAS
230) ELEC/NUKE
231) ELEC/OIL
232) NRG CONSUM
233) FUEL_IMP
234) ENERGY INV
235) $DIESEL
236) $GAS
237) WATER/CHEM
238) WATER/CLAY
239) WATER/FOOD
240) WATER/MET
241) WATER/OTHR
242) WATER/PULP
243) WATER/TEXT

244) WATER/WOOD
245) MA:CLIMATE
246) MA:BIODIV
247) MA:RIGHTS
248) MA:KYOTO
249) MA:POPS
250) MA:WTO
251) ENVIR.REG
252) ENVIR.EFF
253) ENVIR.CMPT
254) STABLE.POL
255) RULE.LAW
256) ENVIR.ACC
257) ELECTRIC80
258) ELECTRIC01
259) GREENHS80
260) GREENHS00
261) GLOBAL:EC
262) GLOBAL:PER
263) GLOBAL:TEC
264) GLOBAL:POL
265) GLOBAL
266) ECON.FREE
267) FREE.TRADE
268) PROPERTY
269) BUS.REGS
270) INF.MARKET
271) INCOME.TAX
272) CORP.TAX
273) CORP:ILL
274) CORP:LEG
275) CORP:ETHIC
276) PUB:ETHICS
277) LEGAL:EFF
278) CORP:GOV
279) CORRUPT%
280) COURT CF%
281) COURT %
282) CRIME %
283) ELCTRC %
284) FINANCE %
285) TAX_CORP
286) TAX_INDIV
287) TAX %
288) VOICE-A:04
289) VOICE-A:96
290) POL.STB:04
291) POL.STB:96
292) EFF.GOV:04

293) EFF.GOV:96
294) REGL.QT:04
295) REGL.QT:96
296) RULE LAW04
297) RULE LAW96
298) CORRUPT 04
299) CORRUPT 96
300) PRESS.FREE
301) INDX:CORPT
302) LEVEL:DEM
303) FREEDOM
304) LEVEL:CMPT
305) CIV LIBS04
306) CIV LIBS
307) CIV LIBS95
308) CIV LIBS90
309) CIV LIBS85
310) CIV LIBS80
311) CIV LIBS75
312) POL RIGT04
313) POL RIGHT
314) POL RIGT95
315) POL RIGT90
316) POL RIGT85
317) POL RIGT80
318) POL RIGT75
319) HEALTH EXP
320) HEALTH SP
321) EDUCAT SP
322) DEFENSE SP
323) ARMS EXP
324) ARMS IMP
325) MIL/BUDGET
326) MIL %GDP
327) MIL %LABOR
328) MIL PERSON
329) SEC_EDUCAT
330) P-SEC EDU
331) HEALTH RES
332) PUB EDUCAT
333) HEALTH_CAP
334) HEALTH_PRV
335) PUB_HEALTH
336) HEALTH_TOT
337) HEALTH PAY
338) M/F EDUC.
339) EDUC INDEX
340) PUB HEAL90
341) PUB HEAL01

342) GENDER EQ
343) FEM POWER
344) %FEM.HEADS
345) %FEM/LEG95
346) %FEM/LEG99
347) %FEM.LEGIS
348) LIT:MALE90
349) LIT:FEM 90
350) NET USERS
351) PRIM MALE
352) PRIM FEM
353) KID LABOR
354) BOY LABOR
355) GIRL LABOR
356) KID WED
357) KIDWED URB
358) KIDWED RUR
359) LITYOUTH:F
360) LITYOUTH:M
361) LITYOUTH
362) PRIM FIN:F
363) PRIM FIN:M
364) PRIM FIN
365) PUPILTEACH
366) UNIVRSTY
367) UNIV:FEM
368) UNIV:MALE
369) SEC:FEM
370) SEC:MALE
371) PRIM:FEM
372) PRIM:MALE
373) PRIM.SCH
374) TRAINTEACH
375) EDUCATION
376) ANTI-SEM.
377) ANTI-FORGN
378) ANTI-MUSLM
379) RACISM
380) ANTI-GAY
381) SPOUSE SEX
382) HAPPY SEX?
383) CHORES?
384) FRIENDS?
385) LEISURE?
386) WORK IMPT?
387) UNIONIZED?
388) UNIONS?
389) MERIT $
390) POOR LAZY

391) INJUSTICE
392) WORKER OWN
393) TRUST?
394) TRUST CITZ
395) CHEAT GOVT
396) CHEAT BUS$
397) CHEAT TAX
398) TAKE BRIBE
399) LYING
400) HOT BUY
401) LITTERING
402) COP CONFID
403) EX-MARITAL
404) MINOR SEX
405) GAY SEX
406) PROSTITUTE
407) RELIG HOME
408) VOL@CHURCH
409) LIFESATIS
410) TWOPARENTS
411) SEX FREE
412) HOUSEWIFE
413) TWO INCOME
414) MEN POLLDR
415) WOMEN EARN
416) BOY EDUC
417) CHURCH CON
418) GOV CONF
419) LIFE MEAN
420) GOOD EVIL
421) RELIG KID

422) GOD BELIEF
423) AFTR DEATH
424) SOUL
425) DEVIL
426) HELL
427) HEAVEN
428) SIN
429) RELIG COMF
430) DO SPORTS?
431) VERY HAPPY
432) NATL PRIDE
433) WILL FIGHT
434) FAMILY IMP
435) KID MANNER
436) KID INDEPN
437) KID OBEY
438) KID THRIFT
439) INTERESTED
440) %MUSLIM
441) %CHRISTIAN
442) %CATHOLIC
443) %HINDU
444) %BUDDHIST
445) %JEWISH
446) JEHOV.WITN
447) MORMONS
448) ELECT04
449) ELECT FMLY
450) GOVERNMENT
451) COMMUNIST
452) COMMTYPE00

453) ISLAMPOL
454) ISLAMLEGAL
455) IND DATE
456) IND PERIOD
457) NO CORRUPT
458) WAR
459) WAR2
460) NUKES
461) MULTI-CULT
462) C.CONFLICT
463) REGION
464) REGION2
465) POPGR15-20
466) POPGR10-15
467) POPGR05-10
468) POPGR95-00
469) POPGR90-95
470) PETITION
471) SIT-IN
472) BOYCOTT
473) DEMONSTR
474) STRIKE
475) %TURNOUT
476) POL INTRST
477) TALK POL
478) ECON.FREE2
479) COMMTYPE06
480) FREEDOM2
481) IND GROWTH
482) GDP CAP 5

• DATA FILE: HISTORY •

1) Date
2) IND NATION
3) IND/DECADE
4) %COMMGM
5) %COMMFR
6) %COMMSW
7) %SOCIALFR
8) %LABOURUK
9) %SOCDEMSW
10) %SOCDEMGM
11) %GREENFR
12) %GREENSW
13) %GREENGM
14) %FREEDEMGM

15) %LIBRLSW
16) %LIBDEMUK
17) STS.LIB.UK
18) %CENTERFR
19) %CENTERSW
20) %CHDEMSW
21) %CHDEMGM
22) %CONSERVFR
23) %CONSERVSW
24) %CONSERVUK
25) %EXRIGHTFR
26) %EXRIGHTGM
27) INFMRT.USW
28) INFMRT.MAU

29) INFMRT.EGY
30) INFMRT.SAB
31) INFMRT.SAW
32) %LIBDEM.JA
33) %SOCIAL.JA
34) %CLNGOV.JA
35) PROTEST.JA
36) PROTEST.US
37) RIOTS.JA
38) RIOTS.US
39) RIOTS.GM
40) PROTEST.GM
41) GROW.EASIA
42) GROW.WORLD

♦ DATA FILE: HISTORY cont'd ♦

43) GROW.SASIA
44) GROW.AFRIC
45) GROW.MEAST
46) GROW.LATIN
47) GROW.EU/CA
48) GR:RUSSIA
49) GR:POLAND

50) GR:S.KOREA
51) GR:INDIA
52) GDP:KOREA
53) GDP:INDIA
54) GDP:EASIA
55) GDP:SASIA
56) ARM CONF

57) WARDEAD:GL
58) WARDEAD:AF
59) WARDEAD:AM
60) WARDEAD:SA
61) WARDEAD:EA
62) WARDEAD:EU
63) WARDEAD:ME

♦ DATA FILE: LATIN ♦

1) COUNTRY
2) AREA
3) POPULATION
4) POP GROWTH
5) LIFE EXPCT
6) HUM DEVLP3
7) EDUCATION
8) MULTI-CULT
9) GDP PPP
10) GDPCAP PPP
11) ECON GROW
12) ECON DEVEL
13) % AGRIC $
14) $ RICH 10%
15) FORESTLAND
16) FREEDOM

17) IND DATE
18) IND PERIOD
19) COLONIZE
20) LANDOWNERS
21) PAST LAND
22) LANDDISPUT
23) INSURGENCY
24) HUMAN RTS
25) VIOLENCE
26) TERRORISM
27) POL RIGT04
28) POL RIGHT
29) CIV LIBS04
30) CIV LIBS
31) GOVT 1978
32) DEBT PAYMT

33) EXT. DEBT
34) WORLDS.7
35) FREEDOM2
36) GOVERNMENT
37) CIV LIBS75
38) POL RIGT75
39) CORRUPT 04
40) CORRUPT 96
41) PRESS.FREE
42) INDX:CORPT
43) DEATH 70
44) BIRTH 70
45) LIFE EX 70
46) BIRTHRATE

♦ DATA FILE: PEW GLOBAL02 ♦

1) COUNTRY
2) WORLDS.7
3) CORRUPTLDR
4) CORRPTGOVT
5) HAVE ELCTR
6) HAVE TV
7) HAVE WATER
8) HAVETOILET
9) HAVE CAR

10) GLOBALZATN
11) ANTI-GLOBL
12) US-TERROR
13) IM:CRITGOV
14) CRIT GOV
15) ETHN CONF
16) MORALDEC
17) WATERQUAL
18) TERRORISM

19) HIV/AIDS
20) SCHOOLQUAL
21) LEAVECNTRY
22) RELIG&POL
23) AMERICN TV
24) RELIG&POL2
25) WEIGHT

♦ DATA FILE: PEW GLOBAL04 ♦

1) COUNTRY
2) WORLDS.7
3) GENDER
4) AGE GROUP6
5) OPINIONUS

6) OPIN AMER
7) UN APPROV
8) GW BUSH?
9) BIN LADEN?
10) US SINCERE

11) US WAR&OIL
12) USWAR&MSLM
13) USWAR&ISRL
14) USWAR&RULE
15) WEIGHT

◆ DATA FILE: PGAP02-GHANA ◆

1) ETHNICITY
2) GENDER
3) ETHNOCENTR
4) INTL ORGS
5) NGOS
6) GOVTCONTRL
7) GOVT DUTY
8) GOVTWASTE
9) BENEFITALL
10) RELIG&GOV
11) CORRUPTLDR
12) OURCOUNTRY
13) CORRPTGOVT
14) WEIGHT

◆ DATA FILE: PGAP02-NIGERIA ◆

1) ETHNICITY
2) GENDER
3) ETHNOCENTR
4) IGBO GRP
5) HAUSA GRP
6) YORUBA GRP
7) INTL ORGS
8) NGOS
9) GOVTCONTRL
10) GOVT DUTY
11) GOVTWASTES
12) BENEFITALL
13) RELIG&GOVT
14) CORRUPTLDR
15) OURCOUNTRY
16) CORRPTGOVT
17) WEIGHT

◆ DATA FILE: WVS02all ◆

1) COUNTRY
2) WORLDS 7
3) TRUST PEOP
4) TRUST CITZ
5) LT-RT-3
6) INCOME EQ2
7) SOCIET CHG
8) CITZ:BRIBE
9) PRE REGIME
10) RELI IMPT?
11) DEMOCRACY
12) DEM DEVLP
13) DEM:ECONOM
14) DEM:BETTER
15) INTRST POL
16) JUNTA

◆ DATA FILE: WVS02-ANALYZER ◆

1) COUNTRY
2) PROUD
3) TRUSTPEOP2
4) DEMOCRACY
5) DEM DEVLP
6) DEM:ECONOM
7) DEM:DECIDE
8) DEM:ORDER
9) DEM:BETTER
10) CHEAT TAX
11) BRIBERY
12) HOMOSEXUAL
13) PROSTITUTE
14) ABORTION
15) DIVORCE
16) EUTHANASIA
17) SUICIDE
18) TRUST PEOP
19) LT-RT-3
20) GENDER
21) AGE GROUP3
22) OBJ CLASS
23) INCOME LEV
24) EDUCATION
25) WORLDS 7

◆ DATA FILE: WVS02-BRAZIL ◆

This is a sample of a typical WVS country file. To conserve space, the author has prepared an unabridged codebook with every country file included with the textbook at:
http://www.thomsonedu.com/politicalscience/Le_Roy
Select the "Student Companion Page" for the complete listing of all variables included in this data set.

1) FAM IMPT?
2) FRND IMPT?
3) LEIS IMPT?
4) POLI IMPT?
5) WORK IMPT?
6) RELI IMPT?
7) HAPPY?
8) HEALTH?
9) RSPECT PAR

10) PAR RESPON
11) IND. KIDS
12) HARD WORK
13) RESPONSIBL
14) IMAGINE
15) TOLERANCE
16) KID THRIFT
17) DETERMINAT
18) RELIG FTH
19) UNSELFISH
20) OBEDIENCE
21) MANNERS
22) TRUST PEOP
23) TALK POLIT
24) ENV: TAX
25) ENV:PRICES
26) ENV:INT'L
27) ENV: WATER
28) ENV:MEETGS
29) ENV:GIVE$
30) ENV/ECON
31) NAT-HUM
32) OTHER/OWN
33) VOL:CHURCH
34) VOL:SPORT
35) VOL:ART/ED
36) VOL:UNION
37) VOL:PARTY
38) VOL:ENVIRO
39) VOL:PROF
40) VOL:CHAR
41) VOL:OTHER
42) NB:CRIME
43) NB:RACE
44) NB:DRINKER
45) NB:UNSTABL
46) NB:MIGRANT
47) NB:AIDS
48) NB:ADDICTS
49) NB:HOMOSEX
50) NB:DIF REL
51) NB:EXTREME
52) MAN'S JOB
53) JOBS NATIV
54) $ SATIS
55) LIFE SATIS
56) FREEDOM
57) WK:LEISURE
58) IMP:JOB1

59) IMP:JOB2
60) JB:GOODPAY
61) JB:PRESSUR
62) JB:SECURE
63) JB:RESPECT
64) JB:GOODHRS
65) JB:INITIAT
66) JB:HOLIDAY
67) JB:ACHIEVE
68) JB:RESPON
69) JB:INTERES
70) JB:ABILIT
71) SECY PAY
72) BUS MGMT
73) FOLLOW INS
74) WK:SAT RES
75) WK:GOALS
76) WK: LATE
77) IDEAL FAM
78) BOTH PAR
79) WOM CHILD
80) MAR OUTDAT
81) SNGL MOM
82) SEX FREE?
83) BOY/GIRL
84) PAR PROUD
85) FRIENDS
86) WORKNG MOM
87) HWIFE FILL
88) DBL INCOME
89) MEN POLS
90) EDUC BOYS
91) WOMEN EARN
92) NATLGOAL1A
93) NATLGOAL1B
94) NATLGOAL2A
95) NATLGOAL2B
96) NATLGOAL3A
97) NATGOAL3B
98) FIGHT WAR?
99) LESS MONEY
100) LESS WORK
101) MORE TECH
102) AUTH RESPC
103) MORE FAM
104) SCIENCE OK
105) INTRST POL
106) SIGN PETN
107) BOYCOTT

108) DEMONSTR
109) STRIKE
110) OCCPY BLDG
111) LFT-RGHT
112) SOCIET CHG
113) INCOME EQ
114) BUS OWNSHP
115) RESPONSIB
116) COMPETITN
117) HARD WK
118) WEALTH ACC
119) MAK CHANGE
120) NEW vs OLD
121) IMPORTS
122) IMMIGRANTS
123) CONF:CHRCH
124) CONF:ARMY
125) CONF:PRESS
126) CONF:UNION
127) CONF:COPS
128) CONF:PARL
129) CONF:CIVIL
130) CONF:TV
131) CONF:GOVT
132) CONF:PARTY
133) CONF:COMP.
134) CONF:ENV
135) CONF:WOMEN
136) CONF:LEGAL
137) CONF:UN
138) CONF:MERC.
139) PRE REGIME
140) NOW REGIME
141) FUT REGIME
142) AUTOCRAT
143) TECHNOCRAT
144) JUNTA
145) DEMOCRACY
146) DEM:ECONOM
147) DEM:DECIDE
148) DEM:ORDER
149) DEM:BETTER
150) INCUMB SAT
151) WHO RULES?
152) PV:FOR AID
153) PV:HOWMCH?
154) PV:WHYNEED
155) PV:ESCAPE
156) AID OTHER

157) WATCH TV
158) LL GROUP
159) LL OFFICE
160) LL TEACH?
161) LL DEMONST
162) CORRUPTION
163) VIOLENCE
164) THINK LIFE
165) GOOD/EVIL
166) MEMB RELIG
167) WHCH RELIG
168) ATTND SERV
169) RAISD RELG
170) RELIGIOUS?
171) BLV:GOD
172) BLV:DTH/LF
173) BLV:SOUL
174) BLV:HELL
175) BLV:HEAVEN
176) BLV:SIN
177) BLV:DEVIL
178) GOD IMPT?

179) COMF:RELG
180) BENEFITS
181) AVOID FARE
182) CHEAT TAX
183) BRIBERY
184) HOMOSEXUAL
185) PROSTITUTE
186) ABORTION
187) DIVORCE
188) EUTHANASIA
189) SUICIDE
190) HOT GOODS
191) GEO GROUP1
192) GEO GROUP2
193) PROUD
194) WHEREBORN?
195) YR. ARRIVE
196) GENDER
197) MAR. STATS
198) CHILDREN?
199) AGE EDUC 2
200) FORMAL EDU

201) EDUCATION
202) LIVEPARENT
203) EMPLOYMENT
204) OCCUPATION
205) WHO CWE?
206) CWE EMPLOY
207) CWE OCCUP
208) SAVINGS
209) CLASS
210) INCOME
211) MAT/PMAT12
212) MAT/PMAT4
213) AUTON-4
214) AGE
215) AGE GROUP3
216) AGE GROUP6
217) ED LEVELS
218) INCOME LEV
219) WHCH REL 2
220) WHCH CHRST

SOURCES

AFRICA

The data in AFRICA are from a variety of sources. The variable description for each variable uses the following abbreviations to indicate the source.

ALLEN: Paul Allen, *Student Atlas of World Politics*, 3rd edition, Connecticut: Dushkin/McGraw-Hill, 1998.

FITW: *Freedom in the World*, published annually by Freedom House, www.freedomhouse.org

HDR: *Human Development Report*, published annually by the United Nations Development Program.

KIDRON & SEGAL: *State of the World Atlas*, 5th edition, London: Penguin, 1995.

PAWP: Dan Smith, *Penguin Atlas of War and Peace*, 2nd edition, London: Penguin, 2003.

SAUS: *Statistical Abstract of the United States*, published annually by the U.S. Department of Commerce.

SMITH: *State of the World Atlas*, 7th edition, London: Penguin, 2003.

STARK: Coded and calculated by Rodney Stark.

SWPA: Dan Smith, *The State of War and Peace Atlas*, 1st edition, London: Penguin, 1997.

TWF: *The World Factbook*, published annually by the Central Intelligence Agency.

TWW: *The World's Women*, published by the United Nations, 1995.

WCE: *World Christian Encyclopedia*, David B. Barrett, editor, Oxford University Press, 2001.

WDI: *World Development Indicators*, published annually by the World Bank.

ASIA

The data in ASIA are from a variety of sources. The variable description for each variable uses the following abbreviations to indicate the source.

ALLEN: Paul Allen, *Student Atlas of World Politics*, 3rd edition, Connecticut: Dushkin/McGraw-Hill, 1998.

CNS: Center for Non-proliferation Studies, Monterey Institute for International Studies. http://cns.miis.edu.

FITW: *Freedom in the World*, published annually by Freedom House.

HDR: *Human Development Report*, published annually by the United Nations Development Program.

KIDRON & SEGAL: *State of the World Atlas*, 5th edition, London: Penguin, 1995.

SAUS: Statistical Abstract of the United States, published annually by the US Department of Commerce.

SMITH: *State of the World Atlas*, 7th edition, London: Penguin, 2003

STARK: Coded and calculated by Rodney Stark.

SWPA: Dan Smith, *The State of War and Peace Atlas*, 1st edition, London: Penguin, 1997.

TWF: *The World Factbook*, published annually by the Central Intelligence Agency.

WCE: *World Christian Encyclopedia*, David B. Barrett, editor, Oxford University Press, 2001.

WDI: *World Development Indicators*, published annually by the World Bank.

WDR: *World Development Report*, published annually by the World Bank.

CSES

The data in all files with the prefix CSES come from data collected by the Comparative Study of Electoral Systems Study Group. The Comparative Study of Electoral Systems (www.cses.org). CSES MODULE 2 FOURTH ADVANCE RELEASE [dataset]. April 10, 2006.

These materials are based on work supported by the American National Science Foundation (www.nsf.gov) under grants SES-0112029 and SES-0451598, the University of Michigan, and the many organizations that fund election studies by CSES collaborators.

Any opinions, findings, and conclusions or recommendations expressed in these materials are those of the author(s) and do not necessarily reflect the views of the funding organizations. Thanks to David Howell, Director of Studies. Selected variables have been collapsed or recoded by the author.

EUROPE

The data in EUROPE are from a variety of sources. The variable description for each variable uses the following abbreviations to indicate the source.

AI: *Amnesty International Report,* published annually.

EU: European Union Official website http://europa.eu/abc/index_en.htm

FITW: *Freedom in the World*, published annually by Freedom House www.freedomhouse.org

HDR: *Human Development Report*, published annually by the United Nations Development Program.

HF: *The Index of Economic Freedom*, published annually by The Heritage Foundation and The Wall Street Journal.

IDEA: Institute for Democracy and Electoral Assistance. Turnout data are from the institute's *Global Report on Political Participation*. (Stockholm, 2006) Electoral system data and coding from *The International Handbook of Electoral System Design* (Stockholm, 2006).

KIDRON & SEGAL: *State of the World Atlas*, 5th edition, London: Penguin, 1995.

LE ROY: Coded and calculated by Michael K. Le Roy. The number of parties is coded and calculated by counting the number of parties that received greater than 5% at the last election.

NATO: "Euro-Atlantic Partnership Council Member Countries, January, 1998," http://www.nato.int/pfp/partners.htm.

P&E: Parties and Elections in Europe, Wolfram Nordsieck, University of Dusseldorf, Germany. http://www.parties-and-elections.de/index.html. Coding into party categories by Michael K. Le Roy.

SAUS: *Statistical Abstract of the United States*, published annually by the U.S. Department of Commerce.

STARK: Coded and calculated by Rodney Stark.

TWF: *The World Factbook*, published annually by the Central Intelligence Agency.

UNMID: United Nations Millennium Indicators, 2004.

UNPD: United Nations Population and Development Indicators.

UNSD: *United Nations Statistical Database*, published annually.

WDI: *World Development Indicators*, published annually by the World Bank.

WVS: World Values Study Group, WORLD VALUES SURVEY, 1981–1984, 1990–1993, 1995–1997, AND 2000–2002 (Computer files). ICPSR version. Ann Arbor, MI: Institute for Social Research (producer), 2004. Ann Arbor, MI: Inter-university Consortium for Political and Social Research (distributor), 2004.

GLOBAL

The data in GLOBAL are from a variety of sources. The variable description for each variable uses the following abbreviations to indicate the source.

AQUASTATS: Food and Development Organization of the United Nations Annual Statistics on Food and Water.

CA: *Church Almanac*, published biannually by the Salt Lake City Desert News.

FAO: Food and Agriculture Organization of the United Nations, *Food Security Report*, published annually.

FITW: *Freedom in the World*, published annually by Freedom House www.freedomhouse.org

HDR: *Human Development Report*, published annually by the United Nations Development Program.

HF: *The Index of Economic Freedom*, published annually by The Heritage Foundation and the Wall Street Journal.

IBWR: *Illustrated Book of World Rankings*, 2001.

IDB: International Data Base, 1998, U.S. Bureau of the Census.

IDEA: Institute for Democracy and Electoral Assistance. Turnout data are from the institute's *Global Report on Political Participation*. (Stockholm, 2006). Electoral system data and coding from *The International Handbook of Electoral System Design* (Stockholm, 2006).

IP: *International Profile: Alcohol and Other Drugs*, published by the Alcoholism and Drug Addiction Research Foundation (Toronto), 1994.

JWY: *The Yearbook of Jehovah's Witnesses*, published annually.

KEARNEY: *Globalization Index*, published annually by AT Kearney

KIDRON & SEGAL: *State of the World Atlas*, 5th edition, London: Penguin, 1995.

LE ROY: Coded and calculated by Michael K. Le Roy.

McCORMICK: Coded by John McCormick, Comparative Politics in Transition, New York: Wadsworth, 1995, p. 9.

NBWR: *The New Book of World Rankings*, 3rd edition, Facts on File, 1991.

PON: *The Progress of Nations*, UNICEF, 1996.

RWB: *Reporters Without Borders*, annual ranking of press freedom published annually.

SAUS: *Statistical Abstract of the United States*, published annually by the US Department of Commerce.

SOWC: *State of the World's Children*, published annually by UNICEF.

SWPA: Dan Smith, *The State of War and Peace Atlas*, 1st edition, London: Penguin, 1997.

STARK: Coded and calculated by Rodney Stark.

TI: *Corruption Perceptions Index*, Transparency International, published annually.

TWF: *The World Factbook*, published annually by the Central Intelligence Agency.

TWW: *The World's Women*, published annually by the United Nations.

UNCRIME: United Nations. The Sixth Annual United Nations Survey of Crime Trends and Operations of Criminal Justice Systems, 1997 (Computer files). Vienna, Austria: Crime Prevention and Criminal Justice Branch, United Nations Office at Vienna.

UNMID: United Nations Millennium Indicators, 2004.

UNPD: United Nations Population and Development Indicators.

UNSD: *United Nations Statistical Database*, published annually.

UNSY: *United Nations Statistical Yearbook*, 1997, United Nations.

WBI: *World Bank Governance Indicators*, published annually by the World Bank.

WCE: *World Christian Encyclopedia*, David B. Barrett, editor, Oxford University Press, 2001.

WDI: *World Development Indicators*, published annually by the World Bank.

WDR: *World Development Report*, published annually by the World Bank.

WHO: *World Health Organization*, Annual Statistical Report.

WRI: *World Resources Institute*, published annually.

WVS: World Values Study Group, WORLD VALUES SURVEY, 1981–1984, 1990–1993, 1995–1997, 2000-2002 (Computer files). ICPSR version. Ann Arbor, MI: Institute for Social Research (producer). Ann Arbor, MI: Inter-university Consortium for Political and Social Research (distibutor).

HISTORY

The data in HISTORY are from a variety of sources. The variable description for each variable uses the following abbreviations to indicate the source.

HSC: The Human Security Report, Oxford University Press, Oxford, 2005. Data published by the Human Security Centre, http://www.humansecuritycentre.org

IHS: Brian R. Mitchell, International Historical Statistics, 1988–1995. A reference guide of historical statistics published on the Americas, Africa, Asia, Europe, and Oceania.

P&E: Parties and Elections in Europe, Wolfram Nordsieck, University of Dusseldorf, Germany. http://www.parties-and-elections.de/index.html. Coding into party categories by Michael K. Le Roy.

TAYLOR: *World Handbook of Political and Social Indicators*, Yale: 1983.

TWF: *The World Factbook*, published annually by the Central Intelligence Agency.

WDI: *World Development Indicators*, published annually by the World Bank.

LATIN

The data in LATIN are from a variety of sources. The variable description for each variable uses the following abbreviations to indicate the source.

ALLEN: Paul Allen, *Student Atlas of World Politics*, 3rd edition, Connecticut: Dushkin/McGraw-Hill, 1998.

FITW: *Freedom in the World*, published annually by Freedom House, www.freedomhouse.org

HDR: *Human Development Report*, published annually by the United Nations Development Program.

KIDRON & SEGAL: *State of the World Atlas*, 5th edition, London: Penguin, 1995.

LE ROY: Coded and calculated by Michael K. Le Roy.

RWB: Reporters Without Borders, annual ranking of press freedom published annually.

SAUS: *Statistical Abstract of the United States*, published annually by the U.S. Department of Commerce.

SOWC: *State of the World's Children*, published annually by UNICEF.

STARK: Coded and calculated by Rodney Stark.

SWPA: Dan Smith, *The State of War and Peace Atlas*, 1st edition, London: Penguin, 1997.

TWF: *The World Factbook*, published annually by the Central Intelligence Agency.

WDI: World Development Indicators, published annually by the World Bank.

WDR: *World Development Report*, published annually by the World Bank.

WRI: *World Resources Institute*, published annually.

PEW GLOBAL02, PEW GLOBAL04, PGAP02-GHANA, PGAP02-NIGERIA

The data in all files entitled PEW GLOBAL02, PEW GLOBAL04, or with the prefix PGAP come from data collected by the Pew Global Attitudes Project, a series of worldwide public opinion surveys that encompasses a broad array of subjects ranging from people's assessments of their own lives to their views about the current state of the world and important issues of the day. More than 90,000 interviews in 50 countries have been conducted as part of the project's work.

The Pew Global Attitudes Project is co-chaired by former U.S. Secretary of State Madeleine K. Albright, currently Principal, the Albright Group LLC in Washington, DC, and former Senator John C. Danforth, currently Partner, Bryan Cave LLP in St. Louis, MO. The project is directed by Andrew Kohut, president of the Pew Research Center, a nonpartisan "fact tank" in Washington, DC, that provides information on the issues, attitudes, and trends shaping America and the world. The project is principally funded by The Pew Charitable Trusts. The William and Flora Hewlett Foundation provided a supplemental grant for the 2002 survey.

WVS

The data in all files with the prefix WVS come from data collected by the World Values Study Group. Ronald Inglehart et. al., World Values Study Group. WORLD VALUES SURVEY, 1999–2002 computer file]. Ann Arbor, MI: Institute for Social Research [producer], 2004. Mexico City, Mexico: Siglo XXI Editores, Mexico [distributor/publisher].

The 1999–2002 study is the fourth wave of the WVS and includes more than 80 surveys, representing a majority of the world's population and ranging from societies with per capita incomes as low as $300 per year, to societies with per capita incomes as high as $35,000 per year; and from long-established democracies with market economies, to various types of authoritarian states; and from societies with market economies to societies that are in the process of emerging from state-run economies. The surveys cover societies that were historically shaped by a wide variety of religious and cultural traditions, from Christian to Islamic to Confucian to Hindu.